THE NEW FORCES
OF DEVELOPMENT

Territorial Policy for
Endogenous Development

THE NEW FORCES OF DEVELOPMENT

Territorial Policy for Endogenous Development

Antonio Vázquez-Barquero

Universidad Autónoma de Madrid, Spain

World Scientific

NEW JERSEY · LONDON · SINGAPORE · BEIJING · SHANGHAI · HONG KONG · TAIPEI · CHENNAI

Published by

World Scientific Publishing Co. Pte. Ltd.

5 Toh Tuck Link, Singapore 596224

USA office: 27 Warren Street, Suite 401-402, Hackensack, NJ 07601

UK office: 57 Shelton Street, Covent Garden, London WC2H 9HE

British Library Cataloguing-in-Publication Data

A catalogue record for this book is available from the British Library.

THE NEW FORCES OF DEVELOPMENT
Territorial Policy for Endogenous Development

ISBN-13 978-981-4282-50-5
ISBN-10 981-4282-50-2

Typeset by Stallion Press

Email: enquiries@stallionpress.com

Printed in Singapore.

Preface

The first decade of the 21st century is ending with a very serious economic and financial crisis that has enveloped the developed economies in a great recession and has provoked a strong contraction in the growth rates of emerging and developing economies. Productive activity has been seriously affected by industrial and service firm shut-downs, a decrease in both domestic and foreign demand, and a rising unemployment rate. Because of this, sustainable development continues to be a vital question in all countries seeking to achieve fundamental objectives such as increased productivity, job creation, eradication of poverty, and the improvement of economic and social well-being.

Since the late 1980s, the change in the political scenario — symbolically represented by the fall of the Berlin Wall in 1989 — has accelerated the integration of the international economic system. The introduction of new technologies has given way to the appearance of new goods and services and new productive processes, has facilitated changes in firm organization (now more flexible and integrated within the territory), and has altered the firm location pattern. In turn, the introduction of new technologies in the transport and communication systems has facilitated the articulation of national and international markets, has stimulated exchange and commercial relations between firms and territories, and has transformed the spatial organization of development.

Thus, the economy is continuously evolving and transforming, and the introduction of new technologies fosters the spatial re-organization of production and markets. New city networks, new forms of organization of the urban systems, and new places where the investment and location decisions are made are emerging. Institutional development facilitates these changes, and many countries have introduced a political and administrative decentralization process that allows cities and regions to acquire new competences in the regulation of the international division of labor. In this atmosphere of growing economic integration, changes in the spatial organization of production, and institutional development, there emerges a demand for a new development policy, in whose design and implementation the local actors and civil society actively participate.

New activities, the economic diversity of the territories, and the emergence of local development initiatives begun in the early 1980s have defined a new scenario. This book considers development as a territorial process of growth and structural change in which the local actors and communities are committed, and proposes the theory and practice of endogenous development. It argues that this approach is an interpretation capable of analyzing the ongoing dynamic and the economic changes, and is a valid instrument for action in a context of continuous economic, organizational, technological, political, and institutional change.

The book begins with a discussion on globalization, productive and territorial diversity, and economic and social inequality, and the question of economic recession in the new scenario is described. It argues that the focus of the discussion lies in the understanding of the development process, which is a concept that has evolved through time. The new reality calls for a view that goes beyond the standard neoclassical model, and that explains growth by focusing on resource endowment and technology. Following this, the book develops its premise based on the concept of endogenous development, which is an interpretation of the economic dynamic based on the dynamics and interactions of the forces of development.

The central part of the book analyzes the dynamics of the economic development process in environments that are increasingly competitive and characterized by greater economic integration. It argues that territorial development is a systemic process in which the most flexible forms of organization of the production systems combine with the formation of polycentric urban region systems and the strengthening of regional innovation systems. The interaction between the forces of development creates synergies between the factors and forces of development and reinforces the effect of each of them on productivity, and makes the development process of cities, regions, and nations more efficient. Therefore, the interaction of the productive systems, the urban systems, and the innovation systems stimulates the generation of increasing returns, improves the productivity and competitiveness of firms and territories, and contributes towards economic and social progress.

The spontaneous appearance of local development policies in cities and regions of Asia and Latin America raises the question of a new development policy. During the last three decades, the economic reality has changed: the organization of companies is more flexible; value chains are becoming global; cities in polycentric urban regions of different countries are establishing connections; and innovation is encompassing business services, financial services, and cultural arts industries. All of this has led to a change in the theories and interpretations of development, abandoning the neoclassical market fundamentalism and instead adopting a more complex interpretation known as the territorial development approach. The new reality, the new processes, and the new interpretations call for an efficient development policy that is capable of using the local development potential of places and territories, as occurs in territorial development policies.

Territorial development policy is a policy with multiple objectives, and its actions are directed at improving the competitiveness of cities and regions and supporting sustainable social progress. This policy favors the convergence of governmental and market actions by coordinating public and private actors who are involved in the process of development. The book ends with a discussion on the general guidelines of the territorial development policy; and maintains that it is a useful policy precisely for activating the mechanisms and forces of endogenous development and for encouraging economic recovery in times of crisis, and should be designed and implemented by private and public actors and the local community.

The book is based on research completed at the Centre for Development Studies of the Universidad Autónoma de Madrid (UAM). I should, in particular, underline three projects whose conclusions have benefited the book: the SMEPOL project (SME Policy and the Regional Dimension of Innovation), the IKINET project (International Knowledge and Innovation Networks for European Integration, Cohesion and Enlargement), and the POLYREGIONS project (Polycentric Regions: A Strategic Space for Economic Development). I wish to thank the European Commission and the Xunta de Galicia, who funded these research projects; and also the members of the UAM Centre for Development Studies, namely Javier Alfonso-Gil, Antonia Saez-Cala, and Mari Cruz Lacalle, with whom I discussed relevant questions for the book.

This book has benefited from comments made by friends and colleagues that have enriched my work. I wish to thank Juan Carlos Rodriguez Cohard of the University of Jaén, Gildo Seisdedos of the IE Business School in Madrid, Francisco Alburquerque of the Council of Scientific Research in Madrid, Alberto Enriquez of FUNDE in El Salvador, Sergio Boisier of the ECLA, Clemente Ruiz of the National Autonomous University of Mexico, and Oscar Madoery of the University of Rosario. Special mention and gratitude must be made to Elena Saraceno of the EU, Giancarlo Canzanelli of the UNDP, Giuseppe Canullo of the University of Ancona, and Gioachino Garofoli of the University of Pavia, who discussed parts of the manuscript with me and made helpful comments. I also wish to thank Henning Schwardt for his help in the translation and his comments during the various revisions of the manuscript.

Antonio Vázquez-Barquero
Madrid
October 2009

Contents

ix

Illustrations

Chapter 1

Integration, Development, and Global Economic Crisis

In a world of ever greater integration, in which the new information and communication technologies facilitate and reinforce the functioning of, and the interaction between, firms and organizations, production systems and markets gradually acquire a global dimension. Globalization is a multidimensional process characterized by the increase of international economic and financial flows, as well as by cultural, political, and institutional exchange.

In contrast to what is frequently claimed, deeper economic integration has expanded the diversity of paths of growth that economies can follow. Countries, regions, and cities differ from each other in the quantity and type of economic, human, and cultural resources and strategic assets they have at their disposal. However, the process of economic growth and structural change as well as the level of well-being depend, above all, on the forces and mechanisms through which the process of sustainable development is fostered.

The current global crisis has brought into question the development processes that liberalization and economic integration have stimulated since the mid-1980s. The global recession has brought out the fact that productivity growth and economic progress do not affect all countries to the same extent. Inequalities in the standard of living have progressively increased, as has the income gap between rich and poor countries. Even the differences among less developed countries have increased in such a way that for emerging countries the income level is situated ever closer to that of developed countries and the level of poverty is gradually declining (mainly in the case of China), whereas less developed countries see absolute poverty increase and suffer from international exclusion. The ongoing global crisis is raising poverty levels and widening income differences among countries and regions.

Globalization and Economic Integration

Since the mid-1980s, the process of integration has accelerated progressively as a consequence of the end of the Cold War, the gradual liberalization affecting international economic exchange, and the strengthening of economic regions. All of this has led to a new paradigm: globalization.

Globalization is a process whose emergence some authors, such as Ferrer (1996), place at the beginning of the modern age, but that was truly consolidated during the period 1870–1914 (O'Rourke and Williamson, 1999). The present stage began around the mid-1980s, with a progressive increase of international trade, growth in capital flows, a new spatial organization of multinational corporations, and strong progress in information and communication technologies. Therefore, globalization means a remarkable increase in the integration of economic and financial markets.

International trade and economic integration

Beginning in the mid-1980s, an important expansion of global exports took place, with a fivefold increase of international trade during the last 30 years of the 20th century, due in great part to the reduction of trade and investment barriers. The newly industrializing Asian countries (Korea, Hong Kong, Singapore, and Taiwan) significantly strengthened their positions in global trade, to the extent that they have doubled their share of manufactured exports on a global scale. Latin America also enjoyed a high growth rate between 1990 and 2002, at a yearly rate of 9.1%, surpassed only by China and Southeast Asian countries. The opening of markets produced a rise in the exports of manufactured goods from developing countries, which in

1998 made up 80% of their total exports (compared to 25% in 1980); in China and also in low-income countries such as Bangladesh and Sri Lanka, manufactured products even exceeded the share of 80% of total exports.

At the same time, as a result of digging more deeply into the liberalization and economic integration processes, the dependence on international markets increased, particularly for the developing countries (UNCTAD, 2008). Between 1995 and 2007, the exports-to-GDP ratio practically doubled from 26.1% to 51.8%. Particularly striking was the increase in integration in Africa (the ratio rose from 21.9% to 49.7%) and in Asia (from 33.9% to 60.8%), and above all the levels reached in Central Africa (132.8% in 2007), Southeast Asia (100.3%), and East Asia (58.9%). In the developed countries, the dependence on international markets has not increased significantly in recent years (the ratio rose from 21.2% in 1995 to 28.4% in 2007), except in the case of Canada (where it rose from 32.5% to 48.0%) and the European Union (from 30% to 55%). Japan and the U.S. have little exposure to the international markets, since exports represented only 13.5% and 10%, respectively, of the GDP in 2007.

Development strategy based on growth led by international trade has given good results, with increased economic and social progress in many developing countries. Their more important markets continue to be the more developed countries, as shown by the fact that in 2007 almost 50% of their exports went to the U.S. (21%), the European Union (18%), and Japan (8%). Yet, the most significant fact may be the increase in South–South merchandise trade that grew threefold between 1995 and 2007 and that has contributed to the diversification of production, the attracting of investment flows, and the creation of new markets.

The worldwide economic boom from 2002 to mid-2008 contributed to the expansion of international markets and to an improvement in the living standards of the population. Increase in international demand also produced a boom in the price of commodities exported by developing countries, which gave way to gains in the terms of trade, which in turn improved the economic situation of the exporting countries of agricultural, mineral, and petroleum products.

Internationalization of production

The short-term and long-term capital flows have intensified, enabled by the international banking system and new financial intermediaries such as pension funds, investment banks and funds, and insurance companies (Eichengreen, 2000). Nevertheless, financial expansion has been subject to constant fluctuations in recent decades, which produced great turbulence in the economies of developing countries, as analysts and international organizations have pointed out. External financing has oscillated from one period to the next, reaching its peak during the periods 1977–1982 (2.3% of the GDP of developing countries) and 1993–1997 (2.8%), and its minimum in 1983–1990 (0.5%) and 1998–2000 (0.7%).

One of the most striking facts is the growth of foreign direct investments. Over 79,000 multinational corporations (MNCs) operate in the global economy through 790,000 foreign affiliates, and they have developed new organizational and territorial strategies that have stimulated mergers and acquisitions of companies. In 2007, their foreign direct investment (FDI) stock was US$15.211 trillion (from US$789 billion in 1982), total sales amounted to US$31.197 trillion (from US$2.741 trillion in 1982), and the number of employees in the foreign affiliates was 81.615 million (from 21.524 million in 1982). Cross-border mergers and acquisitions contributed to the increase in FDI; in 2007 this kind of transaction amounted to US$1.637 trillion, while in 1990 the value at current prices was US$200 billion.

The flow of foreign direct investments has risen from an annual average of US$73 billion during 1980–1984 to US$735 billion during 1995–2000 and to US$1.833 trillion in 2007, the all-time record. Even though the most important flows are registered between developed countries, in the developing countries they have grown considerably, increasing more than 15-fold between 1980–1984 and 2004–2007 (UNCTAD, 2008). The principal recipients of direct investments among the developing countries are China and the 12 main emerging countries, amongst which Argentina, Brazil, Chile, Malaysia, Mexico, the Russian Federation, and Thailand stand out.

As a result of the economic boom and good firm results, direct investment grew in all groups of countries between 2003 and 2007. In developed countries, the FDI inflows reached US$1.248 trillion (68% of the total) in 2007; the U.S. received the most investments, while in the EU it reached two thirds of the total of direct investments. Developing countries increased their participation in investments received (from 25.6% in 1995–2000 to 31% in 2004–2007). Among the most important receptor countries, China, Hong Kong, and the Russian Federation stand out.

Another prominent feature is the growing importance of multinational corporations (MNCs) in developing countries, which represent 15% of the companies in the Fortune Global 500 list (Casanova, 2009; Athukorala, 2007). Since the fall of the Berlin Wall in 1989, Southern MNCs have experienced remarkable growth as developing countries have become more important as sources of FDI, which in 2007 reached a record US$253 billion. The expansion of direct investments from developing countries is reinforced by the growing importance of the sovereign wealth funds, which in recent years have made important investments in cross-border mergers and acquisitions from the developed countries.

According to the UNCTAD World Investment Report 2008 (UNCTAD, 2008), the presence of transnational firms has increased in recent decades. The manufacturing and petroleum firms (such as General Electric, Toyota, Ford, Shell, and British Petroleum) maintain the highest positions in the UNCTAD ranking, although the presence of firms devoted to the service sector is growing. Most notable is the growing presence of MNCs in emerging countries, which in 2006 increased their foreign assets by 21% with respect to the previous year. The category of "the top 25 non-financial MNCs from developing countries, ranked by foreign assets in 2006" is dominated by firms from East and Southeast Asia (six Chinese firms; four each from Hong Kong, in particular Hutchison Whampoa Ltd., and Korea; and two each from Singapore and Malaysia), but the presence of Latin American firms is also growing (three from Mexico and two from Brazil). The most important activities are devoted to electrical and electronic equipment goods, telecommunications, motor vehicles, petroleum, and the industrial chemical industry.

Integration: an incomplete process

Thus, globalization is a process of integration that is associated with greater exchange of goods and services, the internationalization of capital, and an increase in the international production of multinational companies. For many, however, the feature that most characterizes the current stage of the globalization process is the fact that the internationalization of markets, capital, and production is linked to the introduction of new technologies, especially information and communication technologies (ICT). This is in clear contrast to earlier periods, which focused more on the search for raw materials and new markets for products.

Which factors are responsible for the acceleration of the process of economic integration since 1980? The OECD (1996) argues that the most important factors are the following: the new trade and investment policies, which have liberalized the markets for goods, factors, and services; the new spatial strategies of multinational corporations, which make use of the opportunities for location that economic and social integration provide them with; and the introduction of innovations in information, transport, and communication technologies, which facilitate the integration of markets and multinational production as well as reduce the cost of production and exchange.

The current period of globalization has established a new international order and a new international division of labor. The leadership position in the global economy is held by the OECD countries and some newly industrializing countries in Asia (South Korea, Singapore, and Taiwan), which have liberalized their markets and privatized a good share of their public companies, which have opened their economies to international capital, and whose production systems are highly integrated internationally. To them should be added a group of late developed and emerging countries that have increasingly globalized and integrated in the international markets. These include around 24 countries, among which are Argentina, Brazil, Chile, China, Hungary, India, Malaysia, Mexico, the Philippines, the Russian Federation, South Africa, and Thailand. The remaining countries, especially the extremely poor African countries and some that were part of the former Soviet Union, remain excluded from globalization unless they show themselves to be capable of opening their economies to international markets.

Is globalization really such an important and relevant phenomenon for the national economies? The available information shows that its dimension has probably been exaggerated, particularly when compared to previous periods in the process of globalization. As suggested by Ferrer (1996), globalization is a phenomenon that is not as extended as it appears to be. Although economic integration has increased during the last decade, there remain important areas of the national economies that are only indirectly affected by this integration. According to the United Nations, 75% of the global production has been sold in local markets, 90% of investments have been financed by domestic savings, and 9 out of 10 workers worked for national markets during the 1990s.

The international trade and foreign investments of developing countries have increased spectacularly, but the flows of international money and finances as well as labor have not yet reached the levels attained during the period 1880–1914 of the globalization process. According to Maddison (2001), in 1998 the stock of international capital represented 22% of the GDP of developing countries, a value quite inferior to the 34% reached in 1914. Between 1870 and 1910, around 10% of the global population migrated to other countries; while during the middle of the current decade, only 2% (120 million) of the global population lived in foreign countries. Therefore, once the ongoing global crisis is over, it is likely that the globalization process will increase but under a different pattern.

Lastly, the diffusion of information and communication technologies has had a significant economic and social impact, but it seems relatively less important than the innovations of the period 1870–1914. It has facilitated the production and exchange of information between firms, financial institutions, and clients and suppliers; but there is less potential for increasing its effects on global productivity and for achieving the creation of new consumer products and investment goods, as did the electric engine from 1870 onward. Furthermore, even though the diffusion of information and communication technologies has favored changes in the firms' organization and management, mainly in the systematization of administrative and routine tasks, its contribution to the transformation of hierarchical organization models of large enterprises and to improvements in the quality of human resources has been rather limited until now. In the area of transport and communication, the period 1870–1914 was substantially more innovative than the current one, with the substitution of wind-powered navigation by steam-powered navigation, the development of automobile and aviation industries, and the expansion of the railroad. Therefore, there is plenty of room for new developments in the near future.

The Global Economic and Financial Crisis

The ongoing crisis is a global financial crisis that has spilled over into the real economy. It started in the United States during the first quarter of 2007, with the lack of liquidity and the decline in solvency in the financial markets when the banking system incurred important risks because of the default on an important part of the subprime mortgages. After the collapse of the investment bank Lehman Brothers and the nationalization of the insurance company AIG in September 2008, the crisis spread to international markets through the stock exchange, the international banking system, and the monetary standard (Bordo, 2008).

The financial crisis has contaminated the functioning of the economy, generating a decline in GDP during the last quarter of 2008, and this contraction continued throughout 2009 (IMF, 2010). According to the IMF *World Economic Outlook* of October 2009, the "global economy is expanding again.... It will still take some time however until the outlook for employment improves significantly" (IMF, 2009a). Global activity contracted by 0.6% in 2009. GDP, in real terms, declined by 2.4% in the United States and by 4.1% in the euro-zone; it fell by 5.0% in Germany and by 3.6% in Spain. Latin America experienced a GDP growth rate decline of 2.2%; specifically, 1.5% in Chile, 0.2% in Brazil, and 6.5% in Mexico. Growth estimates in the most dynamic emerging economies were revised for 2009 (GDP growth rate of 8.7% in China and 5.7% in India); while for Russia, a significant fall of 7.9% in 2009 was foreseen.

The advanced economies are experiencing a strong restructuring process in their service sectors. Financial activities were re-dimensioned following the shutdown of investment banks and their absorption by commercial banks. As a consequence of the reduction of financial activities, job loss has increased and branch networks are being restructured. It is estimated that up to January 2009, about 325,000 jobs were lost in the global banking system, and 20 banks have declared themselves bankrupt in Europe. In the U.S., 25 banks failed in 2008 and 140 in 2009, while only 11 banks failed in the five years prior to 2008.

At the heart of the crisis is the restructuring of industrial activities in developed and emerging countries. In the eurozone, a rapid decline in industrial production took place during the second semester of 2008 and continued in 2009. Eurostat reported that in April 2009, compared to the same period a year ago, European industrial production fell by 21.6% in the eurozone. Industrial production declined in all EU member countries: 24.2% in Italy, 23.2% in Germany, 21.2% in Sweden, and 19.7% in Spain. In the U.S., on a year-to-year basis, industrial production fell by 13.4% in May 2009 and manufacturing output declined by 15.3%. Activities in sectors such as automobiles, office and telecommunication equipment, consumer electronics, construction, ceramics, textiles and garments, and food processing have sharply reduced their production.

In emerging economies, industrial restructuring is also taking place because of the sharp contraction of international demand, foreign trade, and direct investment. In China, a noticeable slowdown in the growth of industrial production can be seen, dropping from 22.9% in 2007 to 9.3% in 2009. Furthermore, thousands of companies have closed down, especially in the provinces of Guangdong and

Zhejiang; and the steel, car, petrochemical, and textile sectors are, as the Chinese authorities recognize, in need of profound restructuring. In Korea, industrial production has fallen since October 2008, as indicated by the reduction in car sales and exports.

According to the International Labour Organization, unemployment is increasing as a consequence of the recession of the international economic system, and an increase in global unemployment of over 20 million was expected for late 2009. The IMF (2010) report stated that the unemployment rate in the United States was 5.8% in 2008, and was estimated to worsen to 9.3% in 2009 (and 9.4% in 2010). Unemployment also rose in the eurozone during the second semester of 2008, and this trend was estimated to continue throughout 2009, reaching 9.4% at the end of the year (and 10.5% in 2010). In Spain, which has the highest unemployment rate in the eurozone, the unemployment rate was forecasted at over 18% in 2009 (and 20% in 2010). In the emerging economies, unemployment is on the rise because of plant shutdowns. In China, the unemployment rate was 9.2% in 2007, and the situation was expected to worsen if the growth rate of the economy fell below 8% in 2009 because the capacity of the economy would be reduced for the absorption of new workers in the labor market.

The global crisis is having a significant effect on international trade, reducing exchange not only between developed and developing countries, but also in the South–South trade that was so dynamic in the previous decade (particularly intra-Asia trade). According to the IMF *World Economic Outlook* of April 2010, exports were estimated to fall in advanced economies by 11.7% during 2009; whereas in emerging and developing economies, exports were expected to fall by 8.2%, with variations from country to country (IMF, 2010). The OECD (2009) forecasted that exports would fall by 10.5% in Brazil and by 5.6% in the Russian Federation, whereas they would grow by 5.4% in China and by 3.1% in India.

The fall in international demand and the financial restrictions have reduced trade in all productive activities, mainly in manufacturing, and have provoked a fall in commodity prices and therefore in the terms of trade. Among the activities most affected are automotive parts, office and telecommunication equipment, electronics, and textiles and clothing. According to UNCTAD (2009), commodity prices have fallen since mid-2008, particularly for vegetable oil and seed oil (with a fall of 48% between the peak of 2008 and January 2009), agricultural raw materials (36%), and crude oil (petroleum) (67%). Yet, the terms of trade vary from one country to another, according to the merchandise trade balance; thus, the terms of trade were foreseen to increase in India by 1.8% during 2009, while decreasing in the Russian Federation by 22.5%.

If the spread of the worldwide crisis through the fall in commercial exchange is important, then the impact of direct investments is also important since many firms are revising their investment plans. UNCTAD (2009) stated that FDI inflows in 2008 fell by 15% with respect to the previous year. The developed countries were particularly affected, with a fall of 25% with respect to 2007, as a result of the credit crunch and the liquidity contraction of the financial system. In developing countries, however, direct investment inflows grew in 2008, albeit at a lower rate than in 2007.

The forecasts for 2009 indicated that direct investments would continue to fall, particularly in developing countries. These estimates and previsions are not, however, generalized for all countries and territories, given that much depends on the strategies and objectives of each of the firms (UNCTAD, 2009). As a result of the world economic recession, many large MNCs have cut back their plans for expansion and have stopped investing in order to improve the availability of the firm's liquidity. In contrast, other firms have shown a different behavior due to the investment opportunities that the fall in prices of assets and industrial restructuring have presented, as well as the spread of new activities related to the energy and environmental industry.

Direct investments from developing countries have shrunk, although less than in developed countries, due to the growing presence of Southern MNCs, the availability of large sums of foreign currency, and the resources of the sovereign wealth funds (Casanova, 2009). Chinese firms have not suffered any important crisis thus far, although they have diminished their foreign investments or, as Hutchison Whampoa Ltd. has done, announced the suspension of new investments abroad. In fact, China is taking advantage of its large reserves to insure the supply of natural resources from Africa and Latin America, and so has given Petrobras a loan of US$10 billion for prospection and explorations in new petroleum fields in Brazil.

Latin American firms are continuing their internationalization process, especially those in Mexico and Brazil, who are competitive in cement, steel, oil and gas, biofuel, software, petrochemical, and food industries. At the present time, many of these firms are taking advantage of market opportunities, as in the case of the Mexican firms América Móvil and Telmex, who bought under good condition the assets in the area of Bell Canada International, MCI WorldCom, and AT&T Latin America. Their investments in their own Latin American markets are also increasing. Thus, the Chilean group Luksic, who had sold Banco de Chile to Citibank, has bought it again; and the Brazilian bank Unibanco has merged with Banco Itaú, thus becoming the 10th largest bank worldwide.

Economic and Territorial Diversity

As we have just seen, during the past 25 years, the process of economic integration has accelerated and the competition between firms, countries, and regions has increased. This has induced the adjustment of productive systems, the transformation of labor markets, an increase in income, and an increase in the population's standard of living in many of the territories. However, this type of generalization is scarcely valuable, for there is in fact a multitude of situations in localities and territories that reflect the complexity of the economic, social, and institutional systems, as shown by the discussion on the ongoing global crisis.

The economic dynamics of cities, regions, and countries are very different from each other. Each locality or territory has a set of material, human, institutional, and cultural resources that jointly constitute its development potential. Therefore, at any given territorial level, one can find a determined production system, labor market, entrepreneurial capacity and technological knowledge, natural resources, social and political system, and historical and cultural heritage. Every economy articulates its processes of growth and structural change based on its development potential. Moreover, as a consequence of market exchange between firms and the other economic actors, very different results are obtained, which establish a great variety of economic, political, and social situations as well as projects and processes.

The economic, institutional, and technological changes of the last quarter of the 20th century have led to an in-depth transformation of the production system. The changes in taste and demand have meant a divergence from the existing range of products supplied by firms, altering the competitive capacity of regions and cities in poor and rich economies alike. The relative increase of production costs (above all, of labor and energy) has affected the firms' production functions and provoked the shutdown of industrial firms, the change in location of production activities, and the increased competitive advantages in some of the local productive systems. The deconcentration of productive functions, the increase in subcontracting, and the expansion of financial and business services have in turn introduced new changes in the economies and production systems of cities, regions, and countries.

The results have differed from one economy to another, depending on the capacity of each territory to respond to these new challenges. Research studies suggest that the factors which have determined the processes of structural change and economic growth are the diffusion of innovation through the productive fabric; the skill of human resources; the learning capacities of entrepreneurs; the transformation and adaptation of institutions; and the integration of firms, cities, and regions into competitive and innovative networks on a national as well as international level.

Globalization is accelerating productive adjustment and the processes of economic development, creating a new territorial system in the new global economy that some have termed "the economy of the archipelago" (Veltz, 1996) and that others prefer to call a new international division of labor. This spontaneous process that economic, social, and political actors engage in has made the economic and territorial systems more diverse. New products have appeared, some production lines have differentiated themselves, and the territories have adopted new economic and productive functions. The urban and regional system is becoming increasingly polycentric, and regional and urban hierarchies tend to be reduced to the degree that relations and networks of firms and cities intensify, precisely as a consequence of the effects of globalization.

The production system of the most dynamic cities and regions, on which the global economy rests, is more diversified now than during the years of the Cold War. It is formed by high-technology industrial activities (such as microelectronics, biotechnology, robotics, and aerospace industries) — those manufacturing activities that in the 1950s and 1960s were characterized by their standardized production methods, but were subsequently restructured and their production differentiated through the introduction of innovations (such as in the garment and car industries), advanced service activities (such as marketing, design, and technical assistance), financial services, and cultural and creative industries (including leisure, the performing arts, museums, and the print and electronic media).

The increase and diversification in the production of goods and services, and hence in those activities that foster and stimulate the production system, have diversified the territorial system. There are two processes that explain this. On the one hand, the conversion of national urban systems into a European or Latin American urban system (i.e. into global urban systems) has introduced a change in inter-urban relations that has transformed the systems of prices and costs, as well as a change in entrepreneurial and political relations at the global level. As a consequence, the conditions are created for a greater diversity of economic, political, and organizational functions of the cities and regions within a more closely related and interactive system. On the other hand, the increase in the variety of products and activities has reduced the capacity to concentrate productive and commercial functions in one city or urban region due to diseconomies of agglomeration. This dynamic generates the formation of more flexible urban systems and a reduction in the hierarchy of already-existing ones.

The increased diversity of territories and production systems can be appreciated particularly in the dynamics of the rural areas, in both developed and developing countries, which have experienced a period of ever-more complex adjustments as a result of the crisis in traditional agriculture, depopulation, the lack of basic infrastructures, and the pollution and contamination of the environment. Rural development presents a special problem in a world where the international division of labor is changing. In this new framework, everything seems to indicate that for the rural areas the best option is to specialize in productive activities, including non-farm businesses and specific services, in which they have a competitive advantage in national and international markets.

When the differentiation of rural territories is analyzed as a function of their integration into the international economic system, of the distance to markets and the capacity to learn on behalf of the local society, a great variety of situations appear. Remote rural areas, such as the Amazon, Tibet, and Sub-Saharan regions, made up of isolated territories with fragile production systems, frequently show a low-density population (sometimes aged) which relies on natural resources and a historical and cultural heritage that are constantly deteriorating. Therefore, the possibilities of entering into a path of self-sustaining development, using their own resources, are very limited. In the marginal zones of metropolitan areas, such as some peripheral districts of New York City or Caracas, which are physically well integrated into the international markets, insufficiencies in terms of the knowledge accumulated in institutions and firms and in terms of the citizens' and enterprises' capacity to learn are notorious. This limits their development potential and restricts the process of development. On the other hand, in those regions which are not well connected to markets but have a significant development potential, such as the Orinoco region in Venezuela, local actors can make use of the resources and capacities that exist in the territory and integrate the territory into the global economy. Lastly, in rural regions with a high innovative capacity that are integrated into the global economy through multiple network systems (productive, commercial, and technological), entrepreneurial capacity and the flexibility of their institutions allow for the generation of a large number of entrepreneurial projects and, therefore, the articulation of development processes that have their own dynamic.

Likewise, industrial spaces are very diverse, as pointed out by Markusen (2000), among others. If cities and industrial regions are analyzed as a function of the organization of the production system (large firms vs. networks of firms) and of the degree of integration of the enterprises into the production system of the territory where they are located, one can identify a variety of development patterns showing very different paths of growth. Among these, the following stand out:

- Local production systems formed by firms that are connected with each other and whose productive activities are integrated into the production chain of the city or region where they are located. The production system has a labor market that adheres to its own rules, and innovation and technical knowledge emerge and are diffused easily and well within the industrial district; the interaction between firms, in turn, creates externalities that link the local production system to the territory and whose effects on the firms' costs and profits are not reflected in the market prices. This scenario describes such innovative milieus as the Swiss Jura region and Silicon Valley in California, where local firms today enjoy an increasing competitive capacity in national and international markets.

- Local production systems whose firms carry out activities linked to production chains in other cities or regions, and where some of the important stages of the production chain (such as research and development or strategic business services) are produced outside the territory in which the companies are located. Good examples are the industrial districts such as Montebelluna in Italy, known for its production of footwear for mountaineers and plastic ski boots. The adoption of technological innovations has induced changes in the organization of the production process and the decentralization of some stages of production to countries in Southeast Asia. The entry of capital and companies from outside has driven the location of economic decision-making centers to other regions and cities so that, even though local production maintains its position within the chain, it has lost its independence.

• Local production systems formed around big enterprises that carry out all functions (or the most important ones) in the place where they are located, and whose activities are integrated into the local production chain. The leading companies buy from local and foreign providers and sell, mostly, to external markets. The labor market of the production system and the diffusion of technical knowledge are controlled by the dominant enterprise, and the main investment decisions are made locally. Turin, the seat of Fiat, is a good example of this type of production system. Another example is Vigo, a Spanish metropolitan area of less than 500,000 inhabitants located in Galicia, a region north of Portugal, where Citroën — whose plant is well integrated within the local productive system — and Pescanova — a local company specializing in frozen food products — lead the growth and structural change processes of the metropolitan area.

• Local production systems articulated around companies which are parts of external production chains and which lack significant local production links. The production system is dominated by big companies that use the space in which they are located like an enclave that allows them to carry out their own production and to maintain a system of economic and social relations. This is the case for independent companies or subsidiary plants, which produce for a multinational corporation. The relations within local firms are of little importance; the labor market is controlled by the foreign company, as is the diffusion of innovation and knowledge. Two good examples are the "Gran ABC" in the state of São Paulo, Brazil, where since the 1930s, with the arrival of General Motors, the car industry has been concentrated around one of the biggest multinational companies of this sector; and the Research Triangle Park in the United States.

In sum, in a world characterized by the increased integration of economies and countries, the productive systems of both regions and cities have marked differences in their capacity for overcoming the global economic crisis. The progressive increase of competition stimulates the economic actors to make investment decisions that upgrade the local development potential with the objective of improving their market position and, at the same time, increasing the standard of living of the population. Economic diversity leads to different paths of growth for every one of them, taking them to different stages and levels of development. Globalization, therefore, establishes an open and undetermined game with a variety of paths of development, and this widens the possibilities for response and strengthens the diversity of the development processes of territories. This poses a challenge for economic recovery.

Inequality and Poverty

The process of economic integration has increased market competition and, for decades, has stimulated the economic growth and structural change of countries, regions, and cities immersed in the globalization dynamics. This has paved the way for the formation of an ever-more diversified productive and spatial system. However, economic progress does not affect all countries and territories to the same extent: income inequality continues to exist in developing countries, and seems to have worsened in Latin America and Sub-Saharan Africa during the 1980s and 1990s.

Inequality is an age-old problem that appeared on the international scene with all its severity during the 1980s, when, with the Soviet Union in full disintegration, society and the scientific community openly discussed the question of the standard of living of the population. For decades, traditional economic thought and international organizations had maintained the assumption that the income level of less developed countries would converge towards that of richer countries, supported by the idea that the growth rate of less developed countries was higher than that of more developed countries. Studies undertaken since the 1980s, however, show great inequality in the standard of living between countries and between regions, as well as the existence of large pockets of poverty in the less developed countries, especially in Sub-Saharan Africa, South Asia, and Eastern Europe, which are incapable of integrating their productive systems into the international economy.

Therefore, at present, it is largely accepted that, within the world economic system, an unequal distribution of income exists. The human development indexes published by the United Nations Development Programme show that the richest, most developed countries enjoy a development level that is more than two times that of the poorest countries (0.901 vs. 0.444 for 2006), a life expectancy at birth that is much longer (76.2 years vs. 48.4 years), a population with a much higher enrollment in education (87.6% vs. 46.5%), and a GDP per capita that is 20 times higher (US$25,100 vs. US$1,199 using the adjusted index).

The information and data presented by Summers and Heston (1991) and Maddison (2001) show that the differences in income have tended to increase in the long term, leading to a growing divergence between poor countries and rich countries. At the beginning of the 19th century, the GDP per capita in the richest countries was roughly three times higher than in the poorest countries, while currently it is about 20 times higher. Since the mid-1970s, the differences in the countries' GDP per capita levels have continuously increased. Between 1960 and 1990, the countries in which the richest 20% of the global population live increased their participation in the gross world product from 79.2% to 82.7%, while the countries in which the poorest 20% live reduced theirs from 2.3% to 1.4%.

Therefore, everything seems to confirm that a convergence between countries has not taken place, except in the case of developed countries and the most globalized emerging countries like China. The study by Milanovic (2001) on disparities of the per capita income, weighed by the population, shows that, if India and China are excluded, a convergence in the levels of per capita income occurred between the mid-1950s and the early 1970s — precisely during those years in which the level of economic integration diminished — and divergence has progressively increased since then.

At the same time, it seems clear that convergence between the regions in the developed countries has taken place, as shown by the information regarding Japanese prefectures and the regions of the European Union (Barro and Sala-i-Martin, 1995). This allows us to speak of conditional convergence when economies share factors such as political, social and economic institutions, the level of education, infrastructures, and macroeconomic policies. However, amongst the developing countries, the situation differs greatly from one country to another. In Malaysia and the Philippines, the income inequality between households has diminished. But in Latin America, it has increased and continues to be very unequal, as shown by the Gini coefficient; in Brazil it was 0.590 in 2007, and in Mexico it was 0.506 in 2006. In China, where the number of poor people fell from 835 million in 1981 to 208 million in 2005, income distribution has worsened sharply since the beginning of the reforms in 1978, as the Gini coefficient — an increase from 0.33 in 1980 to 0.49 in 2005 — shows.

The disparities in income levels and the divergence between poor countries and rich countries conceal a very serious fact: in 2005, a total of 1.4 billion people lived below the international poverty line (on less than US$1.25 per day), according to Chen and Ravallion (2008). Poverty incidence is uneven across regions. It is most highly concentrated in South Asian countries (43.3% of the poor population in developing countries), in East Asia and the Pacific (23%), in Sub-Saharan Africa (28.4%), and, to a lesser degree, in Latin America (3.4%).

Absolute poverty reached close to 1.9 billion people in 1981, but has begun to decrease since then, especially in the most globalized emerging countries. In East Asia and the Pacific, poverty in absolute terms was reduced by more than 755 million people as a consequence of the effect of an improvement in the income levels mainly in China, whereas an increase of 47 million people took place in South Asia as a consequence of India's rising poverty. In Latin America, however, poverty increased during the 1990s to such an extent that in 2002 the level of absolute poverty surpassed that of 1981 by more than 16 million people, yet during the economic boom poverty declined.

In short, if the developed countries and their regions are excluded, one can conclude that the countries' standard of living tends increasingly to diverge. Since the early 1980s, the number of poor people in less developed countries whose economies have grown at a rapid pace and are more integrated within the global economic system has been reduced, whereas it has increased in the case of less integrated countries with low growth rates. This divergence also remains in other dimensions of poverty, such as the life expectancy at birth, the degree of literacy, and the rate of school attendance.

The economy's incapacity to absorb new workers and the increased unemployment rate are having a negative effect on the living conditions of people, especially in those territories with a low per capita income. Over the last 30 years, poverty has decreased spectacularly throughout the world, and the number of poor people has fallen from 51.8% of the developing world's population in 1981 to 25.2% in 2005 (in Latin America, it fell from 11.5% to 8.4%). Nevertheless, the tide may turn in the near future if international demand is reduced, if the slowdown of global economic growth continues, and if the labor absorption capacity worsens. According to UN estimates, poverty was expected to increase to 150–200 million people during 2009 as a result of the impact of the crisis on the weakest economies.

Development and Economic Crisis

The ongoing global crisis emerged from the U.S. financial system and has progressively spread to the real economy, and its impact on advanced and emerging economies is impeding development processes. Thus, in order to foster economic recovery and promote sustainable development, public policy aims and strategies should be revised. Therefore, some questions should be answered. Which are the factors that explain the global economic and financial crisis? How did the diffusion from one place to another occur?

The current crisis follows a pattern similar to previous crises. Romer (2009) points out that, even though there are big differences between the current crisis and the Great Depression of 1929, mainly with respect to magnitude, there also exist noticeable parallels such as the decline in asset prices and the failure or difficulties of financial institutions, the contraction of production and greater unemployment, as well as the spillover to other developed countries and emerging economies. What is more, after the stock market crash of the 1930s, financial crises have been repeated in a systematic way and have intensified since 1971, when the Nixon administration decided to leave the Bretton Woods system of fixed exchange rates by ending the fixed dollar–gold convertibility rate.

In October 1987, an important stock market crisis took place, and in 1994 the Mexican crisis — known as the "Tequila crisis" — occurred. In July 1997, a significant exchange rate crisis originated in Thailand, with currency speculation spreading to Malaysia, the Philippines, South Korea, and Indonesia, leading to a strong recession that was associated with the rapid financial and capital market liberalization as well as with these countries' policies; it later spread still further to Turkey, Russia, and the Latin American countries. In 1999, the "dot-com bubble" burst as a consequence of speculation that developed around new information and communication technology companies. More recently, 2002 was the period of the Argentine *corralito* crisis.

A financial crisis results from the fact that, during a business cycle upswing, economic agents take excessive risks in the markets for goods, stock markets, foreign exchange markets, and in general for economic assets, leading to an investment boom financed with bank money (Minsky, 1977; Bordo, 2008; Ocampo, 2009). Stimulated by the availability of easy profits, investors turn to operations in which the price of assets goes above their real value, and their financial operations exceed their current income, leading to the formation of "bubbles" in markets and the overindebtedness of agents. The crisis leads to a collapse in asset prices, and the fall pulls economic agents and financial organizations down as well, leading to bankruptcies, the closure of banks and companies, and economic recession.

The ongoing crisis shows some unique features. The fall in housing prices in the United States during the first quarter of 2007 brought an interesting fact to light: the great expansion of credit occurred as a consequence of the creation of new credit instruments and the deficient regulation of financial markets. Perhaps the central point of the crisis was the fact that the collateralized debt obligations and the multiplication of assets coming from new financial intermediaries, which were not subject to the banking sector's regulatory controls, led to a strong expansion of credit, which in turn fueled speculation in financial markets. Moreover, financial liberalization changed the prerequisites that investment banks had to fulfill and allowed more financial intermediaries through non-bank agents; this increased the expansion of credit as the capital ratios of these entities were lower than those of commercial banks, which in turn enabled the former to dispose of more resources for engaging in speculative market activities.

In all, major changes in regulation and the lax oversight of the financial system permitted the formation of the financial and housing market "bubbles" (Tamames, 2009) in which a complex network of agents was involved. Lenders granted mortgages with great ease; investment banks and hedge funds transformed these into products that were attractive in financial markets; and fund managers bought these new assets with borrowed capital. This pyramid scheme, the fruit of speculative activities, collapsed as a result of the fall in housing prices, which left the mortgage value above the true value of real estate, leading the mortgage takers to stop their payments and return the assets to the financial entities instead.

The bursting of the real estate "bubble" led to a strong contraction of credit. On the one hand, the fall in the housing market and the collapse of the bonds' and assets' prices and returns affected banks, funds, and other agents who helped finance the boom. Additionally, the toxic assets had spread through a good part of the financial system, affecting not only the non-bank entities that participated in the network of agents who sustained the financial bubble, but also the commercial banks that were directly or indirectly contaminated by the toxic assets. The problem was made worse as the contamination of commercial banks spread mistrust and uncertainty in the interbank market, and so the price of interbank lending increased. The reduction of credit contracted liquidity and money in circulation, affecting the ability of companies and households to finance their investments and spending.

In market economies, the banking system is the cornerstone for the functioning of the real economy. The relation of companies with their suppliers and customers becomes more efficient due to bank-financed operations and transactions; also, households seek bank credit not only for their mortgages, but also for financing some of their consumer spending. Therefore, the contraction of credit caused by the financial crisis has provoked a reduction in the investment and consumption demand, leading to a contraction of production activities, the closure of companies, a rise in unemployment, and an increase in inequality and poverty, as pointed out before.

The financial crisis has led to a global recession because developed and emerging countries are closely linked to the global economy by trade and direct investment. The banking and stock market systems of developed and emerging economies were affected by the financial crisis, to a greater or lesser degree, through the interbank market, the activity of financial fund managers, and the flow of direct and portfolio investment in international markets. Furthermore, the crisis has had a strong impact on emerging economies through other channels that connect their economies to those of the developed countries. Ocampo (2009) points out that in Latin America the remittances of migrants are diminishing as a consequence of the contraction of international production activities, and the terms of trade are deteriorating in those countries that export agriculture, mining, and energy products.

Chapter 2

Economic Development of the Territory

The concept of economic development evolves and transforms, as does society. This is because countries, regions, and cities must offer solutions to new problems, in the process spreading innovation and knowledge through the economic and social fabric. This occurred in the time of Adam Smith (1776) and the classical economists from the latter part of the 18th century onward, during the Industrial Revolution; this also happened to Schumpeter (1934) in the early 20th century, when inventions and innovations transformed the manufacturing economy, giving rise to a profound restructuring of production activities. During the last quarter of the 20th century, the question arose again in a new period of the process of economic dynamics with the eruption of new information and communication technologies.

As in the past, the question of the increase in productivity and the mechanisms that favor the processes of growth and structural change, as Simon Kuznets (1966) liked saying, is at the heart of the discussion on economic growth. In the new theories of economic development, the accumulation of capital, innovation, and institutional change play a central role in the explanation of the development process. Yet, the cornerstone of the current explanation of territorial development are the forces whose interactions generate investment multiplier effects — those mechanisms, hidden in the "black box" of development, that transform investment into a self-sustaining growth of income, and that give rise to economies in the production system and to increasing returns to scale in production factors.

Development: A Concept in Evolution

The new facts that have characterized the international system since the 1980s, such as the fall of the Berlin Wall, the recognition that the market economy is more efficient, and the generalization of economic integration, have given way to a state of mind that is favorable to a change in the notion of economic development and to proposing more operative concepts. This new mindset allows for a better understanding of the dynamics of the economic reality in order to be more efficient in policies and actions (see Figure 2.1).

The strong process of economic integration that characterized the period between 1870 and 1914 provided the basis for two interpretations of development. The first is that of Schumpeter, who published the German edition of his book, *The Theory of Economic Development*, in the autumn of 1911, when the previous period of globalization reached its peak, and which proposes that the entrepreneur and innovation are the main forces of economic development. The second is that of the Soviet economists of the 1920s, during the Great Depression, who considered growth to be proportional to the investment in capital goods — an interpretation that, as Easterly

Development Model

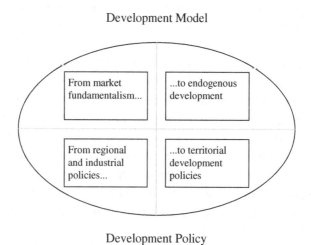

Development Policy

Figure 2.1   The New Development Economics.

(2001) points out, inspired the thoughts of economists from the 1950s to the 1990s.

Following World War II, despite the diffusion of the belief that the Soviet system was superior in its conception of industrial development to the market economy countries, among politicians, economists in international organizations, and academics, a different doctrinal body of economic development was created by, among others, Abramovitz (1952), Arrow (1962), Kuznets (1966), Lewis (1954), and Solow (1956). Essentially, this conceptualization of development refers to the processes of growth and structural change that aim at satisfying the needs and demands of the population and at improving their standard of living, specifically through an increase in employment and a reduction in poverty. Thus, the objective of countries consists of achieving an improvement in the economic, social, and cultural well-being of specific populations through a stimulus to increase the competitiveness of the economy and its enterprises in international markets.

To achieve this, it is necessary to increase productivity in all economic sectors, i.e in agriculture, industry, and service activities. Such improvement in the return to the production factors is what allows the diversification of production and satisfies the new demand for manufactured products and services. When the evolution of the productive structure of an economy is analyzed, one generally observes that industrial and service activities are acquiring more and more importance in overall production. But this phenomenon is only a symptom of the changes in the productive system, where the truly relevant factor, from the point of view of development, is the increase in productivity and the enlargement and continued diversification of the range of goods and services produced.

The increase in productivity depends on how labor and the other production factors are combined, using the equipment, machinery, and production methods required within the production process. Through these mechanisms, knowledge is introduced and energy is applied. This process is usually called the "mode of development" by sociologists. Ultimately, development is a matter of the application of energy and knowledge by human capital in order to generate the final product, using the existing and available raw materials and capital goods.

In short, a long-term increase of production (per capita) is possible due to the application of technological innovation in the production process. Technological change allows for the introduction of new combinations of production factors, which result in an increase in the productivity of labor, which in turn generates an increase in income.

The beginning of the new period of economic integration, from the mid-1980s onwards, opened a new development scenario insofar as the growth models inspired by the fundamentalism of the market were accepted to be unworkable. This was not only because the decomposition of the Soviet Union and the fall of the Berlin Wall testified to the superiority of market economies when compared with planned economies, but also because the policies that were implemented in many developing countries, supported by international aid from developed countries and international organizations, proved to be a great failure (Boone, 1996; Hudson, 2004).

Since the 1980s, the ideas of Schumpeter and those who contributed during the postwar years to the creation of what Krugman (1990) called the "high development theory" (Young, 1928; Rosenstein-Rodan, 1943; Myrdal, 1957; Hirschman, 1958) have been revived. Among the different interpretations that emerged during the last 20 years, and of great importance, was the revitalization of Solow's ideas thanks to a new generation of thinkers, spearheaded by Romer (1986) and Lucas (1988), as Solow (1994) himself recognizes. At the same time, since the early 1980s, an interpretation has developed that we can call "endogenous development". It considers development as a territorial process (and not a functional one) that methodologically rests on case studies (and not on cross-sectional analysis), and that considers development policies to be more effective if designed and implemented by local actors (and not by the central administration).

Giorgio Fuá (1994), intellectually close to Abramovitz (1952), maintains that the capacity of an economy to develop depends on the immediate sources of growth, such as the size of the active population, the number of hours worked, and the availability of equipment and social overhead capital. However, what is most decisive for sustained and durable development are the factors that Fuá calls "structural", such as the entrepreneurial and organizational capacity, the skill and education of the population, the environmental resources, and the functioning of the institutions. As cases like Argentina, Nigeria, and Venezuela show, abundant natural and human resources are not sufficient; once resources run out, the entrepreneurial capacity weakens, technology becomes obsolete, and governance and institutions no longer facilitate transactions among actors, it is no longer possible to reach the desired level of development, and the economy may even enter a process of depression characterized by the destruction of physical capital and loss of human capital. The examples of Zambia, Jamaica, Mauritania, and Zimbabwe, on the other hand, show that high levels of investment (and the concurrent foreign aid) do not necessarily produce the desired results in terms of long-term growth, as Easterly (2001) points out.

Philippe Aydalot (1985), a follower of Perroux (1955) and Schumpeter (1934), adds that development processes have three fundamental features. One, instrumental in character, refers to the fact that the development agents should be flexible productive organizations. For example, small- and medium-sized enterprises are capable of overcoming the rigidities of large organizations, such as big enterprises that are organized hierarchically (Fordist), and can achieve better results especially in periods requiring a response to changes in the environment and the market. The second, more strategic in nature, defends diversity in technology, products, tastes, culture, and policies, as it facilitates the opening of multiple paths of development for different territories, depending on their development potential. The third feature, more operative in nature, maintains that development processes are the result of the introduction of innovation and knowledge through the investment of economic agents, a territorial process resulting from the interaction of the actors who form what Aydalot has termed the "innovative milieu".

From this perspective, development is not concentrated but diffused within the territory, as Giacomo Becattini (1979), who is very knowledgeable on Marshall's (1890) work, argues. The entrepreneur (as an individual or as a collective) plays a unique role in the development processes and becomes the motor force of growth and structural change, due to his creative capacity and innovative nature (Fuá, 1988). However, Fuá and Becattini add that firms are not isolated entities that exchange products and services in abstract markets, but rather they are located in specific territories and are part of productive systems which are firmly integrated within the local society. The society is self-organized for producing goods and services in a more efficient way, and this gives rise to industrial districts and local productive systems, which lead to the appearance of network economies in the territory, which in turn contribute to the development of the economy.

John Friedmann and Walter Stöhr take a broader view, and approach the development and dynamics of production systems from a territorial perspective, attaching great importance to the initiatives of local actors through their investment decisions and participation in the design and implementation of development policies (Friedmann and Weaver, 1979). Likewise, they argue that the economic progress of a territory is only possible when firms and other local actors interact among themselves, organize, and carry out investments aimed at the development of the local economy and society. Following this line of thought, they propose bottom-up development strategies that allow mobilizing and channeling the resources and capacities of the territory (Stöhr and Taylor, 1981).

Boisier (2003) sums up some of the features that characterize "endogeneity", according to the territorial development approach. First, he points out that endogeneity is understood as the capacity of the territory to save and invest the profits generated by the productive activity in the territory, and to promote the diversified development of the economy. Furthermore, endogeneity refers to the capacity of the territory to foster the technological progress of the productive fabric within the territorial system of innovation. Alternatively, endogeneity is understood as the capacity of cities and regions to adopt their own development strategy and carry out the necessary actions for achieving the objectives set by society, which is associated to processes of decentralization. Lastly, Boisier maintains that all of this is only possible when a culture of territorial identity that allows strengthening the competitiveness of local firms and the local economy exists, through the stimulation of intangible assets (such as brands, property rights, certificates of origin, and organizational quality).

The Functional Approach to Development

The notion of development, as we have seen, has profound roots in the theory of economic growth. Having been outside the sphere of interest of the main currents of economic thought for more than a century, with the exceptions of Marx and Schumpeter, development discourse was revived at the end of World War II (Fei and Ranis, 1997). The revitalization of the theory of economic growth took place as a consequence of the sensitivity to the postwar problems of unemployment and economic instability in the developed countries, as well as the interest among less developed countries in reaching the same living standards as the advanced countries, by which the former had been subdued during the colonial period that had just ended.

Capital accumulation and economic growth

Harrod's model (1939, 1948) served as the reference point for policies that attempted to make the processes of structural change more dynamic until well into the 1970s. Harrod and his followers argue that savings and investment are the forms that the process of capital accumulation takes. We can agree that the part of the income generated in an economy that is not dedicated to consumption purposes constitutes the savings of the productive system. The application of these savings to the acquisition of machinery and capital goods in more profitable activities and industries would increase productivity and, consequently, production and income.

As argued by Harrod (1939, 1948), the growth in output and income demands an increase in the capital stock and, therefore, new investment. If one accepts a fixed relation of capital/output

($k = k^*$), given by the state of technology, one can say that an increase in investment will produce an increase in the gross domestic product (GDP). Likewise, accepting that savings are a fixed proportion of total income (Y) and that new investments are determined by the level of savings, one can construct a simple growth model in which the growth rate of internal output (g) is directly related to the savings rate (s) and inversely related to the capital/output ratio. In other words, the growth rate has a direct relation with the productivity of capital.

$$g = s/k.$$

Under the additional hypothesis that all profits (B) are saved and that all wages are spent on consumer goods, if $s = B/Y$, then it follows that the rate of profit of capital is equal to the growth rate of capital and the growth rate of output.

Therefore, for an economy to grow, it has to save and invest a share of its income; the more it saves (and invests), the faster it grows. But, the actual rate at which it can grow for each level of savings depends on how productive investments are made. On the other hand, the rate of growth of output (and income), and therefore of employment, is limited by the growth rate of capital (that is, by the rate of profit). Therefore, the stimulus to investment and to the increase of income and employment is determined by the financial returns to capital.

However, as Harrod says, the path of growth that is determined by the growth of output does not imply that full employment of all production factors will result. In the long term, the expansion of output has a limit that is given by the rate of growth allowed for by the rate of population growth (the size of the labor force), capital accumulation, technological improvements (the state of technical knowledge), and the endowment of natural resources — this is called the "rate of natural growth" by Harrod (1939, p. 30). Put simply, this can be expressed as being equal to the growth rate of employment (l) and the increase in productivity due to technical progress (t). Thus, balanced growth with full employment can only result when the rate of growth is equal to the rate of growth of employment and of technological progress; but, as Harrod assumes that s,k,l,t evolve independently, this equality is only produced by chance.

This conclusion implies that the stability of economic growth is not guaranteed, as firms may invest above or below the savings rate of the economy; and neither is full employment, as the growth of the economy may lie below its natural growth (which generates unemployment) or tend to lie above it (leading to inflation). This conclusion calls for state intervention through economic policies using public investment and the monetary policy to neutralize the effects of the business cycle in developed economies. In the case of developing countries, their governments would intervene, especially, to increase savings when they are insufficient for achieving increased productivity, which is a requisite for increased income and employment.

The success of the Harrod–Domar model

Harrod's model had great success given that it inspired the restructuring policies of the European economies in the postwar period, and, especially, because the planning commissions that were constituted in many developing countries at the time turned to its conclusions when launching policies for growth promotion that would allow them to reduce the income gap with respect to developed countries.

Harrod's approach appears often in the economic literature (Ray, 1998) as the Harrod–Domar model, as a consequence of its similarity to an article published by Domar (1946) about economic growth, where he proposed that the production capacity was proportional to the stock of capital goods (buildings, plants, and machinery). According to Solow (1994), Domar's contribution has the advantage of focusing on the requisites necessary for reaching an equilibrium between supply and demand in the steady state.

The use of the Harrod–Domar model and its success is due to "its power of prediction, its amenability to statistical implementation, and its feasibility for theoretical extension" (Fei and Ranis, 1997). Its power of prediction allows it to propose that, given that GDP growth is proportional to the investment in capital goods, when an economy saves more (the higher s is) and/or the higher the productivity of capital (the lower k is), the faster its economic growth will be, which would increase the well-being of the population and their consumption, assuming population growth is controlled. Furthermore, given that the values of those parameters can be quantified easily, it is possible to identify the necessary amounts of savings and investment to reach the desired rate of growth. If, for instance, a country wishes to grow at an annual rate of 7%, it would require that both the investment rate and the savings rate stand at 21% of GDP, if it is supposed that the capital/output ratio is 3. But if savings only reach 15% of output, the "financial deficit" (as it is known in the economic literature) can only be covered by external aid or private investment from international organizations or other countries.

The weaknesses of the Harrod–Domar model

The new theory of development shares with the Harrod–Domar interpretation the idea that capital accumulation is one of the cornerstones in the development process, but shows profound differences with those currents of opinion present in universities and international organizations that call for freer markets and increasing investment in capital goods. Those currents of opinion, which maintain that the investment in buildings and machinery is the fundamental determinant of economic growth, have imposed their criterion on the development and aid policies of developing countries in Africa, Asia, and Latin America over the last four decades, but the results are not satisfactory (Easterly, 2001).

Above all, as economic thought has recognized since the time of Adam Smith and as Solow's contribution took up in an extraordinary way, the law of diminishing returns that affects all production factors makes the proposal for capital-intensive investment unfeasible. An economy's long-term growth on the basis of an increase in the proportion of one productive factor — in this case, capital — is limited by decreasing returns to scale. Therefore, the investment in equipment and capital goods is necessary but not sufficient for development, as the experiences of developing countries and the Soviet Union show.

The theory of endogenous development, on the other hand, takes a position that differs from the financial deficit interpretation, as it concedes a strategic role to local savings and the use of resources that are part of the economic development potential in the territory, leaving a secondary role in the development process to external savings. From the perspective of endogenous development, it is understood that development processes have to be anchored in the territory; local entrepreneurial capacity and investment, using local savings and resources, are strategic factors in development projects, as without them long-term growth would soon reach its limits. This aspect seems a crucial factor in less developed economies where, if local firms are scarce and, therefore, local savings are not converted into local investment projects, for all the "water falling from the sky" (in the form of international aid and foreign investments), "the earth won't bear fruit" (development will not take place).

Likewise, foreign savings that are channeled from other economies in one of the different forms of internationalization can suffer leakages, which diminish their long-term impact on the growth of the recipient economies (Todaro, 2000). In the case of capital inflows, in the form of loans or the acquisition of stocks and bonds, the external resources do not always produce a long-term increase in the volume of investment in the recipient country, principally so if the interest and dividend payments that have to be made are high. In the case of investments from multinational corporations, even though in the short-term the flow of investment brings an increase in income and employment, the results may be less stimulating than hoped for if the transfers of profit abroad are sizable, if national savings are the main basis for investment projects, or if oligopolistic practices are very developed in product and factor markets.

This type of surplus leakage has been interpreted as the explanation for the low growth rates and underdevelopment of the poorest economies by structural theorists during the 1960s and 1970s. Defenders of the dependency theory (such as Cardoso (1972), Frank (1966), and Furtado (1964)), who, as North (1990) points out, explained the bad results of the Latin American economies in the 1960s and 1970s, argued that the fundamental characteristic of the peripheral economies is their dependent structure which inhibits their autonomous growth. The Economic Commission for Latin America and the Caribbean (ECLAC) argued in its 2002 report, *Globalization and Development*, that the inequalities in the levels of development between countries are fundamentally due to international factors, among which the "extremely high concentration of technological progress in the developed countries" stands out (ECLAC, 2002).

The "Discovery" of Technological Change

Solow (1956) gave a convincing answer to the question of economic growth when he asserted that increased investment in equipment goods does not, by itself, produce economic development. It is technological progress that increases the productivity of labor, which is equivalent to saying that it allows for savings of the scarce factor: labor. For this, he constructed a growth model, probably in response to the ideas of Harrod (particularly those that concern the instability of the development process), and, using the instruments of marginal analysis, made a seminal contribution to the neoclassical theory of growth and introduced technology as an independent variable into the growth equation.

In this way, in the mid-1950s Solow (1956) and Swan (1956) could present the question of economic progress in a simple fashion that analyzed the behavior of income as a consequence of the use of disposable quantities of human resources and equipment goods. In the simplest version, an aggregate production function is used that considers only two production factors: K_t, capital; and L_t, labor. If one assumes that the production function is of a Cobb–Douglas type, where $0 < a < 1$, the expression would be

$$Y_t = AK_t^a L_t^{1-a},$$

where a is the share of capital in the GDP, $(1 - a)$ is the share of labor, and A is the level of technology that picks up technological innovations and all institutional and environmental elements which favor their generation.

Assuming that technological progress is not produced, output growth is only possible as a result of an increase in factor endowment. Given that the amount of labor per worker is fixed, the per capita production function shows decreasing returns in the accumulation factor, K_t. This means that, as the share of capital per worker increases, the per capita output grows at a decreasing pace (Valdés, 1999).

The assumption of diminishing returns to capital implies that in the long term the growth rate of productivity tends towards zero, as investment is directed towards activities which are less and less productive and which, therefore, produce lower and lower returns, thus discouraging the investor. In other words, the neoclassical model tells us that economies tend towards the steady state, in which only the reproduction of installed capital and the replacement of labor are covered, all variables grow at a rate close to zero, and economic growth therefore comes to an end.

The only way to make this result compatible with the empirical evidence of the growth of the more advanced economies during the 1950s and 1960s is to accept the fact that the production system changes (the production function is shifted upward over time, in economic jargon) as a consequence of technological advancement. Therefore, in the neoclassical growth models, A grows exogenously, which generates an exogenous increase in productivity.

During the transition of an economy to the steady state, the growth in output and income is associated with the investment in machinery and capital goods and, hence, with savings; but once the steady state has been reached, economic growth will continue as technological knowledge extends over time. There would exist a synergetic relation between technological change and investment to the point where the latter would act as the transmitter of growth, particularly when capital goods incorporate knowledge and new ideas.

This interpretation has two main weaknesses. One is technical in nature, as the Solow–Swan model does not explain how innovations are created, what their origin is, or how they are introduced into the productive system, but rather simply accepts that technological progress is external and at the disposal of all enterprises which together make up the production system. This is an important limitation, as innovations are the principal explanatory element of the argument. This weakness can be overcome by making endogenous technological progress, as Arrow (1962) proved when he considered learning effects or "learning by doing" as the source of technological change. The other is more ideological and affects the neoclassical interpretation, as the hypothesis regarding the existence of diminishing returns to scale leads one to predict that poor countries would grow at a higher rate than rich countries, causing a convergence in their income levels. As previously discussed, empirical evidence shows that this conclusion cannot be generalized for all types of economies, as the appearance of increasing returns to scale neutralizes the tendency towards the steady state.

The endogenous growth models that have appeared since the publication of the work by Romer (1986) are a variant of the Solow model and signify a step forward in the effort to accommodate formalization and reality, as they maintain the thesis that the existence of diminishing returns is, in fact, only one of the possible alternatives in the growth process. Furthermore, this view of growth considers that technological knowledge should be included within the production system because it should be considered as a product depending on the companies' investment decisions and, therefore, conditioned by the profits expected by the companies. Hence, this approach overcomes the limitation of accepting that technology is external to the growth process.

Thus, Romer, based on Arrow's model, argues that growth is produced as a consequence of an increase in the aggregate stock of capital and knowledge that firms' investment generates, producing economies of scale that are external to the companies. Lucas (1988) presents another variation of Solow's model, pointing out that an increase in productivity is also the result of an increase in human capital stock which generates externalities in the production system, interacting with the knowledge generated within the company. Grossman and Helpman (1994), following Schumpeter and Solow, argue that technological progress is the force behind improvements in the standard of living and consider industrial innovations to be the engine of growth, whilst the quest for monopoly returns provides an explanation for the introduction of innovations. The introduction of capital goods and the diffusion of knowledge within the production system are fostered by the investment in R&D; therefore, costs are reduced and productivity is increased.

Economic growth can continue through time as long as investment in capital goods, in human capital, and in R&D generates increasing returns to scale through the diffusion of innovations and knowledge within the production system. An improvement in the quality of human resources by training and education, the introduction of capital goods that incorporate new technology, and the accumulation of knowledge from the investment in R&D produce an innovation effect that spreads through the entire milieu (spillover effect). Knowledge is transferred from some companies to others through a network of formal and informal relations that exist between them, through the interaction between clients and suppliers, and through the labor market. All firms, even those competing with more innovative firms, benefit from the diffusion of knowledge without increasing their production cost. Therefore, the whole economy profits from the increasing returns to scale that the individual investment decisions of enterprises generate.

The idea of obtaining increasing returns to scale in the economy through the diffusion of innovation and knowledge was introduced by Alfred Marshall at the end of the 19th century, when he defined the external economies of scale that are generated as a consequence of the interactions between the enterprises which form the productive system. Its current application allows the possibility to keep the classical economic analytical instruments, such as the supply and demand curves, in order to explain how increasing returns to scale are generated by investments.

The endogenous growth models show important differences with the neoclassical growth model as used since the 1950s. First of all, they maintain that there is no single development path which economies would necessarily have to take, as Rostow (1960) claimed, but rather that different paths of growth exist for economies to follow, as their growth rates may be decreasing, increasing, or constant. Furthermore, the transition to the steady state is not an irreversible process for all economies, as it depends on the entrepreneurial and innovative capacity within the production system and on institutional change. Finally, the growth rate and the per capita income level of the economies are not inversely related, so endogenous growth models do not predict the convergence of different economies, as research undertaken in the last quarter of the 20th century proves.

What distances the endogenous growth models from the traditional growth models brings the former closer to the endogenous development approach. The viewpoint, perhaps optimistic, that productive systems assemble a collection of material and immaterial factors that allows regional and local economies to follow a differentiated path of growth is shared by the theories of endogenous growth and endogenous development. They also agree on the interpretation that growth is a result of productivity increases generated endogenously by the gradual introduction and diffusion of innovation within productive processes.

The endogenous development approach is not necessarily opposed to the new growth theory and, based on case studies of territorial development, has attempted to analyze the mechanisms of capital accumulation and the forces that lay behind what Nelson (1999) calls "the immediate sources of growth". Economic growth is a process that is characterized by uncertainty and chance, and is subject to the changing market conditions and the actors' investment decisions; therefore, it should be understood as an evolutionary process. Companies make their investment decisions keeping in mind their own capacities and the opportunities that the territory where they are located offers them, which is why growth analysis can be enriched when it also includes the territorial dimension.

Furthermore, long-term economic growth depends not only on the resource endowments of a territory and the capacity of an economy to save and invest, but also on the functioning of mechanisms through which capital accumulation is expanded (the organization of the productive system, the diffusion of innovations, the urban development of the territory, and the changes in the institutions) and the interaction produced between these forces. Therefore, in order to interpret and explain economic growth, it is necessary to specify that the behavior of productivity also depends on the results of forces and processes that the production function does not explicitly capture. This means that the law of diminishing returns to scale needs to be amended to include increasing returns to scale resulting from the interaction of the forces of development.

Finally, the analysis of cases of territorial development shows that the decisions made by public and private actors reflect the local framework of interests and institutions, and have very important effects on the forces of development. Therefore, this approach gives preferential treatment to the "bottom-up" actions in development processes, as opposed to the "top-down" approach which characterizes traditional policies.

Territorial Development: An Evolutionary Approach

The endogenous development approach is a useful interpretation in this sense. It argues that economic development comes about as a result of the processes and mechanisms determining capital accumulation: the flexible organization of production, the diffusion of innovation, a territory's urban dynamic, and the change and adaptation of institutions (Vázquez-Barquero, 2002).

How do the forces that facilitate long-term growth of productivity and economic development work? What are the mechanisms through which the tendency towards the steady state is neutralized? How can the determinant forces of the accumulation of capital and knowledge be activated? How do the hidden economies that exist within productive and urban systems emerge? What about the reduction of transaction and production costs caused by the institutional model?

One of the central forces of the capital accumulation process is the organization of the productive system, as seen in advanced countries and in late developed economies over the last 30 years (Garofoli, 1983; Scott, 1988). The question lies not in whether the productive system of a locality or territory is formed by large or small firms, but rather in the organization of the production system and its effects on the behavior of productivity and competitiveness.

Thus, local productive systems, clusters, and industrial districts are a production organization model based on the division of labor between firms and the creation of a local exchange system that produces greater productivity and economic growth. Furthermore, it is an organization model that generates increasing returns when the interaction between firms permits the emergence of scale economies which are concealed in the productive systems, ultimately one of the development potentials of the local economies (Courlet, 2008).

The backbone of a local productive system (particularly in the case of industrial clusters) is the existence of a network of industrial firms. An industrial network (Hakansson and Johanson, 1993) is made up of actors (the firms in the local productive system), resources (human, natural, and infrastructural), economic activities (productive, commercial, technical, financial, social, and legal), and their interrelations (interdependence and exchanges). The relations within the network are conducive not only to the exchange of products and services among the actors, but also to the exchange of technological knowledge and behavioral codes (Becattini, 1997).

Furthermore, the adoption of more flexible forms of organization in large firms and groups of firms makes them more efficient and competitive, and new territorial strategies involving networks of subsidiary plants make them more autonomous and more integrated within the territory. The enhanced organizational flexibility of large firms allows them to make more efficient use of the territorial attributes and so obtain a competitive advantage within the markets (Bellandi, 2001; Vázquez-Barquero, 1999). Furthermore, multinational corporations have embedded themselves as leading partners in knowledge-intensive clusters of developed regions and cities (Dunning, 2001).

The formation and expansion of networks and flexible firm systems, the interaction of the firms with local actors, and strategic alliances allow the productive systems to generate economies of scale (external and/or internal, depending on the case) not only in production, but also in research and development (when the alliances affect innovation). In this way, firms reduce their transaction and production costs.

The introduction and diffusion of innovation and knowledge is another mechanism for increased productivity and economic development, since it stimulates economic growth and a structural change in the productive system (Schumpeter, 1934). Economic development and the dynamics of production depend on the introduction and diffusion of innovation and knowledge, which foster the transformation and renovation of the local productive system. Aydalot (1986) maintains that local firms are the instrument through which innovations and knowledge are introduced into development processes. Firms' creativity is conditioned by the territory's experience and tradition. In other words, knowledge — accumulated in firms and organizations — is one of the mainstays of development, and the local milieu may serve as an incubator of innovation (Camagni and Maillat, 2006).

From this perspective, innovation is a collective learning process among the actors within the milieu in which firms make investment and location decisions (Cooke and Morgan, 1998). Thus, we are dealing with learning processes, rooted in society and the territory, in which coded knowledge (or production "recipes") and tacit knowledge incorporated into human resources are diffused within the network as a result of relations among the actors. Consequently, processes of technological change and innovation are interactive, and regional systems of innovation play a strategic role in both the learning process and the diffusion of innovation (Asheim *et al.*, 2003; Lundvall, 1992).

The adoption of innovations allows firms to widen their range of products, create larger groups, and construct smaller plants in a more efficient or economical manner, and so reinforce internal economies of scale. Furthermore, innovations allow firms to define and carry out strategies that are focused on exploring and widening new product and factor markets. The adaptation of technologies favors differentiation of production and creates scope economies. In short, the introduction and diffusion of innovations and knowledge leads to an improvement in the stock of technological knowledge of the productive system — which creates external economies — for the benefit of all types of firms in the system. To sum up, the diffusion of innovation and knowledge by the productive fabric allows each and every firm within the cluster or productive system to obtain economies (both internal and external) of scale and scope. Thus, the adoption of innovations is stimulated, and the productivity and competitiveness of the local firms and economies are increased.

In today's scenario, which is characterized by the globalization of production and exchange as well as greater service activities, cities continue to be a preferred space for economic development, given that these are where investment decisions are made and where industrial and service firms are mainly located (Lasuen, 1973). Historical evidence shows that sustained per capita income growth is accompanied by higher levels of urbanization, specifically in its initial phases. Particularly after the Industrial Revolution in England, increasing productivity and expansion of urban production are driven by the introduction of innovations. Changes in firm activities and city systems can be understood as the temporal and spatial effect of adopting innovations. It was Perroux (1955) who, by means of the growth pole theory, argued that economic development and urbanization are the consequence of innovation. Economic development and urbanization are, therefore, two sides of the same coin.

Cities are a place for endogenous development. They generate externalities that lead to increasing returns; they have a diversified productive system that propels the economic dynamic; they provide space for networking, in which relations among actors lead to the diffusion of knowledge; and they stimulate the innovation and learning processes of firms. Cities are places for the creation and development of new industrial and service spaces, due to their capacity to generate externalities and allow hidden economies to emerge (Hall, 1993).

Development acquires significance within the territory and, in organized societies, is articulated through the urban system. A well-structured urban system, made up of city networks, encourages the exchange of goods and services, stimulates the performance of firms, and promotes a satisfactory evolution of the labor market; while the presence of adequate economic (transportation, communications, and energy) and social (health and education) infrastructure facilitates the appearance and development of external economies and, therefore, sustainable development. As suggested by Camagni (1992), at the present time this can be conceived in terms of polycentric urban models, a sort of urban armature which tends to function more and more as a network.

Last of all, development processes are not isolated, but rather have deep institutional and cultural roots (North, 1990, 1994). The development of an economy is always led by the local actors who organize themselves in order to carry out their projects. Thus, cities and regions stimulate the development of specific forms of organization and institutions that respond to the needs of economic and social actors, and that will either facilitate or obstruct economic activity.

The emergence and consolidation of local productive systems have come about in areas where social and cultural systems are strongly rooted in the territory. Moreover, increased competition in the markets requires efficient responses and the strategic cooperation of actors and local organizations; and, as pointed out by Cooke (2002), the development of clusters in "knowledge-based" economies requires social capital (norms of reciprocity and trust) and collective learning. Thus, the emergence of multiple institutions from the plurality of actors has led to effective strategic responses to the new needs posed by the economic, social, and political dynamics. In the most innovative cities and regions, institutional relations have become more complex and the number of actors and institutions has multiplied. This has led some authors (Amin and Thrift, 1993) to refer to this phenomenon as "institutional thickness".

Economic development, therefore, takes strength in those territories with evolved, complex, and flexible institutional systems. The strategic relevance here lies in the fact that institutional change and development allows for the reduction of transaction and production costs, strengthens trust among the economic and social actors, improves entrepreneurial capacity, strengthens networks and cooperation between actors, and potentiates learning and interaction mechanisms. In other words, institutions condition the behavior of productivity and, therefore, the economic development process.

Finally, the diffusion of innovations and knowledge, a flexible organization of production, and urban and institutional development generate increased efficiency in the performance of the productive system. Each one of these mechanisms becomes an efficiency factor in the process of capital accumulation to the extent that it stimulates economies of scale, external economies, and reductions in transaction costs, all of which bring about increased productivity and returns.

Development: A Systemic Process

The forces of development are not autonomous mechanisms that directly exert their influence on the functioning of capital accumulation and on increased productivity. On the contrary, these processes are related among themselves and mutually affect each other to the extent that they may reinforce combined effects or neutralize the other. A malfunction in the organization of production or in the diffusion of innovation and knowledge negatively affects and weakens the capacity of other forces to develop, thus limiting the impact on productivity growth and development. Therefore, the sustainability of development depends on the direction and strength of the effects generated by the interaction between the development forces.

The effect on the organization of production

As previously pointed out, the way in which production is organized conditions the mechanisms that facilitate increased productivity and economic progress. The organization of the production system is more efficient when the diffusion of innovations, the urban and infrastructural development, and the local institutions respond to the needs of firms and organizations.

Innovations condition the internal organization of firms and the organization of production systems. The introduction of new products and new production methods requires new forms of internal organization of firms that make them more efficient. This has happened in the car industry, from the early 20th century when Ford invented the assembly line to the present era where we see subcontracting and outsourcing of parts of the production process to suppliers located in an industrial park. The application of new technologies allows for the separation of the production process into parts, the specialization in their production by enterprises, and the reengineering of the configuration of the production system for the final product; this is true in the case of industrial districts as well as in that of networks of firms located around a big firm.

Cities are the physical space of firms and local productive systems, as they supply the resources, goods, and services necessary for them to function. The city is the space in which an innovative and entrepreneurial atmosphere is created, technological knowledge is spread, and the meeting points for the company network are located. This results in the emergence of all kinds of economies and a reduction in firm costs.

Finally, the institutional development of the territory in which enterprises carry out their activities also conditions the form of organization of production in the production system. Where strong connections between the population and firms are developed, trust between organizations arises; this favors the exchange of products and information as well as fosters the spread of knowledge and information among local companies, which reduces transaction costs and activates the capacity to create and diffuse technological knowledge. Moreover, on the basis of contracts and formal agreements between enterprises, economic transactions and exchanges are carried out and the organizational dynamic takes shape. When strategic agreements between firms are reached, mechanisms that lead to economies of scale in the production and commercialization of goods and services, to economies of scope through the differentiation of production, and to a reduction in production costs multiply due to the enlargement of the innovative capacity.

The stimulus to the diffusion of innovations

As pointed out, the diffusion of innovations and knowledge is a determining mechanism for the increase in productivity and competitiveness of firms and territories. In order for the creation and diffusion of innovations to occur, it is necessary that all of the forces of development create an environment favorable to innovation and change.

The organization of production in the territory conditions the functioning of the processes of innovation. When the production system is organized in networks of firms, the exchange of knowledge and technology is made easier, and, as a result, so is the access to innovations through exchanges and formal and informal contracts. Furthermore, the value chain, on the basis of which production activities are organized, conditions the relations between enterprises and the type of innovation introduced into the production processes in such a way that technological changes adopted by some companies condition the others' innovations. Finally, resistance to the diffusion of innovations is introduced into the production system when the organizations are not very flexible and firms show a scarce capacity for learning.

The introduction and diffusion of innovations is also conditioned by the characteristics of the institutional system: the more flexible and proactive the networks of actors are, the stronger the mechanisms of innovation will be. It is worth remembering that the creation and diffusion of innovations is an interactive phenomenon, based on the collective learning of firms, that depends on the creative capacity and culture of the social and institutional systems of a territory. Additionally, the creation and diffusion of innovations is determined by the disposition of a favorable socio-institutional environment for innovation and by the functioning of the territorial system of innovation. Lastly, the institutional environment determines how the mechanisms of cooperation will work together via contracts and formal agreements, and therefore also conditions the creation of innovations and the diffusion of knowledge. In this sense, North (1990) points out that strong interactions exist between institutions and innovations that determine the development path of an economy.

Landes (1998) argues that the institutions in China during the Middle Ages limited the diffusion of knowledge and technology, pointing to the all-encompassing power of the Imperial Court and the mandarins who not only suffocated political dissidence but also hindered innovations (including technical innovations) when these threatened the status quo. This explains why China has not led the European countries in industrial development, even though it spawned many advancements such as, for instance, the application of hydraulic machines for hemp spinning in the 12th century, 500 years before England did; the production of 125,000 tons of iron at the end of the 11th century, a volume not reached in England until seven centuries later; and other great inventions such as the wheelbarrow, the compass, paper, the printing press, and gunpowder.

In Silicon Valley, as pointed out by Saxenian (1994), the U.S. Department of Defense has stimulated the liberalization of licenses whenever a product or process is developed with the support of public funding, assuring that the invention can be used by anyone possibly connected to the government-financed programs. In addition, Stanford University has fostered cooperation between firms, supported young entrepreneurs such as Hewlett and Packard, and created a scientific park to stimulate the creation and diffusion of innovations and knowledge.

Finally, cities are and have historically been the space in which innovations are created, the learning processes take place, and the processes of the diffusion of knowledge and technology are put forth. Agglomeration, in turn, allows the necessary economies of scale for the production of innovations.

The forces of urban dynamics

Cities are the central space for endogenous development. Cities contain hidden economies that are associated with agglomeration and externalities, which favor the increase of productivity and growth. Empirical research and historical studies show that a direct relation exists between agglomeration and growth. Ciccone and Hall (1996) established that, when doubling the occupational density in a county in the United States, the average productivity per worker increases by 6%; and that by doing so in Europe at the NUTS 3 level (Nomenclature of Territorial Units for Statistics at the third level), a 4.6% average increase results. During the Industrial Revolution in Europe in the 19th century, growth increased significantly whilst the rate of urbanization increased and industrial clusters were formed.

The economic efficiency that urban development brings is reinforced by the effect which the mechanisms determining the accumulation of knowledge exert. The spread of innovations through the production, organizational, and institutional systems creates a new economic and urban dynamic. The introduction and spread of innovations through the production system leads to an increase in productivity and income, which generates an increase in the demand for urban services among companies and citizens. Consequently, innovations in organization, processes, and transport stimulate the urbanization process and diversify the urban functions within the network of cities; therefore, the urban system becomes more polycentric.

Furthermore, the organization of production and the changes involved also condition urban development. When more flexible forms prevail in the organization of production, such as industrial districts or new organizational models of big enterprises, the rules governing the firms' location change and the urban system becomes more dynamic and tends to be more polycentric. In this sense, the organization of production has a direct effect on the process of urbanization.

History, culture, and institutions characterize a city and exert a strong conditioning role in urban development. The existence of an institutional context (norms, behavior, and organizations) that is flexible and adequate for the needs and demands of the economic, political, and social actors reduces uncertainty and attracts investment, which fosters the process of urbanization. The dynamic of economic development requires changes in the local institutions; this signifies both increase and change in the public and social services and the attraction of private service enterprises, which generate and stimulate urban development. However, these processes are not linear and frequently encounter institutional and social resistance to change, which has an effect on the process of urbanization. Finally, cities can be understood as a network of actors who interact among themselves and in which the institutions create the necessary conditions for reaching agreements that favor cooperation. These institutional mechanisms favor the processes of investment and urban development.

The conditions for institutional change

The development of institutions and their changes are one of the basic mechanisms of the processes of economic growth and institutional change, as they facilitate the interaction between firms and actors as well as reduce the risk and uncertainty in exchange, which help the functioning of the economic system. So, institutions emerge, change, and transform as a result of the historical, cultural, and associative conditions during each period of the process of economic development. Institutions are therefore, among other factors, determined by technological change, the organization of production model, and the specific conditions of the territory.

Technological change directly affects the growth process, creating new needs and demands for institutions in order to ease the capital accumulation process. Innovations transform the environment in which production activities are carried out, and permit the emergence of new business opportunities and new paths for firms' development; this situation demands adequate institutions and new regulatory controls. When innovations lead to new activities that result in changed power relations and new agreements between firms and actors, an adequate regulation for the new undertaking is needed.

A good example of such changes is the transformation that resulted in new norms and regulations for the new activities which emerged as a result of the introduction of new information and communication technologies in Europe. During the 1980s and 1990s, in Spain as well as in England, France, and Italy, the production of services using information and communication technologies — such as in the information and informatics, telecommunications, financial and banking service, and business service industries — increased at a fast pace. This growth was accompanied by the adoption of new laws and norms that regulated both the old and new sectors, and their implementation was accompanied by an intense struggle for market share among companies. Even as we speak, the introduction of new telephones and personal computers is changing the norms, conventions, and codes of behavior among populations and organizations.

Consequently, the forms of organization and their transformation determine the appropriate institutions that facilitate relations between firms and organizations. In cases where the production is carried out by Fordist enterprises and groups of firms, i.e. the hierarchy determines the relations and exchange between production units, norms and contracts are used to guarantee the agreements. But in cases where production is organized through industrial districts, custom and trust shape the relations between the firms within the network. Lastly, in agreements and strategic alliances between enterprises, explicit and codified relations require them to be arranged through contracts that do not exclude mechanisms of trust.

Furthermore, institutions adopt specific forms in each territory owing to the differences in their respective technological and economic history, to cultural differences, and to differences between actors and forms of association. The city is a constructed space in which modes of development have historically sedimented over time, just as norms of behavior and cultural traits have conditioned the evolution and dynamic of the institutions as the growth process evolves. The city is a space of networks of actors whose interactions and exchange activities have shaped the codes of behavior as well as the establishment of rules based on trust. As the behavior of the actors takes on strategic forms, agreements tend to be formal and relations are increasingly subject to explicit, previously agreed upon rules. Finally, changes in the urban system facilitate the emergence of new demands for rules and norms of behavior that regulate local and international relations between cities.

Chapter 3

Endogenous Development

Since the early 1980s, the use of the term "endogenous development" has spread successfully, and it is now widely accepted by academics and economic and social actors. What is perhaps most attractive about the term is its usefulness for interpreting the development process of cities, regions, and countries at a time when, as a result of increased economic integration, great transformations in the economy and society are taking place.

At the same time, endogenous development should also be recognized as a concept that is used by authors who work in different fields of the social sciences as well as by public actors, all coming from different schools of thought, and so the term has acquired a broader significance. Many of these authors and actors probably share in their criticism of the traditional neoclassical growth theory, the approach which provided the arguments for the actions of international organizations devoted to development in the 40 years following World War II. Yet, their conceptual differences should not be ignored, since policy actions are conditioned by the conceptual view of development.

The purpose of this chapter is to discuss some issues associated with the endogenous development approach. How did this interpretation of development emerge? What are the different views of endogenous development? Are they converging into a general interpretation of endogenous development? What are the strengths and weaknesses of this approach? Is it useful for the analysis of the economic reality? What is the relation between endogenous development and the new development policy?

Emergence of the Endogenous Development Paradigm

In the early 1980s, two research programs converged that gave rise to the formation of the paradigm known as endogenous development. One focused on theoretical and policy matters, and was based on studies originally designed to search for a development concept that would help define and implement public actions in backward countries and regions (Friedmann and Douglas, 1978; Stöhr, 1981, 1985). The other was the outcome of the analyses of both the industrial clusters in Italy (Becattini, 1979; Brusco, 1982; Fuá, 1983) and the endogenous industrial development in Southern European late developed countries (Courlet, 2008; Garofoli, 1992; Konsolas, 1990; Reis, 1987; Vázquez-Barquero, 1988). The interpretation was improved with such important contributions as the "discovery" of more flexible models in the organization of production (Piore and Sabel, 1984; Porter, 1990; Scott, 1988), the introduction of networking within the economic analysis of the territories (Johannisson, 1995; Hakansson and Johanson, 1993), the understanding of innovation as an evolutionary process (Dosi, 1988; Maillat, 1995), and the acceptance that culture and institutional change play a strategic role within development processes (North, 1981, 1986).

Endogenous development is an interpretation with distinguishing traits. When a comparison with the endogenous growth theory is made, analogies and differences appear. Both of them share important analytical conclusions: there are differences in the economies' path of growth when the available resources, the capacity for savings and investment, and the social and institutional environment are different; it is possible to obtain increasing returns to scale in the economy through the introduction and diffusion of innovations; technical progress and innovation are endogenous to the growth process; and there is room for industrial and regional policies in order to stimulate the processes of economic growth and structural change.

However, the endogenous development approach involves a more complex analysis of the process of capital accumulation than does the theory of endogenous growth. The former argues that the process of growth and structural change should be analyzed as a territorial process, and not as a functional one. Growth is a process in which the institutions and social organization of the territory play a strategic role. The forces of development interact within the development process and their synergetic effect conditions economic returns, productivity, and growth. Finally, the endogenous development approach argues that policy is important in development processes, and that local actors should play an important role in designing and implementing policy actions.

Endogenous development is a complex concept that tries to analyze the process of development from different perspectives. The propositions of self-centered development and bottom-up development are a reaction to the dissatisfaction of the development model prevalent during the 1960s and 1970s. The human development approach became increasingly popular during the 1990s, thanks to the support given by international organizations through their development initiatives in backward localities and regions. The new forms of international cooperation and aid helped to implement projects that were focused on fighting against poverty and on fostering entrepreneurial development through the use of the population's capabilities.

The self-centered development view and the human development approach are probably optimistic (and, certainly, utopian) interpretations. The evolutionary approach to development, however, analyzes economic growth and structural change within places and territories in an attempt to explain the process of capital accumulation and the competitiveness of cities and regions; thus, this approach makes the theory of endogenous development more robust. But, perhaps, the development policy actions have been better received by local actors because they permit better identification of the ways for fighting against poverty, for job creation, and for the improvement of local firms' competitiveness.

The endogenous development approach argues that the territory is no longer simply a place where resources and economic activities are located. Its analysis explains how economic viability is possible due to the generation of a surplus, and how it is affected by the external

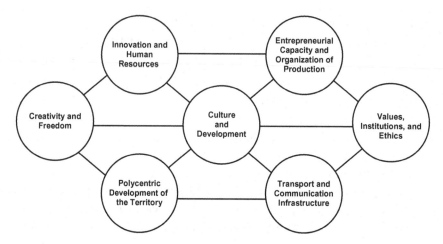

Figure 3.1   Endogenous Development of the Territory: Explanatory Factors.

economies of scale and the reduction of production and transaction costs. On the other hand, the territory can be understood as an agent for transformation because local firms and other actors interact in order to develop the economy and society. In this way, endogenous development can be understood as a process of economic growth and structural change that is led by the local community, and that employs its development potential to improve the population's standard of living (see Figure 3.1).

In sum, at least three dimensions are identified by the endogenous development approach. One is an economic dimension characterized by a specific production system that allows local entrepreneurs to efficiently use the productive factors, introduce innovation and creativity, and reach targeted productivity levels, thus making them competitive in the marketplace. Another is an institutional dimension in which economic and social actors are integrated into a system of institutions and create a complex network of relations, thus incorporating social and cultural values into the development process. Yet another is a political dimension, instrumented through local initiatives, which leads to the creation of a local environment that stimulates production and brings about sustainable development.

Self-Development with Local Initiatives

Endogenous development is often associated with the capacity of a local community to use the existing development potential within the territory, and so respond to the challenges at a given historical moment. At present, the challenges are due to the important effects of the globalization process in terms of the spatial division of labor. This view obeys a territorial approach towards development and gives a positive, often optimistic, valuation of the role played by the development potential existing in all types of territories. This allows the local communities to give an adequate economic response, and so satisfy the needs of the population (Vázquez-Barquero, 1993; Alburquerque, 2001).

Autonomous development of the territory

This is a territorial approach, based on the assumption that each local community has been historically shaped by the relations and interests of its social groups, the construction of its own identity, and its own culture which distinguishes it from other communities (Massey, 1984). Thus, the territory can be understood as the network of interests of a territorial community, which allows us to perceive the community as a development agent that maintains and develops the integrity and interests of the territory in the processes of structural change and economic progress. This concept explains the reality in all types of territories, as Scott (1988) recognizes when pointing out the importance of culture and local identity in the development processes of more dynamic metropolitan areas. Saraceno (2000) agrees with this view when analyzing today's transformation and productive differentiation process in rural areas.

Therefore, at a specific moment in time, a territorial community, of its own initiative, may find new ideas and projects that will allow the population to use their resources and find solutions to their problems and needs. The local actors, through their initiatives and investment decisions as well as participation in designing and managing policies, contribute towards the development and productive dynamic of a locality, country, or territory (Friedmann and Weaver, 1979). These "development from below" strategies, which allow for the mobilization and channeling of the resources and existing capacities within the territory, lead to economic progress when the local actors interact, organize themselves, and carry out their initiatives in a consistent and coordinated manner (Stöhr and Taylor, 1981).

This interpretation has received the support of those who believe that development is not imported, but rather produced by the economic and social resources and effort of the local communities. To eliminate poverty and create jobs, the most efficient strategy would be to re-establish an autonomous development pattern that would drive the local development potential and stimulate small agricultural production, small- and medium-sized firms, and handicraft industries. The strategy would detain the massive urbanization process and involve the participation of the population in the development process (Gore, 1984; Kitching, 1982).

Development, solidarity, and democracy

This populist view of development is recurrent, particularly after the three great technological revolutions: in the early 19th century, as a reaction to the dehumanization that industrialization and urbanization represented; in the first third of the 20th century in industrialized economies, which were faced with unemployment and the effects of a financial and industrial crisis following the electrical revolution; and at the present time, as a reaction to the impact of globalization on inequality and social exclusion.

This approach explains why, in recent decades, socially sustainable development has received special attention in the sense that development strategies and policies stimulate, above all, the start-up and development of economic initiatives based on solidarity, the autonomy of local communities and therefore of countries, and the use of the local development potential. Giordani (2004) argues that the social economy approach overcomes the separation between capital and labor and introduces solidarity within the economic process; and he proposes a new development approach for Venezuela that includes the public sector (government), the private sector (business), and the social economy sector. From this point of view, solidarity is at the center of production, accumulation, distribution, and consumption.

The social economy appears spontaneously in answer to social deficiencies (in employment, housing, and quality of life) that neither the market nor the state is able to address (Toscano Sánchez, 2000). In this economy, projects focused on social well-being are carried out by the cooperatives, micro and small firms, savings banks, and non-profit organizations. What counts here is the work done by those members involved in management, and the decisions are made democratically among members. The social economy is a development culture that allows for the integration of population groups at risk of exclusion, takes advantage of the existing development potential within the territory, and spurs on production and employment.

The demand for greater participation on behalf of the local actors and civil society has led to development initiatives based on direct citizens' participation in the decision-making process, of which the "participative budget" of Porto Alegre, in Rio Grande do Sul, Brazil, is a good example. This approach to local development is based on the idea that there is no true development if the citizens — the beneficiaries of the development — do not participate in the design, implementation, and follow-up of the development initiatives. The point, therefore, is to provide a methodology that will facilitate citizen participation, instead of other methodologies that are hierarchical in nature (like regional development planning undertaken by the central administrations).

Self-development and local initiatives

In sum, the populist vision of endogenous development maintains that what is important about development today is its autonomous nature, based on the use of a territory's own resources. Development can therefore occur in any locality or territory, since all territories have a development potential. The point is to use local resources in projects that are designed and managed by the citizens and local organizations themselves in such a way that the process and the local development initiatives would be controlled by the local actors.

This is an optimistic interpretation of the development process. It suggests that the needs of the population would be well served (and the success of the local initiatives guaranteed) when the population designs, takes responsibility for, and controls the projects, no matter how limited the means available and/or investments made. Furthermore, it values the usefulness of all types of resources available in a territory, and considers that the resources and economic potential of the territory constitute the capacities on which the productive process is based. It also suggests that development policies should be implemented by local action groups, as the most efficient public actions are those designed and managed from the bottom, which gives a democratic value to development policy and to citizens' decisions for satisfying their needs.

This approach, however, has important limitations. Above all, it fails to recognize the fact that the development process depends on capital accumulation, and that savings and investment are required mechanisms for assuring long-term economic and social progress. In any case, it does not pay enough attention to the mechanisms that facilitate the economic sustainability of development. The introduction and diffusion of innovations and knowledge within the production processes is not well articulated in this approach, and the importance of the role played by the organization of production for obtaining increasing returns is poorly dealt with. Last of all, it is an autarkic approach to development, and the local economies are not discussed within the context of national and international productive systems; therefore, the policy actions are not well designed.

Human Development and the Population's Capabilities

Development processes are conditioned by the territory's institutions and culture, as acknowledged by sociologists (Weber, 1905; Putnam, 1993; Fukuyama, 1995), historians (Landes, 1998; North, 1990), and economists (Lewis, 1955; Guiso *et al.*, 2006). Culture embodies the values, norms, and principles that are transmitted from one generation to another through the family, religion, and social groups, and can either facilitate or block the economic outcome. Economic development depends on cultural factors such as the work ethic, savings capacity, honesty, tenacity, and tolerance, as well as on the norms and institutions that regulate the relations between people and territorial organizations.

Development of the population's capabilities

Culture leads people's behavior. Nevertheless, culture is more than just an instrument that facilitates and influences the development process, as the mechanisms favoring the development process have to do with the projection and use of individual and collective capabilities as well as with the creative and entrepreneurial capacity of people. In other words, the core of the development process lies in the development of human capabilities and, in particular, in the population's creative capacity, which is key to the capital accumulation process and to the economic progress of societies and territories.

Amartya Sen (2001) proposes an important change in the interpretation of development. He argues that the concept of development should go beyond economic growth and the per capita income of a country or territory, given that these are only instruments for carrying out the capabilities of the population. What is really important is that people carry out the tasks and activities that they wish, and are capable of carrying them out. That is to say, economic development is achieved by using the capabilities that people have developed, thanks to the material and human resources and the culture that the territory enjoys.

This concept shows the strong relationship that exists between development and freedom. Sen (2001) argues that what is important in the development process is the capacity of people to decide what potentials they wish to use in carrying out their life projects and, hence, in their contribution to development. In other words, people can choose: the population has opportunities to undertake those activities that they wish to accomplish with the abilities and knowledge they possess. From this point of view, the citizens' freedom to choose is central to the development process. Therefore, Sen argues that the institutions, norms, and rules (both formal and informal) should contribute to the exercise of citizens' freedom, and that freedom is an intercultural value since it always allows for the use of the population's capacities and abilities.

The United Nations Development Programme has accepted this development approach, and considers human development to be a process through which citizens increase their capacities in such a way as to improve their knowledge and have the necessary economic resources to lead a decent life. Development policies should broaden citizens' possibilities to choose, so that people will become key to all processes which contribute to the development of countries, regions, and cities. Thus, in the local initiatives for meeting today's challenges, emphasis is placed on defining a path of growth that is in accordance with the capabilities of the population, on strengthening the quality of their training and education, and on covering their basic needs, always within a framework of change in culture and institutions.

Development, creativity, and entrepreneurial capacity

As argued by Alonso (2006), Sen's approach (2001) presents development as an open process that feeds on people's opportunities and capabilities, which change and transform as the process evolves. A city, region, or country develops when the necessary mechanisms for development are created and when the institutions that allow its citizens to freely choose the capabilities they wish to develop are available. Development is, therefore, a continuous transformation process of the economy and of society, based on the development potential and the capacities of the individuals, and affects all types of territories regardless of the level of development.

This approach to development places people at the center of the economic and social transformation processes, and this has important implications. Above all, it is understood that the results of human activity, in a material sense, are never an end in themselves, but rather an instrument for achieving the well-being of citizens in general. Furthermore, poverty (and, therefore, low income levels) is no longer a constraint for development, since what is important is not the amount of resources in a territory but rather the capacities of its inhabitants. A known fact, as shown by the migratory flows of the last century, is that people with few economic resources do not necessarily lack entrepreneurial and creative capacity, or the capacity to save and invest. Last of all, this view considers the differentiation between development and underdevelopment to be misleading, and argues that development is a continuous process that changes and transforms the capabilities of the population in relation to the changes in the environment (which they also help transform).

The argument that the use of the population's capabilities is a critical element in the development process leads, inexorably, to the consideration that people's creative capacity is a necessary condition for the development of a country or territory. Without it, the functioning of the economic system as well as the forces that motivate economic and social progress cannot be understood.

Creative capacity has permitted people to create the mechanisms (economic, technological, and institutional) that facilitate increased productivity and the possibility to achieve economic progress, and so change society. Creativity goes hand in hand with the entrepreneurial capacity of individuals and organizations, since the former facilitates the latter's development and, thus, the urban, technological, organizational, productive, and institutional transformations (Lasuén and Aranzadi, 2002). In conclusion, it is through the entrepreneurial capacity that people transform reality and create opportunities for development.

Entrepreneurial and organizational capacity is, therefore, a manifestation of the people's creativity that allows them to produce something new and original within their environment. The creative process is produced with respect to the resources, potential, and attractiveness which characterize a territory, and this changes from one place to another. Because of this, entrepreneurial capacity is always conditioned by the cultural factors that explain the specificity of the territory. Therefore, development is generated by the entrepreneurial creativity of the citizens in a specific cultural environment. In this way, development, creativity, and culture relate differently to each other in each territory. A process of continuous interactions between them is produced as the territorial development process begins.

Culturally sustainable development

Territorial development is clearly an interactive process. The economic and non-economic institutions are important for the functioning of the economy, for the introduction of innovations and technological change, as well as for the transformation of productive and monetary organizations (Polanyi *et al.*, 1957). Yet, the economic development process also transforms the institutions and culture. This is similar to Marxist thought, which argues that the productive structure determines beliefs and culture in general, although Becker (1996) points out that, given that individuals and society have a limited control over culture, cultural change would be slower than that of social capital. Change in culture, institutions, and social capital also influences the mechanisms that make productivity and territorial development more dynamic.

Human development is an interpretation that places people at the center of development, since transformation and change in the economy and society in general are produced thanks to their capabilities (more specifically, to their creative and entrepreneurial capacities), and development makes sense when it benefits people. This allows us to deal with the question of poverty in a more natural manner since, even if the economic resources are few, human capacity may be used and developed so as to improve the well-being of the population. On the other hand, this view of development argues in terms of a culturally sustainable development model that interprets economic and social change as an open and continuous process, and therefore conceptualizes structural change and economic progress regardless of the amount of resources or income levels available.

However, though this view emphasizes the importance of human development, it does not sufficiently consider the relevance of both the development potential and the specific resources of the territory in the economic development process. Furthermore, this approach does not give the true value of the mechanisms and forces of development that condition the capital accumulation process and the competitive position; therefore, the policy actions usually limit the possibilities of self-sustaining growth and structural change. Lastly, the resources for financing human development projects often come from international cooperation and aid, and thus their capacity for promoting development processes that are economically and socially sustainable is limited.

Evolutionary Development and Interaction

From the perspective of the evolution and transformation of a country's or territory's economy, a main subject of development would be to identify the mechanisms that facilitate growth and structural change processes. In this sense, the evolutionary approach to development presents a useful interpretation because it goes farther ahead in terms of the efficient use of available resources and the development potential, and analyzes the mechanisms regulating and controlling the accumulation processes that facilitate increasing returns and thus explain economic development.

Accumulation of capital and knowledge

The growth and structural change process of an economy is the result of the application of economic resources, energy, and knowledge to the production of goods and services sold in national and international markets. Thus, the path of growth and its results are conditioned by the surplus generated within the economy, which facilitates savings and its utilization in productive investments.

The evolutionary view of endogenous development argues that capital accumulation depends on the capacity of the forces of development for fostering increased productivity and improved competitiveness in the territory. In other words, the sustainable development of an economy depends on the capacity of the forces of development to generate increasing returns as well as a surplus to be invested. In this way, it is argued that economic, social, and institutional transformations are possible when the resources used in investment projects affect the forces of development. This means that endogenous development refers not only to the capital accumulation process, but also to the internal mechanisms that allow for the transformation of savings and investment into productive capacity and economic and social progress.

Endogenous development is a process in which the social dimension is integrated with the economic dimension, as Arocena (1995) points out. Economic growth and income and wealth distribution are not two parallel processes, but rather part of a single phenomenon. Public and private actors make investment decisions for the purpose of improving the productivity and competitiveness of firms, as well as for the purpose of solving problems and improving society's standard of living.

Finally, the factors and forces on which the processes of economic development are based are man-made. Cities and urban development are one of mankind's most important achievements, and they allow for the emergence of urban agglomeration and business attraction. The start-up and development of firms and the organization of production come about as a result of people's creative capacity in seeking more efficient forms of production. Norms and regulations are adopted by the communities and society, in general, in answer to the needs and demands of citizens and organizations. Institutions make the productive system more efficient, and help to solve conflicts and problems more efficiently. The creation and diffusion of innovations is one way through which human creativity changes the environment, favors structural change, and helps satisfy the needs of the population.

Dynamics of development forces and increasing returns

The theory of endogenous development discusses growth and structural change in the context of the forces and mechanisms that condition the behavior of the productivity of production factors and the dynamics of capital accumulation. It argues that each and every one of the determining mechanisms and forces in the process of capital accumulation affects and conditions the processes of the transformation and development of cities, regions, and countries.

Economies develop and grow when companies carry out their production activities in cities and dynamic urban regions, which supply them with quality resources, agglomeration economies, externalities and economies of proximity that favor firm efficiency, and an increasing rate of returns. Economies develop and grow when the organization of the production system is more flexible and when networks and alliances are established, which favor internal and external economies of scale and scope, reduce transaction costs, and improve the competitive position of firms and territories. Economies develop and grow when institutions change and adapt to new conditions that allow firms and actors to reach agreements and contracts as well as exchange goods and services while facing low transaction costs. Economies develop and grow when innovations and knowledge spread through firms, territories, and institutions in such a way that production increases and becomes more differentiated, production costs fall, economies of scale increase, and productivity increases.

Therefore, cities, regions, and countries would be more successful in their processes of growth and structural change if all the forces that influence the processes of economic growth act jointly, creating synergies among themselves and reinforcing their effect on productivity and production factors' returns. It can be said that the mechanisms and forces of growth form a system that allows them to multiply their individual effects, resulting in an amplifying effect or synergy (the H factor). Hence, one can argue that increasing returns exist when the H factor is activated (Vázquez-Barquero, 2002).

Territorial development, however, is a process conditioned by the dynamics of development forces. In recent decades, a profound transformation in the organization of production pattern has taken place: the hierarchy has been reduced, and more flexible and decentralized organization systems have been adopted. The present transformation of industrial clusters has been produced as a result of the emergence of global value chains and the firms' territorial strategies, and the exchange of products and knowledge within the global clusters conditions the dynamics of the global economy. Therefore, territorial development is characterized by the evolution of global clusters and value chains, and depends on the new organization of production associated with the globalization process.

These changes and transformations have redefined the relations between cities and regions, and therefore a new territorial organization pattern has appeared. In recent decades, the organization of the economic space has evolved with the globalization process and acquired more flexible forms, giving way to polycentric urban regions (Hall and Pain, 2006). The reduction in transport costs, the information revolution, and the emergence of more flexible forms of organization of production have permitted the formation of interconnected city networks and differentiated spaces, where the exchange of goods and services as well as the productive, technological, and commercial relations have given way to an articulated economic system. This shaping and development of polycentric urban regions has improved the competitive capacity of firms and territories by increasing their scale and by widening the critical mass of their specific resources and potential.

As mentioned above, development is a process associated with the accumulation of knowledge and with the creation and diffusion of innovations through learning. Innovations are adopted by firms, and depend on their objectives and strategies as well as on the interactions between the actors who shape the regional system of innovation. In recent decades, important changes have taken place in innovation processes. The internationalization of value chains associated with the growing economic integration conditions the diffusion of knowledge and know-how within the global cluster of firms. In addition, the nature of innovation is under strong modification as a result of the introduction of innovations in business services, financial services, and the cultural arts industry (Maillat, 2008). Finally, regional innovation systems are strategic in the R&D process, since it is within the region where creativity is most naturally and efficiently fostered, given the cultural and geographic proximity. But, at the same time, innovation is becoming multi-local as a result of the impact of globalization on firms and networks.

The analysis of the dynamics of the forces of development includes norms, codes of conduct, patterns of behavior, and agreements between economic agents, leading us to argue in terms of institutional development. Institutional change, therefore, is a main force of development, as the institutional framework regulates production processes and commercial relations as well as provides the background against which actors make their investment decisions and the rules for the functioning of public policy.

Economically sustainable development

Finally, as mentioned above, development forces shape the economic capacity of the territory. They create an environment in which the economic growth and structural change processes are organized and carried out. Capital accumulation processes require the combined action of all of these development forces, such that the effect of each of them on productivity and returns is conditioned by the behavior of the others. That is to say, the interaction of the forces of development and their synergic functioning stimulate economic development and social progress.

The evolutionary approach to endogenous development is an interpretation that goes beyond the proposals of traditional neoclassical growth theory, by giving to increasing returns an analytical role in economic progress. It considers that the introduction of innovations in productive activities is a necessary condition for economic development, and analyzes development from a territorial perspective. It also proposes a self-sustaining development model, based on the creation of a surplus that allows investment, and guarantees the continuous transformation of the productive system through a constant change in the forces of development. This approach is in itself a model for analysis and action.

Nevertheless, this represents a partial view of the economic dynamic for it does not point out the relevance of the macroeconomic functioning, but rather leans on the assumption that the economy maintains the macroeconomic equilibrium. Furthermore, even if it interprets economic growth under competitive conditions, it does not consider the role of demand in the analysis or the integration of the local economy within the system of international economic relations.

Lastly, it is an interpretation that focuses, above all, on the economic conditions of change and transformation of the economy and society; thus, the analysis does not include the important elements that affect the social, cultural, and environmental sustainability of development.

Local Development

Since the early 1990s, several local development initiatives have emerged in Asia and Latin American countries (Aghon *et al.*, 2001; Altenburg and Meyer-Stamer, 1999; Scott and Garofoli, 2007). Local development initiatives are a spontaneous response on behalf of the local communities and governments, and can be interpreted through the different approaches to endogenous development as discussed above. In some cases, the local community takes on actions focused towards achieving autonomous development and, in this way, overcomes the needs and problems that limit their economic and social well-being. Often, as in the Sierra de los Cuchumatanes in Guatemala, or in Marikina in the Philippines, the social economy plays a significant role through the development of cooperatives. Democratic participation is encouraged in other cases; a good example of this is the citizens' participation in the projects to be included in the municipal budget of Porto Alegre in Rio Grande do Sul, Brazil.

Local initiatives are often directed towards solving the immediate needs of the local population by using the capabilities and the creative and entrepreneurial capacity of its citizens. The objective may be to reduce poverty in a territory, as in the case of the Cuchumatanes. Alternatively, the objective may be to face situations of great need that appear at a specific moment in time, as in the case of Villa El Salvador, Peru, whose growth is the result of a project that came about in order to solve the problem of the victims of the earthquake in the early 1970s; or to remedy some of the "collateral effects" of war, as was the case for the project developed by the United Nations Development Programme in Cartagena de Indias, Colombia, for displaced persons.

Development initiatives are also specifically directed towards affecting the accumulation processes, which favor increased productivity and competitiveness and, thus, foster economic and social progress. In the case of the Penang Development Corporation, in Malaysia, its purpose is to stimulate the formation of firm networks; in the case of the Technological Institute of Novo Hamburgo, in Rio Grande do Sul, its strategic objective lies in the creation and diffusion of innovations; and in Villa El Salvador, the strategic action of the local initiatives is aimed at physical urban development in order to encourage the emergence of agglomeration economies.

The explosion of local initiatives during the end of the 20th and the beginning of the 21st centuries has raised some questions concerning their emergence, content, and objectives followed. A preliminary look into the local development experiences studied shows that the local communities have gone through a pronounced learning process of productive adjustment and restructuring. Faced with problems like unemployment, poverty, a fall in production, and loss of markets, local actors had to consider the necessity of improving the responses on behalf of the local productive systems to the challenges of increased competition and changes in demand.

Even though local response varies widely, the key question is how to integrate local economies within the international economy and how to make their production systems more competitive. The solution includes a restructuring of the economic system and an adjustment to the institutional, cultural, and social systems of each territory in such a way that it allows firms to exploit the opportunities arising from changes in their environment and increased competition. The local development experiences show that the path to be followed should lead towards the definition and implementation of a strategy of entrepreneurial development, enforced through activities which pursue economic objectives as well as those related to equity and sustainability.

It is generally agreed that increased productivity and competitiveness are goals on which the process of structural change of local economies has to be focused. But, these objectives can be met in different ways and, put simply, may belong to one of two strategies: a strategy of radical change, consisting of a number of activities where the priority is on increased competitiveness (efficiency/effectiveness) of the local production system, independently of the associated cost in terms of employment or the environmental impact; or a strategy of small steps, combining actions that pursue the goals of efficiency, equity, and improved environment in the long term.

The first strategy involves a technological leap, the production of new goods, and/or alternative locations. In any case, there should be a radical change in the center of gravity of the productive system of the city, region, or country — sometimes with negative effects (in the short and long run) on employment, the model of organizing production, the environment, and the local culture.

In contrast, the strategy of small steps opts for the use of the know-how and technological culture already existing within the territory. It takes a step forward in structural change by developing new activities related to the existing productive fabric and combining the introduction of innovations with existing jobs, so that the transformations will be better accepted and ushered in by the local society.

This second option combines the objectives of efficiency and equity and, furthermore, gives priority to sustainable development. However, there is a risk that the local economy may fall into an assisted economy model, given the necessity of public support for this strategy, with the subsequent problems for the continuity of the economic development process. Excessive public assistance can suffocate the emerging entrepreneurial capacity of the territory, as demonstrated in the Italian Mezzogiorno during the 1960s and 1970s as well as in Asturias, Spain, during the 1980s and 1990s.

This is a simplification of the problems faced by local communities during restructuring and economic development processes, and the conflict of interests in society is very complex. In fact, development is a process that attempts to improve efficiency in the allocation of public and private resources, to foster equity in the distribution of wealth and employment, and to satisfy the present and future needs of the population through the adequate use of natural and environmental resources, as will be discussed later.

The first strategy — based on radical changes — encounters competitive barriers that are difficult to overcome in the short term, and normally incurs significant social and environmental costs that have to be assumed and that often come at a high political cost in democratic countries. For these and other reasons, best practice recommends that a strategy of small steps which makes use of the specific resources and development potential should be followed, fostering the accumulation of capital and knowledge and seeking support in the strengths of the local production system. Examples of the latter strategy can be seen in the Gran ABC of São Paulo, Brazil; the Cuchumatanes, Guatemala; Marikina, the Philippines; and Penang, Malaysia.

These local initiatives which emerged spontaneously combine a number of characteristic traits that allow us to talk about a new development policy. What are the main features of the endogenous development policies? How are they different from the regional development policies of the 1960s and 1970s? When the local endogenous development policy and the traditional regional development policy of the 1960s and 1970s are compared, differences in the conceptualization of the strategies, in the objectives pursued, and in the mechanisms of the functioning and managing of the policy tools can be identified (see Table 3.1).

The traditional regional development policy followed a supply-side view that was based on the model of uneven development; thus, it was aimed at favoring the spatial redistribution of economic activity, employment, and income by incentivizing firms to locate in the regions to be supported. The local development policy, however, tries to satisfy the needs and demands of the citizens and firms by encouraging the sustainable development of territories that have the potential for competitive development. The new approach, therefore, is based on the belief that economic growth does not necessarily have to be polarized and concentrated in big cities. Economic development can arise in polycentric regions, provided that the resources which exist in the territory are used efficiently (including those factors that attract foreign investment).

The traditional development policy chose a functional approach. The development of a territory was understood as the result of the mobility of production factors, which favored the distribution of income and employment as well as guaranteed convergence between rich and poor regions. The endogenous development strategy, on the other hand, follows a territorial approach. It argues that the economic

Table 3.1　Changes in Development Policy.

	Traditional Development Policy	Endogenous Development Policy
Dominant Strategy	• Functional view • Polarized development	• Territorial view • Polycentric development
Objectives	• Quantitative growth • Big projects	• Diffusion of innovation • Institutional change • Numerous projects
Mechanisms	• Mobility of capital and labor • Functional redistribution of income	• Mobilization of the endogenous potential • Utilization of local resources for development
Organization	• Centralized management • Public financing to companies • Public administration of resources • Administrative hierarchy • Administrative coordination	• Local development management • Rendering of services to companies • Administration through intermediate agencies • Partnership of local actors • Strategic coordination of actors

history of a particular locality, the technological and institutional characteristics of the local environment, and the local resources condition the growth process. Therefore, the local factors are strategic to the development of a territory; and the process of change should be controlled by the local actors, who have the capacity to transform the territory through their participation in the decision-making processes regarding investment and location.

The challenge for the new strategy of local development is to establish a self-sustaining development process for territories within the context of a very competitive and highly turbulent environment. Therefore, the objective is not so much to obtain short-term results, but rather to identify and follow a long-term path of growth. It is about strengthening and fostering the diffusion of innovation and knowledge within the economy and society in order to boost the emergence and development of companies and to increase the flexibility of the productive system, to foster the urban development of the territory, and to transform the institutional framework into a system that is favorable to the emergence and development of firms, as argued above.

Investment in important industrial projects is not a prerequisite for success in the development of a territory, as was implied in traditional development policy, which was based on an approach that believed in the existence of a direct relation between the amount of investment and economic growth. Rather, success in development is about designing and implementing projects that are adequate in size and that drive a progressive transformation of the production system forward by introducing innovations into the productive fabric, and about creating the institutional and spatial conditions that favor self-sustaining growth.

Finally, there are important differences between the two policies in terms of the organization and implementation of the development strategy. The state central administration used to carry out the implementation of supply-side policies through direct financial support to those firms and activities which fulfilled the required conditions. Endogenous development policy, however, is implemented in a decentralized way through intermediary organizations supplying real services, such as technology institutes, business and innovation centers, training institutions, and development agencies. The new policy adopts a self-sustaining growth approach and places the emphasis on endowing territories and productive systems with the services that firms need in order to improve their competitiveness, and not on making funds directly available to the firms.

Thus, the endogenous development policy is a bottom-up policy whose definition and management are under the control of the local actors. In more advanced economies, local actors are organized in networks that serve as tools for stimulating the diffusion of knowledge and learning within the dynamics of the productive system and the institutions, and for agreeing on the initiatives and implementing the policy actions, which together constitute the development strategy.

Economic Recovery and Endogenous Development

The previous discussion leads us to consider that endogenous development is an approach in which different views of development converge. The core of this interpretation lies in the territorial character of the growth and structural change processes, which depend on the territorial resources and the mechanisms on which development is based as well as on the laws that regulate and govern the growth and income distribution processes.

It is impossible, however, to reduce the concept of endogenous development to a single general interpretation. This is because the territorial base of development differs from one place to another, reality changes, and the social and institutional conditions under which development processes take place also change. In this sense, the different approaches to endogenous development are not necessarily incompatible, but rather can be integrated within a more complex interpretation.

The populist approach makes more sense within a wider interpretation of endogenous development, which considers that entrepreneurship and the creative capacity of the population are mechanisms that spur on the economic and social progress of places and territories. In turn, the evolutionary approach to development stresses the mechanical aspects of the development process, and is useful for analysis and policy action; therefore, it helps in interpreting today's development problems and guides the actors' responses to the challenges of globalization. Finally, the human approach to development understands development as a culturally sustainable process; but, its sustainability requires support from the evolutionary approach to development, since the economic development process is stimulated by human capabilities as well as by the territory's specific resources and assets that foster the forces of development.

The concept of endogenous development is helpful in analyzing the evolution and transformation of economies and territories, and in defining strategies and policies that may be implemented by taking advantage of the opportunities brought about by globalization. Hence, this approach can be used for analyzing the effects of the current financial crisis on the real economy. What are the mechanisms through which the crisis affects the processes of capital accumulation? What are the factors on which economic recovery can be based?

When the dynamics of developed and emerging economies in the ongoing global crisis are analyzed, it appears that the companies' shutdowns and lay-offs are due to the fact that the recession has limited the firms' capacity to invest. According to the evolutionary development approach, economic progress depends on the generation of savings within the economy and the transformation in productive investments, a process in which the financial sector plays a key role. Therefore, when, as is currently the case, this mechanism is disrupted — be it as a result of the credit crunch and the malfunctioning of the banking system, the firms' profit reduction, or a slowdown in demand — productive investments are reduced.

The development of savings and investment is key to the processes of growth and structural change, as productive investments generate increasing returns as a result of the combined effects of the forces of development that induce a sustained increase in productivity and improved competitiveness. Therefore, the sustainability of economic development is based on the generation of a surplus that allows for re-investments and that guarantees the continuous transformation of the production system through constant changes in the forces of development. For this reason, when a liquidity crisis or a contraction of credit affects profits, as has occurred in the ongoing crisis, productive activities are reduced and the development process is brought to a halt.

Nevertheless, financial crises are a phase of the business cycle in which the conditions that lead to economic recovery are shaped. Sen (2001) maintains that the creativity of human beings is at the center of all transformations and changes in an economy or society, and that economic and social progress occurs due to human resource capacities (specifically, to the creative and entrepreneurial capacities of the population). When this reasoning is connected to the Schumpeterian view of development, the creation and diffusion of innovations is regarded as the cornerstone of economic development. Hence, economic recovery will only be possible when the innovative capacity is activated and when innovation and knowledge are diffused through-out all of the mechanisms that affect capital accumulation.

This interpretation has important implications for economic policy. It argues that poverty and a lack of natural resources are not necessarily a constraint to economic development (and, likewise, to economic recovery), as the capacities of the population are the basis on which economic progress and the welfare of the population rest. Moreover, it suggests that development depends on the choices made by the citizens of a territory with respect to the use of their resources and capacities, and that their decisions regarding projects open the way for implementing local development strategies. Finally, it main-tains that the citizens' capacity for action depends on the historical development of their production systems, on the accumulation of technical knowledge within the economy and society, and on the rules and norms which characterize their institutional framework at any given moment.

Following this line of thought, the self-development approach goes further and holds that economic recovery depends on the use of the development potential and the initiatives which emerge from civil society, because the processes of development are the result of the application of local resources in projects that have been designed and implemented by the local organizations and citizens themselves. Therefore, the existing resources in a territory do play a strategic role; however, it is, above all, the capacities of the territory, which are con-tinuously transformed as a result of the application of resources and knowledge, that constitute the key to economic and social progress. From this perspective, the effectiveness of development policies and, therefore, economic recovery depend on the public actions designed and implemented by local actors.

The discussion on the processes of growth and crises in the eco-nomic and production systems — from the perspective of the endogenous development approach — permits the identification of some of the factors that are key for economic recovery. For the evolu-tionary development approach, the main question concerns the mechanisms of capital accumulation that affect the generation of a surplus as well as the generation of increasing returns (i.e. the basis for increasing productivity). The human development view adds that, given the fact that development is a culturally sustainable process which uses the creativity and entrepreneurial capacity of the population, the strategic factor for economic and social transformation rests on the application of innovations and knowledge to the economy and society. Therefore, as the self-development approach stresses, success rests on the use of the development potential and the responses on behalf of the local communities to achieve development objectives through their own initiatives.

Chapter 4

The Dynamics of Clusters and Milieus

A renewed interest in the location of productive activities has appeared during the last 20 years. Sociologists, geographers, and economists believe that at the present time the organization of production is experiencing a profound transformation process in which the hierarchical models, so characteristic of the Fordist period, have reduced in hegemony and given way to more flexible forms of organization of production.

A single unique interpretation as to how production is organized within the territory does not exist. Several approaches attempt to identify the factors that explain the emergence of industrial clusters and the mechanisms through which they develop, as well as the reasons for their change and transformation. Gordon and McCann (2000) maintain that the diversity of analytical approaches has led to a certain degree of confusion in the analyses and interpretations. This chapter discusses the question of spatial organization of production from the perspective of economic development.

The spatial organization of production changes as cities, regions, and countries develop. The chapter begins by pointing out the outstanding features of the different forms of organization of production, in light of the different stages of industrial development. Given that innovations are a key element in the economic dynamic, the discussion focuses on the outreach and significance that knowledge networks have today. Next, the diversity and dynamics of industrial clusters are discussed, and the factors and forces in favor of change and transformation are put forth. The chapter ends with comments on the role played by local firm strategies in the ever-changing spatial organization of production.

The Spatial Organization of Production

Only recently has the organization of production been considered a strategic mechanism that determines the economic development process. Three important moments should be considered in the evolution of the economic system, and in the interpretation of which factors condition the economic dynamic.

Adam Smith (1776) and other classical economists in the latter third of the 18th century — during the Industrial Revolution and at a time when the formation and expansion of national markets took place — gave great importance to natural resources and pointed out the appearance of new kinds of firm organization, forming a local productive system. Schumpeter (1934) wrote in the early 20th century, during the electric revolution, when inventions and innovations transformed the manufacturing economy that gave way to a profound restructuring of productive activity, and economic integration consolidated itself with the increase in international trade, the intensification of capital flows, and the expansion of multinational companies; he stressed the role of the innovative entrepreneur as well as that of innovations in product, process, and organization in the development process. Marshall (1890) pointed out the importance of large firms, an organization of production model that allows for scale economies, in local firm systems.

Since the last quarter of the 20th century, the world economy has entered into a new phase of formation and integration due to the spread of new information and communication technologies, leading to the new technological revolution. As in the past, at the core of the discussion remains the question of increased productivity and the mechanisms that favor the self-sustaining growth of economies. However, this discussion also raises a new question: how does the organization of production produce a multiplier effect on productivity, generate increasing returns, and therefore condition economic development? The innovative fact is the formation of global clusters, stimulated by the information revolution.

The spatial organization of production is a process associated with the strategy of the most dynamic firms, the dynamics of development forces, and the process of development. Increased competition in markets and the search for investment returns stimulate the firms to adopt innovations as well as make good use of the resources (including intangibles) and specific assets of cities and regions. Thus, the transformation of the organization of production is conditioned not only by the introduction of innovations and knowledge in the productive systems, in transport and communications, and in the markets, but also by the change in institutions and urban development, as shown below in the analysis of each stage of industrial development.

Industrial districts and the Industrial Revolution

The Industrial Revolution, which began in the mid-18th century, represents one of the great economic transformations that changed the forms of organization of production and gave rise to the formation of national markets (Landes, 1969). For the first time, there was a specific pattern in the location and agglomeration of firms — the industrial district — as theorized by Adam Smith (1776) and Alfred Marshall (1890).

The first Industrial Revolution was characterized by the manufacturing of new goods (textiles, iron) in small factories, where the work was organized by dividing each of the tasks into different parts with the help of new machinery (e.g. the spinning jenny in 1764, the steam engine in 1769, and the steam-powered mechanical loom in 1785), new materials (cotton), and the use of steam. The putting-out system was slowly abandoned and the new firms were located in small cities, provoking migration flows from the rural areas to the cities. With the improvement of transportation through the canal system (the commercial activity of canal boats was at its peak in the 1840s), the beginning of the railroad (in 1830), and the creation of the telegraph (in 1837), an important revolution in transportation and communications took place that allowed for the formation of national markets in the more dynamic economies of Europe and America. Landes (1969) argues that the Industrial Revolution took place in the U.K. at that time not only because of the British effort, imagination, and entrepreneurial spirit, but also because of the transformation of values, culture, and institutions (which had prevailed for centuries) in response to the new needs and demands.

Alfred Marshall (1890) witnessed the economic, social, and technological transformations of the late 19th and early 20th centuries. He analyzed the concentration of specialized industries in specific localities, and based his writings on those of Adam Smith (1776). The basic explanation for the agglomeration of firms in an industrial district lay in the fact that geographical proximity stimulated the creation of external economies of scale, as a result of the creation of a specialized labor "pool", the circulation of ideas and knowledge among the different firms, and the specialization of the different firms in different productive activities.

Becattini (1990) has interpreted Marshall's ideas and tried to explain the good performance in the 1970s and 1980s of some Italian regions (in terms of growth in the number of employees, production, exports, and per capita income), whose productive system was organized around "concentrations of many small businesses of a similar character in particular localities", as Marshall had suggested. To the factors proposed by Marshall, Becattini adds new features that the more developed industrial districts have adopted over time, among which the following stand out: the specialization of different firms in the different phases of the productive process; the incorporation of productive activity in the social life of the city, in which the firm becomes the "interface" between the economy and society; and the relevance of social and cultural factors in the development of the productive system and the local economy. Thus, Becattini understands the industrial district as "a territory, historically and spatially defined, that is characterized by the active presence of the population and the local firms" (1990, p. 39).

The industrial complex and the electric revolution

Between 1870 and 1920, a new industrial revolution took place that was more intense and important than the previous one, and that was characterized, above all, by the introduction of electricity in the production of public and private goods and services (Hall and Preston, 1988). Again, it transformed the way in which production was organized and gave way to the consolidation of international markets.

In the latter third of the 19th century, a variety of new products appeared (such as automobiles and chemical products) that were produced by large factories and industries, which were located in large cities (and in cities close to the raw materials), thanks to the use of new equipment goods (electrical machinery) and electricity (in the 1870s, Edison developed a series of generators related to the system of incandescent illumination). The large firm was born, as a new form of organization of production (with the introduction of the assembly line in 1905) located in large cities, where a great supply of cheap labor and a high demand for local products were found.

Also at the same time, the railroad developed much of its potential (a resurgence took place in the early 1870s) and naval transportation introduced the steam engine (1890s), along with the appearance of automobiles (1895) and aviation (1905) as well as the spread of telephone (an innovation of the 1870s) and radio (the first successful long-distance transmission by Marconi was in 1901). All of this led to the consolidation of national markets as well as the widening and strengthening of international markets for raw materials and commodities.

Industrial development during this period was based on technological innovation and the new organization of production, as well as on institutional change (Chandler, 1990). Innovation depended more and more on laboratory research; industrial education became necessary for economic progress, and higher education and science were essential to industrial development. Changes in business organization and turn-of-the-century merger movement required large financial resources and the development of financial organizations. The enlargement of international markets favored the spatial and strategic development of multinational corporations and the increasing internationalization of the economy. Finally, the role of the state became more and more present within economic life, providing technical education in some cases as well as supporting the emergence and development of big firms in new activities through tariffs, patents, and government regulations.

The organization of production was transformed by the appearance of the large firms and the industrial complexes that settled around them as a result of increased commercial relations between suppliers and clients. Alfred Marshall (1890) understood the large firm to be a new type of organization of production that helped firms obtain internal economies of scale due to optimization in the use of raw materials, intermediate goods, and equipment goods. Nevertheless, it was Weber (1929) who first established the relation between production and spatial organization of industry, and who established the optimum firm location in relation to the transportation cost, the price of inputs, and the demand for finished goods (Gordon and McCann, 2000).

Hoover (1937, 1948) synthesized the advantages of agglomeration of firms, by combining the effects of internal and external scale economies in his interpretation. Following Marshall, he pointed out that internal economies of scale were the result of the efficiency of large firms in the management of inputs for manufacturing a growing number of goods for a wide market. He also added that external economies of scale were produced as a result of the location of the firms of a certain sector in a specific locality, and of urbanization economies associated with the agglomeration of a variety of industries and services in a city.

All of these ideas led to an economic development paradigm that was widely spread over decades by identifying it with the industrialization processes through investments made by both the large firms in large cities and the public administration in large infrastructures. Yet, even though the idea that development is produced thanks to the investments made by industrial firms has been maintained, one of the great contributions of Schumpeter (1934, 1939) has been forgotten, namely that long-term development can only be generated if innovations and knowledge are introduced in the products, processes, and forms of organization.

Fostering the structural change of an economy through the industrialization processes was a well-accepted proposal in the Soviet Union during the 1920s (Lenin was a great admirer of Ford's ideas), and industrial complexes have for decades been considered an instrument for industrial development in planned economies. In market economies, industrial development policies were based on the concept of growth poles, which is Perroux's (1955) version of industrial development, but the importance of the diffusion of innovations and knowledge in development was ignored.

Global clusters and the information revolution

Since the mid-1980s, strong institutional transformations have occurred and a new industrial revolution has appeared, stimulated by the new information and communication technologies. This has led to a new form of organization of production and to the formation of global markets.

With the introduction of the transistor (1947), the electronic computer (second-generation electronic computers using transistors were created in 1958), and the personal computer (1978), a strong process of productive restructuring has taken shape; and the development of more advanced industrial activities (biotechnology, electronics, pharmaceuticals) and services (financial, management, cultural, leisure) has generated a strong structural change in the productive system. It is led by firms of very different sizes, located in large and small cities and in countries with different levels of development. The organization of production has become increasingly flexible, due to changes in the organization of large firms as well as to the formation of firm networks and strategic agreements and alliances between innovative firms. Transport and communication services have become more efficient, and the new technologies speeding up economic integration — thanks to the opening up of markets and profound institutional changes, such as the fall of the Berlin Wall, the opening up of commerce to and from China, and the change in trade policies in Latin America, India and some African countries — have given way to global financial, commodity, and service markets (Dunning, 1998, 1999).

In an increasingly competitive world, the spatial organization of production is taking on new forms. The old regional industrial centers are being restructured, and new centers are beginning to appear in both developing and developed countries. Porter (1990, 1998) includes the concept of clusters in his dynamic competition theory, which recognizes the globalization of good and factor markets, where continuous improvements and innovations in product, process, factor, and organization are made.

Porter understands that, in order to compete under the best conditions, firms and organizations tend to group geographically, linking themselves to each other and so creating a system of relations that stimulates the firms' competitive strategies and, thus, the cluster itself. Clusters are made up of suppliers with specialized inputs (parts, machinery, service, specialized infrastructure). These clusters often extend to clients; firms that produce complementary products; and firms from other industries with whom they share inputs, technology, and skilled labor. Some clusters even include both private and governmental organizations that supply specialized training, information, research, and technical support (see Figure 4.1).

However, what most characterizes this phase of industrial development is the evolution of global clusters and value chains. Globalization of the productive system has given rise to new systems of relations and exchange among firms and clusters (Scott and Garofoli, 2007; Schmitz, 2007): export of finished products to final markets, commerce within multinational networks, and flows associated with outsourcing activity. These types of flows gradually expand as international transport costs decrease, and subcontracting firms adopt network technologies and adjust their production to international standards.

The increase in subcontracting at the international level as well as in combined production among firms located in different spaces and territories creates new challenges because the production of goods on a global scale requires that participating firms share the

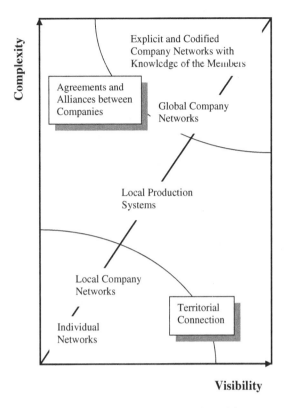

Figure 4.1 Networks for Economic Development (adapted from Bramanti and Senn (1993)).

same technology, entrepreneurial culture, and institutional system. In other words, when the value chain of production is internationalized, linking clusters of firms from several countries, the flow of products among clusters and firms necessarily depends on a common set of ground rules and economic and social relations in order to manage flows and exchange within the global value chain (Gereffi, 1994).

Economic integration, therefore, connects spaces and clusters in advanced economies with spaces and clusters in developing economies. The relations within global value chains can be of different types (Gereffi, 1999; Gibbon, 2001; Sverrison, 2004): *producer-driven* (as in the case of aeronautical and automobile activities), in which large firms control the distribution and marketing of final products; *buyer-driven*, in which final production is sourced from small firms in other countries according to a specified design, and the buyer then distributes and markets the product under his or her own label; or *trade-driven*, in which business and export agents promote relations and agreements between producers and buyers.

Messner (2004) argues that the world is currently witnessing the formation of a global economy based on firm networks and relations among regions and countries. Within global value chains, relations among regions and countries are established through the exchange of products and knowledge. Governance of the relations between the local firm network, the leading firms in the global chain, and the global network of norms based on the enforcement of international standards becomes more complex as firms and local public actors are less capable of acting when immersed in a system of global relations.

Knowledge Networks

As we have just seen, change in the spatial organization of production is a process related to the economic dynamics of countries, regions, and cities. According to Schumpeter (1934), innovation is the key factor explaining both the spatial organization of production and economic development, although, as North (1990) points out, institutions also matter. Furthermore, from the perspective of the functioning of the mechanisms of capital accumulation, the widening and strengthening of markets depends, among other factors, on the introduction of innovations in the transport and communication systems, which in turn influences the spatial organization of production.

Dunning maintains that the following has occurred in the last three centuries:

> [The main source of wealth] has switched from natural resources (notably land and relatively unskilled labour), through tangible created assets (notably buildings, machinery and equipment and finance), to intangible created assets (notably knowledge and information of all kinds) which may be embodied in human beings, in organizations or in physical assets. [Dunning, 2001, p. 186]

He argues that it is precisely the increased contribution of services to GDP that, in most cases, explains why the "created intangible assets are replacing natural and created tangible assets as the main source of wealth", particularly in the case of developed economies. Because of this, when transformation and change is introduced by key elements of the economy of knowledge (the microprocessor and computer), the difference between high- and low-technology industries is less significant. Knowledge in effect becomes heterogeneous merchandise, transforming the economic and social reality.

Nevertheless, innovation has always been at the core of development during each of the key moments of the economic dynamic. Innovation is nothing less than the application of knowledge to the production of goods and services that are commercially relevant. In other words, innovation necessarily encompasses the application of new technology in goods and services that are sold in national and international markets. Therefore, the explanation for today's distribution of economic activity and the interpretation of spatial organization of production lead us necessarily to consider knowledge and information as forces for cluster development.

All of this leads to the idea of associating the cluster with the knowledge economy (Cooke, 2002; Maskell, 2001). Clusters exist because of the advantages that the knowledge generated by those firms which work in an innovative atmosphere can present. Once a firm succeeds with a new product in the market, which is the result of new knowledge, an ever-larger group of imitators will appear to be interested in producing the same product; this gives way to the appearance of a cluster. The formation of the cluster produces a strong attraction on the part of newcomers, who in turn strengthen the cluster even more and expand its knowledge base (Tallman *et al.*, 2004).

Hudson (1999) points out that there is a growing recognition that knowledge is the most strategic resource in the present form of organization of production. Thus, learning has become the most important process, since it is through learning that knowledge is created and transformed. Lawson and Lorenz (1999, p. 307) point out that the process of generating knowledge is based on three basic ideas: knowledge is mostly tacit and is embodied in the organizational routines and procedures of firms; the production of new knowledge within the organizations depends on the combination of diverse knowledge; and firms usually find it difficult to make effective use of new knowledge because they face a resistance to making changes in the organizational routines and procedures where knowledge is embodied.

Thus, learning is "path-dependent" in the sense that the creation of knowledge supposes the existence of acquired knowledge. Yet, learning is to a large extent interactive (Lundvall, 1992), which is why it is necessary for firms — among which ideas circulate — to share a language and culture. As Camagni (1991) points out, learning is not merely the acquisition of information, but rather a process through which information is transformed into knowledge and for which the firms need to develop a "decoding function" that will allow them to incorporate outside information. Therefore, in order for the learning process to be produced, it is necessary that the firms have a collective language, i.e. that learning and language share the same codes.

Although, as Hudson (1999) maintains, it is necessary to recognize that the national context of the innovation and learning system plays an important role, the local learning and knowledge system is, perhaps, more significant (Maskell *et al.*, 1998). Gilly and Torre (2000) point out that physical and organizational proximity facilitates the exchange of goods, services, resources, and information between firms and the other actors of a locality, and stimulates interaction among them as well as the creation and diffusion of knowledge (including tacit knowledge). Furthermore, in the learning processes, it is necessary for firms and actors to share a set of rules and regulations that will allow for the cooperation and diffusion of innovations and knowledge through a collective learning process.

The notion of local environment ("milieu") establishes that the territory plays a strategic role in the creation and diffusion of ideas and innovations. As Maillat (1995) explains, innovations and technological change emerge in a specific territory, and are associated with local know-how, human resource skills, and knowledge institutions which undertake R&D. The creation and diffusion of innovations is a phenomenon based on the relations and interactions of the firms with the milieu. The performance of the firms, the economy and society, the innovative capacity of firms, the milieu's creative and productive culture, and the economic and technological history of the territory are all factors that condition the learning processes and the response of firms and organizations to the challenge of competition.

In an ever-more competitive and globalized world, knowledge and learning are necessary elements for making quality goods and services in order to have a competitive position within the market. Geographical and institutional proximity favors interaction and the diffusion of knowledge, which reduces transaction costs and helps firms improve their investment profits. Thus, the term "learning region" is used when referring to more dynamic economies that lead the structural change process on a global level (Florida, 1995; Maskell *et al.*, 1998).

As Hudson (1999) maintains, there is perhaps too great an obsession in associating the success of a city or territory only with its learning and knowledge capacity. As previously mentioned, the concepts of "learning firm" and "learning region" are not new ideas, since the economic development process has always been carried out through innovative firms and territories. Furthermore, other forces exist that are jointly — with the diffusion of innovations and knowledge and the organization of production — essential for the economic dynamic, such as the urban development of a territory and the change and adaptation of institutions. It is precisely the interaction between these forces that stimulates the territorial development process.

The Cluster's Life Cycle

Continuous waves of innovation, the integration of markets, and progressive changes in the organization of production have created a great variety of clusters and local productive systems. The diversity of clusters and the diversity of their paths are a reflection of the firms' learning capacity. Despite what authors like Martin and Sunley (2003) maintain, the juxtaposition of different forms of spatial organization of production today clearly shows the diversity in the paths of development of the territories as well as the vitality of the development process in all types of economies.

The literature analyzes a great number of cases of clusters and local productive systems that produce all types of goods, and that are located in regions and countries with different levels of development (Altenburg and Meyer-Stamer, 1999; Rosenfeld, 1997; Staber, 1997; Porter, 1998). These include electronics in Silicon Valley (U.S.), Silicon Glen (Scotland), Guadalajara (Mexico), and Penang (Malaysia); optics in Rochester (New York) and Orlando (Florida); the car industry in Detroit (Michigan), Vigo (Spain), and Tianjin (China) where Toyota has helped to create a cluster; ceramic tiles in Sassuolo (Italy), Castellón (Spain), and Criciúma in Santa Catarina (Brazil); the shoe industry in Brenta (Italy), Elche (Spain), León in Guanajuato (Mexico), and Marikina (Philippines); textiles and the garment industry in Reutlingen (Germany), the Itajaí Valley (Brazil), and the Republic of Mauritius; and financial services in New York City, London, Frankfurt, Hong Kong, and Shanghai.

Firm agglomeration, which emerges as a result of increased services and the concentration of activities in large cities, is also becoming more important. Global cities and urban regions hold a strong attraction for financial and business service firms; for example, in New York, the financial hub is on Wall Street and advertising firms are mainly located on Madison Avenue. The most dynamic functions in the advanced service sector (like marketing, design, technical assistance, R&D, and information) have progressed remarkably in their efforts to satisfy the growing demand for business services and — as Simmie and Sennett (1999) point out — tend to focus in global cities (the urban areas of London or Paris and other important commercial nodes), forming innovative multi-clusters (in conjunction with high-technology activities). The integration of world markets has also contributed to the development of service clusters in certain international cities like São Paulo, Buenos Aires, Mexico City, Santiago, Beijing, Kuala Lumpur, Singapore, and Shanghai.

We can see that the geographic concentration of firms — in districts, complexes, clusters or milieus — is constantly experiencing a transformation and change process, which is associated with the creation and diffusion of innovation and knowledge as well as with a change in market dynamics. Thus, like the firms, the clusters and the local productive systems in general are born, grow, and transform (Pouder and St. John, 1996; Porter, 1998; Vázquez-Barquero, 1988). In other words, the introduction of the notion of a cluster life cycle permits us to identify three stages of cluster evolution: emergence, development, and transformation.

The local productive systems emerge as a result of very specific processes. In some cases, the markets may appreciate those production activities in which the local economy has a comparative advantage because of the specific natural resources available, as occurred with the marble industry in Olula del Rio–Macael, Spain, in the early 20th century. At other times, the local community's reaction to a crisis in the former productive system or the loss of traditional markets for agricultural products may spur new initiatives in expanding markets. This occurred in the Valle del Vinalopó in Valencia, Spain, when a phylloxera epidemic destroyed an important part of the vineyard production in the 19th century and so clusters devoted to shoe manufacturing emerged in small cities like Elda and Petrel. In situations where the productive activity loses its markets, it would be replaced by another activity that may or may not be related to the previous one.

Krugman (1990) maintains that the appearance of firms and the formation of a local productive system can be the result of chance, as occurred in Dalton, Georgia, which became the manufacturing center for the production of carpets in the U.S. by accident. Bernabé Maestre (1983) suggests that the emergence of firms and the formation of local productive systems obey imitation mechanisms of industrialization experiences in contiguous or nearby areas, stimulating entrepreneurs in the local economy to imitate them using the resources available in the territory.

As shown by the cases of endogenous industrialization studied in Spain (Vázquez-Barquero, 1988), the start-up which initiates structural change eventually becomes a development and industrialization process due to certain development conditions. These conditions include entrepreneurial capacity, the local awareness of "new" products and markets, the availability of savings from agricultural and/or commercial activities, the supply of a cheap labor force, and the existence of a developed social capital and culture.

Clusters also appear because innovative firms stimulate their emergence and development, or because multinational companies decide to locate in a specific place (Dunning, 2001). As Martino *et al.* (2006) discuss, the optics/photonics industry in Rochester, New York, first developed with the establishment of three firms specializing in imaging and/or optics: Eastman Kodak in 1881, Bausch & Lomb in 1853, and Xerox Corporation in 1906. An industrial cluster was established around these companies; and imaging, optics, and photonics academic programs were created throughout the region, with the support of government funding.

When the emergence of a cluster is conditioned by the strategies of external firms, the attraction factors are relevant for the development process. The location factors that generate an attraction for firms depend on their strategies, which can be based on the existence of expanding markets or on factor costs. In the case of innovative firms, they are concerned with the availability within the territory of specific resources and assets, such as strategic infrastructure, qualified human resources, the technological and entrepreneurial knowledge accumulated within the territory, as well as the local sense of identity and the prestige of the city's or region's image.

The emergence of clusters in recent times also takes place thanks to public support, as has occurred with the Telecom Corridor in Richardson, Texas, and the biotechnology cluster in Cambridge, England. More outstanding, perhaps, is the transformation of Austin, Texas, into one of the leading knowledge economy clusters in the U.S., which came about as a result of the interaction between firms, the government, and the University of Texas at Austin — what has come to be known as the "triple helix". The result was the formation of a high-technology cluster, based on obtaining projects, that included the research consortium in semiconductors between SEMATECH and MCC, as well as companies like 3M, Dell, IBM, and Motorola. Up to 200 high-technology firms were created each year throughout the 1990s, which meant 30,000 new jobs annually and an annual growth rate of over 9% (Etzkowitz and Leydesdorff, 1997).

Once the local firm system begins to take shape, a local network for the exchange of resources, goods, and services between the firms and the local organizations and institutions appears (Pouder and St. John, 1996; Porter, 1998). The firms' economic success generates a strengthening of relations within the system, and favors specialization and the integration of public services needed by local firms. The appearance of new local firms and the attraction of firms from other areas strengthen local networks and productive systems.

In the cluster development phase, the agglomeration process is facilitated by such mechanisms as the diffusion of innovations, urban development, and institutional dynamics. Interaction between firms facilitates the transmission of information and the diffusion of innovation and knowledge; the cluster develops its own learning process, and so the diffusion of innovations becomes very creative. Clusters also react to changes in the environment through job mobility in the local market; the exchange of product, process, and organization technology; and informational flows of all types. Innovation, therefore, becomes a collective learning process, and a culture of innovation and change is spread throughout the territory.

Cities and other localities where the clusters are anchored become a space in which economies associated with agglomeration and externalities favor the lowering of production and coordination costs in cluster firms. The urbanization process makes production and culture more diversified, favors interaction among firms, and encourages innovation and learning throughout the entire local fabric. Thus, urban development stimulates agglomeration economies and cluster dynamics.

Firms within the cluster share a common culture, history, and institutions which emerge spontaneously within the cluster's organization process. They facilitate exchange as well as market and non-market transactions, and reduce production costs. Trust and cooperation develop within industrial networks and milieus, thus providing profits to the cluster firms. New forms of social capital come about in response to the new demands of the cluster and society, and appear only when the mechanisms which guarantee economic efficiency are created.

The emergence and development of a cluster is a process of self-organization based on the firms' strategies, and on the interaction between the firms and the territory. Economies of scale, reduction in transaction costs, and agglomeration economies make clusters an efficient organization of production mechanism and favor the growth of local firms, whose competitive advantage strengthens their presence in the market. Market forces, however, do not guarantee the steady growth of clusters and local productive systems.

Firms may lose their competitive advantage because of the weaknesses of the leading firms' strategic response to the challenges of market competition, and the consequent effect of cumulative causation on the cluster's functioning. The loss of market position by the more dynamic firms, as a result of changes in the clients' requirements that the firms have failed to meet, as well as the surge of new competitive firms and clusters which are more efficient in the use of innovations could give way to the relocation and shutdown of firms. In addition, a diminished innovation capacity due to local firms' stagnation in the creation of new ideas and knowledge — along with a weakening of institutional development and social capital, which reduces cooperation between firms and breaks down the existing social agreements — could have a negative effect on the economic results of the firms and the cluster. Furthermore, failing to upgrade the territory's resources and specific assets or an increase in agglomeration costs would reduce the urban attraction, and so the local firms and the cluster would lose their competitive advantage. Such a breakdown in the functioning of clusters creates the conditions for the transformation of the productive system.

Transformation of Clusters and Milieus

Clusters and local productive systems are efficient forms of spatial organization of production that have spontaneously emerged as a result of firm strategy in response to changes in market competition. They are in constant transformation, continually adapting and responding to the challenges of innovation and to changes in the business environment through productive restructuring and structural change.

Local productive systems last a long time. The industrial district of Prato, Italy, for example, has introduced knowledge and innovations in firms for hundreds of years, adopting new production processes, improving the internal organization of the district, and increasing its social capital (Becattini, 2001). Nevertheless, local productive systems also transform by giving way to new industrial activities, as Rosenfeld (1997) points out. Thus, the semiconductor industry in Silicon Valley gave way to the equipment goods and personal computer industry; and in the Ruhr Valley, Germany, a new cluster specializing in environmental technologies emerged precisely because it had, over the years, acquired specialized knowledge in environmental subjects in order to solve the traditional pollution problems caused by the iron industry.

It can be argued, as Cooke (2002) suggests, that the same thing happens to clusters as to innovative firms in that they change the productive activity continuously, as a result of increased competition in the market. Nokia, for example, began as a forestry firm, after which it specialized in the production of paper, capital goods, and machinery, after which it specialized in wiring, computers, and data services; today, it is the most important producer of mobile phones in the world. Undoubtedly, the transformation of clusters is a more complex phenomenon, since it requires transformations in the organization of manufacturing, innovation development, and institutional adjustment.

The transformation of local productive systems can follow very different paths, as seen by analyzing the present-day behavior of the different cases mentioned above (innovative milieus, industrial districts, industrial complexes, and economic enclaves). In the case of local firm systems which are well integrated in the territory (innovative milieus), the situation will vary depending on the productive system's capacity for response. Saxenian (1994) argues that globalization fosters the creation of innovative firm systems and improves the position of productive systems based on firm networks. Therefore, in this case, the development processes of cities and regions — where the firms are located — tend to continue, and are compatible with the dynamic of the globalization processes.

On the other hand, Markusen (1996) argues that increased competition and the introduction of process and organization innovations can adversely transform the internal organization of the productive system. As shown by the case of Detroit, which at the beginning of the 20th century was an industrial district comparable to Silicon Valley today, the formation of the automobile industry oligopoly and the flight of other productive activities from the city have led to a more hierarchical productive system that has hindered diversification and caused serious problems in productive adjustment. The Rochester cluster; however, as Martino *et al.* (2006) point out, has undergone a significant restructuring process in the past 20 years and positively transformed its internal organization structure. Kodak, Xerox, and Bausch & Lomb no longer play a dominant role within the cluster; instead, the productive system has become an innovative milieu of specialized photonics/optics-related local firms.

In the case of local firm systems which are partially integrated into value chains from other regions (industrial districts), their evolution can also differ considerably. On the one hand, if firms have a weak relation with local value chains (lack of R&D segments or producer-service activities within the locality), the impact of globalization can generate a very different set of dynamics from the endogenous development processes. Increased competition can lead to the disappearance of the district and the absorption of remaining productive factors (labor force, for instance) by other districts, as occurred in the case of the footwear district in La Vall d'Uixó, Spain, whose local resources were absorbed by the ceramic district of Castellón (Vázquez-Barquero and Sáez-Cala, 1997) (see Box 4.1).

Box 4.1

The Ceramic Productive System in Castellón

The production system in Castellón consists of a number of companies that dedicate themselves to the production of ceramic surfaces and veneers. These companies are concentrated in the area of Alcalatén (Alcora), Plana Baixa (Betxí, Nules, Onda, Ribesalbes, La Vall d'Uixó, and Villareal), and Plana Alta (Almassora, Borriol, Vilafamés, Vall d'Alba, Cabanes, and Castellón de la Plana, among other municipalities), which makes the territory highly specialized in the production of ceramic tiles and very competitive in international markets.

The manufacturing of ceramics has a tradition that is over 200 years old in the region. It began at the end of the 18th century with the first small ceramics workshops, *les fabriquettes*, which were dedicated to the manufacture of formed pieces and glazed tiles in Alcora, Ribesalbes, and Onda, due to the influence of the Royal Factory of Conde de Aranda. In the year 2000, a total of 226 companies made up the productive fabric, 92% of which employed less than 250 people. At the forefront of those companies with between 25 and 100 employees — and among the most representative — are Porcelanosa, Venis, Gres de Nules-Keraben, Aparici, Vives, Taulell, Pamesa, and Grespania.

The companies are part of the production system in Castellón and specialize in different activities. Producers of glazed tiles, ceramic surfaces, and ceramic tiles are producers in the strict sense, since they carry out every phase of the production process — from the design to the commercialization of their products — and form the central core of production activities. Extractive industries supply the prime material (clay), which is principally extracted in Teruel, Valencia, and Castellón. The companies producing frit, enamel, and ceramic colors have also been key in the development of the sector since the 1980s, as the technology, design, and quality of the product are their responsibility, and they hold a leading position in the world today.

(Continued)

(Continued)

The last transformation of the production system in Castellón began in the mid-1970s with a crisis in the local system due to the fragility of the production base, which was unable to deal with the increased competition from foreign producers, leading to the disappearance of a large number of companies. The emergence of bigger and better-organized companies — in particular, the adoption of process innovations in the 1970s and product innovations in the 1980s — rationalized the entire production system, which increased the network of contacts and relations throughout the district and made the production system more efficient. With the appearance of new institutional actors, the process of restructuring production consolidated itself, companies and the territory increased their competitive advantage, and the companies' position in international markets improved.

The private and public institutions surrounding the production system have gathered to support the sector, carry out and coordinate R&D&I activities, manage the external promotion of ceramic products, and take charge of specialized human resource training. Among these institutions are the *Instituto de Tecnología Cerámica*, the *Asociación para la Promoción del Diseño Cerámico*, and the Jaume I University, which are dedicated to research and training activities. Important activities are also carried out by the business associations themselves; academic institutions such as the *Instituto de Formación Profesional*; and the *Feria Internacional de Cerámica* (CEVISAMA), the sector's annual exhibition fair. This institutional environment plays an essential role in the generation and diffusion of innovations throughout the productive fabric. It is also a basic support framework for the construction of inter-entrepreneurial networks and for the intensification of relations between companies and institutions.

Source: Carpi *et al.* (1999).

On the other hand, the strengths of these systems — associated with the existence of specialized firms, firm mechanisms of entrepreneurial and institutional interaction, and local learning capability — can attract external firms searching for a milieu with external economies which are not sufficiently exploited. In Montebelluna, Italy, productive restructuring has brought about the decentralization of production to Southeast Asian countries, and the arrival of external economic actors has externalized the decision-making centers.

In the case of productive systems led by firms whose productive activity is well integrated within the local value chain (industrial complexes), several scenarios may take place. In an analysis of the economic dynamics in Seattle, Markusen (1996) found that the formation of technological poles around leading and innovative firms is a common strategic response to the challenges of competition in an increasingly globalized world. The specific characteristics of Boeing in Seattle have contributed to productive diversification in the region with the expansion of new technology sectors, such as computer software, biotechnology, and shipping activities, giving rise to a singular path of endogenous development.

Finally, in the case of productive systems made up of firms which have no local roots and which are integrated in external production networks, i.e. mere enclaves of external firms, their permanence in the region is unpredictable. It depends on whether the cost/price conditions and the value of the resources that led to their initial location in the area continue to exist. It also depends largely on the technological dynamics of the cluster, as occurred with the production of personal computers in Taiwan (Kishimoto, 2004). In the last 20 years, Taiwan has become the third-largest producer of computers in the world (after the U.S. and Japan), no doubt due to the manufacture of product brands from foreign firms which produce computers. Yet, the most important factor behind the success of this computer cluster (located north of Taipei, where approximately 1,200 firms are located) is that local firms have improved their capacity for the design of products (improved knowledge) and logistics, to which must be added the changes in organization of production with a growing externalization (offshore production) towards continental China.

Thus, the spatial forms of organization of production experience continuous transformation, seeking the most efficient form of production in such a way that new forms are added to the previous ones and so form multiple spaces of development. This is a self-organizing process led by the most innovative firms of the cluster, who react to the changing needs and market competition through responses which modify the cluster network (Best, 1990). Saxenian (1994) adds that, when competition is based on continuous innovation, as in the case of computer and semiconductor industries, the strategy of the leading companies is focused on the constant introduction of new products and their application in new markets. The internationalization of local companies does not necessarily imply that the interaction among local firms and local networks weakens; the new firms are reliant on local externalities for their growth and, as in the case of Rochester, local relations and connections may even expand.

In the transformation process as a whole, the behavior of other forces that determine development is very important. Innovations condition the internal organization of firms and the spatial organization of production. The introduction of new products and new methods of production requires new forms of internal firm organization, for reasons of efficiency. An example is the automobile industry, from the time Ford introduced the assembly line in the early 20th century through to the current subcontracting and externalization of parts of the productive process to suppliers grouped in industrial parks. The application of new technologies allows for the division of the productive process into parts, the productive specialization of firms, and the re-engineering of the manufacturing system for final products, whether it pertains to an industrial district or an industrial complex around the large firms. Moreover, local learning and innovation as well as the interaction among local firms evolve due to global competition. The search for production efficiency stimulates new location strategies that favor cluster transformation, especially in the case of innovative firms.

A territory's urban development conditions its own production organization, since cities are the preferred location for industrial and service firms, clusters, and local productive systems in general. Cities supply the resources as well as the goods and services required to make firms more competitive. The city is the space in which industrial and service investments are made, firm networks are established, and meeting points for the firm network are located. Thus, the city's size and urban characteristics as well as its position in the urban system determine the configuration of the local firm network.

The city is the place where innovations are produced — according to Feldman and Audretsch (1999), 96% of innovations in the U.S. were made in metropolitan areas with only 30% of the country's population — and where technical knowledge is disseminated. This explains why firms which share the same scientific base tend to group together in certain cities. The attraction of these intangible assets in cities stimulates the formation and development of firm clusters, and the specialization of firms in specific industrial activities and services. From this point of view, the system of cities forms the territorial side of the spatial organization of production. It is, therefore, in the cities where the location and urbanization economies and the cost reductions for firms take place.

Finally, the institutional development of the territory, where firms carry out their work and where clusters are established, determines the type of organization of production of the productive system (Putnam, 1993). Cities and regions, in which new forms of organization of production have emerged and gradually been embedded, are territories where trust and reciprocity between individuals and organizations stimulate cooperation as well as economic exchange. The economic activity and, thus, the forms of organization of production are immersed within a set of social, cultural, and political structures that either favor or hinder the economic dynamic. The rules of the game — in other words, the formal and informal institutions — change as the society evolves and as the firms and citizens make new demands, leading to an improvement in their standard of living.

In a productive system where globalization is the rule and where clusters form part of a global value chain, the appearance of new rules facilitates ties among firms and clusters. This can be seen in the growing amount of international standards and behavior patterns (environmental regulations, quality control, technical capacity, labor conditions, ethical and social norms) that have surged spontaneously as the networks and clusters organize themselves on a global level (Humphrey and Schmitz, 2004). However, although globalization conditions institutional change, the cultural and historical specificities of the territory continue to determine the development process, since they maintain and regulate the mechanisms of organization of production (Messner, 2004).

Local Productive Systems on the Move

One of the characteristic features of the economic dynamic today is the shaping of a diverse productive space, located in a singular group of cities or regions in advanced and developing countries. The development of the productive forces is speeding up both the productive diversity and the diversity in the forms of organization of production (industrial districts, industrial complexes, clusters or innovative milieus, and firm networks). As discussed above, in each of the technological revolutions of past centuries, the forms of organization of production have changed; and the introduction of innovations in the productive system, the integration of markets, and the firms' quest for economic efficiency explain the change in firm strategies, in investment and location decisions, and in the forms of organization.

As we approach the end of the first decade of the 21st century, a pronounced transformation of productive systems is taking place in late developed and emerging countries as a result of the increased competition within national and international markets. Why are some industrial clusters disappearing? Why are many others internationalizing their activities or entering global value chains? Why is the local economy looking for new production factors and new markets? How is the system of relations changing within the industrial district? Some of these answers can be obtained from an analysis of the evolution of Italian industrial districts.

Solinas (2006) points out that some clusters, such as that of textiles in Lombardy, disappeared because they were low-cost productive activity clusters facing strong international competition from emerging and developing countries. But frequently, under pressure from product markets, leading companies and the entire network of companies in the local productive system react strategically and diversify their production, introduce new processes, change their area of specialization, and enter new markets. This has led to a change in specialization from manufacturing to service activities, a specialization in the construction of machines (for the production of shoes, textiles, and wine, among others), and an improvement in the quality of exports (Rabellotti *et al.*, 2009).

Perhaps the most significant innovation is the internationalization of production through outsourcing, or the relocation of productive activities following different strategies (Solinas, 2006). Occasionally, the leading companies adopt defensive strategies in the relocation of production; this occurred in the shoe and textile clusters, where the relocation process has redirected productive activities towards low-cost production countries, such as Romania, Tunisia, and China. In other examples, as in the case of Montebelluna, the most labor-intensive and low-quality production phases have been relocated while key competences, especially those relating to innovations, are retained within the local productive system, attracting innovative multinational corporations so that a strategic position in international markets is maintained.

The reaction of companies to globalization and to increased competition in markets seems to be transforming the essence of the industrial district (Rullani, 2008; Guelpa and Micelli, 2007). The internationalization of cluster production is, first and foremost, the recognition of the fact that agglomeration economies, associated with industrial clusters, are no longer sufficient for making local companies competitive when the level of competition increases. Therefore, in order to strengthen competitiveness, companies opt for the outsourcing or relocation of production to other places and territories. This change is often made by groups of companies, led by medium-sized companies.

Rabellotti *et al.* (2009) point out that the importance of medium-sized enterprises in industrial districts is increasing in all types of sectors. These include the typical "made in Italy" sectors such as clothing (Benetton), shoes (Tod's), industrial optics (Luxottica), and ceramics (Ragno); as well as the metal manufacturing sector for scooters and motorbikes (Aprilia and Piaggio). Yet the most relevant innovation factor may be the formation of groups of companies in industrial districts, because this increases the size of companies and strengthens their financial capacities, thus improving their competitiveness. The specialized literature points to two options for pursuing this strategic behavior: a strategy of vertical integration, and a strategy of horizontal differentiation.

The internationalization of production and the change in company size introduce significant transformations in the functioning of an industrial district. The companies' new dynamic implies a change in relations among the companies in the district and the appearance of new hierarchies within the district. The mono-production of the original territory is abandoned as industrial production is externalized, the production in the district diversifies, and the provision of services to companies increases. Change in the productive structure of the territory requires the introduction of product, process, and organizational innovations, as well as access to qualified and sufficiently skilled human resources so as to carry out new activities.

All of this leads to an important change in the role of social capital in the development of districts. External economies — the basis of competitiveness for industrial districts — are associated with knowledge of products and markets, skills of the labor force, commercial networks, and services offered to companies which have historically focused in a specific location. But in an increasingly competitive world, companies have to incorporate new knowledge of products and markets, create new networks of production and commercialization, and have access to new business services, for which the social capital in the original territory is not always sufficient.

Hence, clusters and industrial districts are in a process of transformation leading to a new model of organization of production. Industrial districts continue to be an efficient form of the organization of production, whereby the important trait is not the size of the companies, but the network or the system of companies. The following are among the most important changes and innovations:

- A decisive innovation is the internationalization of the value chain so that the production process acquires a local/global character. Phases of the production process are carried out in different locations, while in the original cluster location service activities increase, thus changing the territory's production culture.

- In addition, the entrepreneurial capacity changes, as greater creativity is necessary in order to respond to the challenges presented by global competition. Innovations in production and management are introduced in a way that allows companies to strategically control the risks they take by dealing in global markets.
- Finally, the relation between companies and the territory changes as the location of productive activity widens. The value chain firms, beyond producing within the original territory, are also present in those territories which supply the resources and markets. Therefore, when companies change location, they also change their relations with other companies, agents, and institutions, leading to changes in the culture and governance which have traditionally characterized the district.

Thus, companies and territories are changing their strategies as a result of the effect of the globalization process on their markets. Companies continue to be connected to their place of origin, but economic integration opens up new opportunities by allowing them to internationalize and broaden their production through alliances in different locations and sectors and through integration in different cultures.

Chapter 5

Polycentric Development of the Territory

In the preceding chapters, two questions of particular interest were discussed: the economic and spatial effects of globalization, and the meaning of the relation between development and the territory. I argued that markets for products, resources, labor, and capital are expanding as a result of the reduction of protectionist barriers and the introduction of innovations in the transport and communications systems. The increasing dynamics of exchange stimulate important changes in the location of productive activities and the progressive diversification of production in all types of territories, leading to changes in the geography of economic development.

In this chapter, the transformations in the territorial organization model and the emergence and consolidation of polycentric regions are analyzed. What are the new forms of territorial organization? Are the networks of global cities or city-regions polycentric systems? Are the polycentric models considered useful for analysis and policy actions by urban planners and decision makers? Is territorial development polycentric?

For the purpose of making the meaning of the new models of physical organization of the territory more precise, the theories of central place and core-periphery are discussed. The idea is that the hierarchical view of the spatial organization of the economy has given way to a more flexible interpretation, and the polycentric region has become an adequate concept for understanding the new forms of organizing the territory in times of globalization. The polycentric region is defined as a network of places and territories with differentiated activities that share a common history and culture as well as a network of local actors who interact.

The Formation of New Urban Spaces

As pointed out by Perroux (1955), economic development and urbanization are the result of innovation and, therefore, are two closely related processes. However, urban development is conditioned by history in such a way that the initial models of the settlement of a population are transformed and the population density changed, at times radically, though always within the limits maintained by the earlier urban structures. Because of this, localities and cities that have grown and developed together appear at the present time to be responsible for forming the polycentric system of cities and regions (Batty, 2001; Batten, 1995).

Polycentric regions are formed by a number of localities and urban centers in which capital and labor converge, in which firms and farms that constitute the productive system settle, and in which the population works and lives. In geographic terms, polycentric regions are made up of a number of urban centers, with high or low productive specialization, connected by a grid of transport and communication systems — among which, on the one hand, resources, goods, and services are exchanged, and, on the other hand, interactions between the companies and the organizations take place — and where a well-defined labor market is established. As a result, these are territories that, throughout their history, have consolidated their own culture and have developed their own institutions, which shape the current model of organization of the territory.

The process of globalization has had a strong impact on the evolution of cities, giving an impulse to the formation and development of geographical platforms that facilitate competition between firms in national and international markets (Scott and Storper, 2003). Currently, different ways of organizing the territory can be identified: the global cities, the city-regions, the polycentric urban regions, and the territorial systems of decentralized urban centers (Hall and Pain, 2006; Parr, 2004; Batten, 1995; Fuá, 1983).

The new international division of labor takes shape through the formation of the system of global cities, each of which has a different function and plays a different role in the dynamics of the international economic system (Hall, 1966; Sassen, 1991). A great variety of global cities exists. Some are the centers of international economic power, like New York, London, Paris, or Tokyo; others are national capitals, like Brussels, Berlin, Budapest, Rome, Madrid, Buenos Aires, or Cairo; and others are commercial cities, such as Amsterdam, Milan, Barcelona, Frankfurt, São Paulo, Mumbai, Osaka, Chicago, or San Francisco. A relevant trait common to all of them is that strong competition exists between them based on their specialization in different functions and, hence, on the different roles they play in the global economy, as Hall (1999), Sassen (2006), and Taylor (2004) point out.

Global cities are centers of political power, of international commerce, and of financial, banking and insurance systems; they are centers specializing in the creation and diffusion of knowledge, centers in which information concentrates and also spreads; they are centers of art, culture, and leisure (Hall, 1997). For some (Friedmann, 1986; Castells, 1996), this network of cities obeys a markedly hierarchical structure. Nevertheless, it would seem more appropriate to speak of multiple hierarchies existing among them, as their relations are not uniform. There are different hierarchies in the futures markets for raw materials and agricultural products, while on the other hand the functions for the provision of new strategic business services have grown within the national and commercial cities. Lastly, as the geographer Peter Hall (1997) points out, the recent dynamics and growth of global cities may have provoked the relocation of their activities and functions to neighboring places and territories, giving rise to metropolitan systems that are highly polycentric.

City-regions are platforms that have seen a substantial development as a result of the economic and social influence of a big city. These are cities (with a regional or national character) that differentiate themselves through a number of functions (such as organization and control, property, or public administration) and that seek support in the territory nearby, where different urban centers and localities exist (Parr, 2005). In some cases, these are cities that occupied a strong leadership position during the Industrial Revolution, such as Manchester or Birmingham; in other cases, these are places that were already consolidated as cities before the Industrial Revolution, such as London, Paris, or Frankfurt. Parr (2005) points out the possibility that within a city-region there may be more than one city and proposes some European examples, such as Cologne and Düsseldorf in Germany, Metz and Nancy in France, or Manchester and Liverpool in England, even though he argues that these cases represent the exception to the rule.

Given the complementary nature that exists between a city and its surroundings, strong relations of supply and demand of factors and goods are established between both "components" of the city-region. The development of a great variety of social and economic relations is favored by commercial exchange and by labor and capital flows, facilitated by the existence of a good transport and communications network. Scott (2001) points out that, given that the process of globalization has a spillover effect from the global cities towards their surroundings, it is more appropriate to talk of city-regions that are global in nature in order to refer to the mosaic of big cities whose functions lead the transformation of the international economic system. In any case, as with the concept of the global city, the dynamic of the city-region refers to a region whose strong polycentric network seeks support in the system of relations and exchange that has historically been developing between the urban centers within a region.

Network cities — as Batten (1995) calls the polycentric urban regions, which is the term most often used — constitute modern urban agglomerations that refer to a plurality of centers which enjoy more creativity and diversity, less congestion, and more freedom than monocentric cities of the same size. Among the classical polycentric urban regions, Batten points out two: the Randstad region in the Netherlands, which is formed by the cities of Amsterdam, The Hague, Utrecht, and Rotterdam, as well as additional minor cities such as Delft, Haarlem, and Zandstad; and the Hansai region of Japan, which includes the ancient Japanese capital cities of Nara and

Kyoto, the port cities Kobe and Osaka, and other cities such as Wakayama, Himeji, and Ohtsu, where the area of the Osaka coastline has become an international business center based on trade and indus trial activity. Further examples could be added, as Parr (2004) suggests, such as the Ruhr Valley (from Bochum to Düsseldorf and Bonn) in Germany; the Katowice district in Poland, whose productive activity is supported by the availability of energy resources (such as coal and hydraulic energy) and natural resources in general; and the Research Triangle in North Carolina, which is articulated around the urban centers of Raleigh, Chapel Hill, and Durham, with their training facilities, research centers, and governmental institutions. Finally, as Hall and Pain (2006) indicate, polycentric regions have been rediscovered in Eastern Asia, in areas like the Pearl River Delta region, the Yangtze River Delta, and Greater Jakarta.

As Meijers (2005) argues, one of the ideas behind the concept of the polycentric urban region is that the economic functions, urban facilities, residential services, and business environment are provided jointly by the region's cities and settlements, and not by a single city. Therefore, firms, citizens, visitors, and tourists can choose between a broader and more specialized set of urban functions and services. This model of spatial organization is distinct and specific because economies of agglomeration are based on the complementary productive systems that have increasingly been established among cities and settlements in a region, as well as on the cooperation among actors and decision-makers of a region. In short, the development of urban network structures, such as those which characterize polycentric regions, provides increasing efficiency to this type of spatial organization model as a result of the synergies that arise between localities and cities.

Finally, territorial systems with polycentric development have a specific form of territorial organization that is rooted in the system of economic and social relations which evolve between the firms of an industrial district (Dematteis, 1991). Multiple cases of local production systems have been studied in late developed countries of Southern Europe. In Italy, industrial districts are found all over the country, especially in the Northern regions such as Lombardy,

Tuscany, Emilia-Romagna, and Marche. The same occurs in Spain, where at least 83 local production systems have been identified and are located in specific cities and localities such as the Mediterranean coast (Alicante and Murcia), the Balearic Islands, the axis of the Ebro River valley (Navarra and Rioja), and Galicia (Pontevedra).

The territory is organized around a grid of urban centers that are very different in size, and whose dominant activities have traditionally been handicrafts and manufacturing until industrial production was internationalized in many of those territories in recent decades. In this process, a continuous transformation of the urban centers has taken place: localities and cities went from being rural service centers to being industrial centers, and ultimately became business services centers. The territory is structured by a road and infrastructure network that allows for exchange between firms and that provides services to its citizens. Local production systems, anchored in the city network, have emerged and evolved thanks to their culture, values, institutions, and social capital which is specific to that local community. Their work ethic is based on effort, social mobility is strengthened, and this stimulates the functioning of the labor market. Thus, trust becomes a factor that regulates the relations within the production system.

The Polycentric Organization of the Territory

At present, there is a great variety in the spatial organization of the territory, with each form having its own characteristics and differentiating traits that show the complexity of the territory. But, as argued above, the transformation of the spatial structure of each territory is strongly linked to the urban system that existed in the past, and to the specific resources of the territory that attract the location of firms and that change and transform the transport and communications systems.

In fact, one of the most important conclusions of the above discussion is that, despite the diversity in organizational forms, no matter which concept is used, all interpretations agree in pointing out that the economic and spatial dynamics of recent decades have reinforced the polycentric character of the territory. As Batten (1995) maintains, important transformations in the form of organization of the territories that are now taking place favor the change in paradigm. In this sense, the hierarchical view of the organization of the economic space, based on the central place theory and the core-periphery model, has given way to a more flexible approach of multiple hierarchies such as the system of network cities or polycentric urban regions. The new paradigm rests on a historical and territorial interpretation which argues that development is a territorial phenomenon that emerges in a differentiated manner in multiple places as a result of their own resources, history, institutions, and culture.

The central place theory (Christaller, 1933) argues that the territory is organized in a hierarchical manner with the specialization of cities according to their size, and predicts the functions of each city in a region as a result of its size. The regulating element here is the demand of each locality: while the smallest localities and cities have a demand for basic products that can be supplied by their own production, only a small number of cities can produce those high-quality goods and services that require a specific and high demand. This means that the hierarchy of cities and products is associated with the conditions of production and demand. Production locates in a specific territory as a function of economies of scale and transport costs, in such a way that the higher the economies of scale and the lower the transport costs, the higher the probability of a concentration of production. Therefore, a number of localities and cities of different levels exist within a region, each of which tries to supply to the specific demand as a function of its size. The urban settlements, villages, and small cities produce simple goods and services to supply the demand of the local population; whereas large cities, beyond the goods and services for general and basic consumption, produce high-quality goods for their citizens and for those of other, lower-ranked localities and cities.

The research carried out regarding the relation that exists between the size of a city and its position in the urban system supports the conclusion of this theory. However, it only provides an adequate interpretation for the explanation of the behavior in health, education, and cultural services markets, for instance, where the transport cost tends to be relatively important in relation to the production cost and where the final consumer is willing to take it on, in the same way as when the consumer moves in order to buy a durable consumer product or seek specialized medical service. The theory's usefulness is limited when the production cost is higher than the final product's transport cost, as in the mining, textiles, and car industries.

Yet, the transformations that arose as a result of the introduction of innovations in economic activities and in the system of transport and communications, as well as the increase in the income and welfare levels of the population, have changed the assumptions on which the interpretation was based. Competition between cities based on market areas defined in terms of population size is no longer a good argument, given that the rise in income has changed the purchasing power of the population and consumers' preferences vary throughout the territory. In addition, innovations applied to transportation have changed the market areas as they allow for rapid long-distance displacements and, furthermore, the availability of modern transport infrastructure within a territory has changed the firms' location pattern. Lastly, the central place theory does not permit us to argue in terms of the effects of economies and diseconomies of agglomeration.

The arguments regarding the hierarchical organization of the territory gain more strength when reasoning in terms of the core-periphery model, which in the final analysis is a proposal that considers economies of agglomeration as the main mechanism in the development processes (Fujita *et al.*, 1999; Scott and Storper, 2003). The core-periphery model is a broader version of the cumulative causation approach (Myrdal, 1957; Friedmann, 1973). In its original version, it tried to explain the processes of industrial development that follow differentiated paths in different territories. It establishes a typology as a function of the positional differences as reflected in economic and spatial indicators, thus differentiating between core and periphery regions.

The core regions are those urban regions in which activities that benefit from economies of agglomeration, external economies of scale, and diversification economies are located. The structure of the productive activity has changed with the crisis of the 1970s and

1980s. What at one time was the production of industrial goods and consumer services has changed, in the post-industrial era, to the production of high-technology goods and advanced business services (Precedo Ledo, 1996).

The peripheral regions are at a great disadvantage in competing for investments, visitors, and tourists, in comparison to other places and territories, owing to the high cost of transport, the *de facto* absence of agglomeration economies, and the dispersion of human resources (mainly skilled workers) (Copus, 2001). Their productive structure — initially associated with the supply of raw materials and a first transformation of local resources — currently includes those routine phases in the production processes where high-technology content is low as well as tourism and leisure services, which are derived markets that depend on the main decision-making centers.

The core-periphery model is a simplification of the economic and spatial reality (Precedo Ledo, 1996; Copus, 2001). It basically reduces the development of the territories to two dominant causal factors, i.e. the high cost of transport and the absence of economies of agglomeration. But, even if one accepts that space is continuous (as this interpretation assumes), the reality is more complex, as other systems with a broad diversity of centers and peripheries that are internal and external to regions and countries exist. Moreover, as Lasuen (1973) argues, inverted core-periphery phenomena may arise in cases where the economic core is not the political core (and the economic periphery may not be the political periphery), leading to situations in which the economic core is the political periphery (and the economic periphery is the political core). This would place us in a situation of multiple hierarchies that is very difficult to analyze using the core-periphery approach.

Furthermore, in recent decades a noticeable improvement in transport and communication infrastructures has taken place. This has drastically reduced transport costs and has changed the perception of what "far" or distance signifies, leading many manufacturing industries which are sensitive to transport costs to make their location decisions based precisely on cost reduction. In the developed countries, and specifically in the countries of the European Union, the costs of transport are decreasing at a time when the economies are experiencing intense structural change, with a progressive increase in services and light manufacturing and a prolonged decline in traditional basic industrial activities. If technological change (especially that concerned with information and communication technology) is also considered, more possibilities as to the location of tertiary activities and light industry are opening up for non-metropolitan areas, including rural areas which are distant from the great consumer centers.

Lastly, as Friedmann (1973) himself had anticipated (Richardson, 1978), the core-periphery relation has broken down over the last three decades, and the territorial system has become progressively more polycentric. The expansion of markets, the improvement of the transport system, the progressive diffusion of innovations, the new forms of organization of production, and administrative decentralization have made the spatial reality more polycentric. Thus, the cities and localities in the periphery have become more attractive for the location of productive activities.

The Italian and Dutch cities of the 11th century show that cities were always organized in networks. The notion of a network city refers to a flexible and polycentric structure of the urban system that facilitates the exchange of goods and services between the different centers or nodes of the network; it stimulates the flow of information and, from an economic perspective, allows for the functioning of imperfect-competition markets. The network city theory goes even further, and understands that the space is a discontinuous concept in which the processes of development are interactive processes between the nodes. It also argues that development, beyond a system of spatial relations, is a process that includes economic, social, and political relations; in other words, it is a process that has more to do with the decisions of agents and social groups and with structural change than with the position held within a given organization of the territory.

This view of a polycentric development of the territory is reinforced by the endogenous development approach. The latter argues that each economic space appears with its own configuration, which is defined as a function of the dynamics of the production systems, the introduction and diffusion of innovations, the emergence and development of networking, the transformations in economic and trade relations, and the changes in the economic, political and social institutions. Historically, each local community has changed as a result of the population's capability and creativity, the relations and connections between the interest groups and social actors, and the construction of its own identity and culture. At the center of the territory's development process are the cultural dimensions, and its development and transformation are enhanced by culturally sustainable processes.

Development, therefore, is a territorial process that affects local and territorial differences in a specific way. But given that culture as well as economic and social institutions condition the development processes, which in turn transform culture and institutions, we see that spatial structures and the models of the organization of the territory are strongly determined by its history, the people's creative capacity, and the complexity of institutions, norms and rules of the game, codes of conduct and existing conventions in each territory.

Relations and Interactions in Polycentric Regions

Globalization, as pointed out above, has continuously incorporated cities and urban systems by means of the flows of labor, capital, and commodities. Thus, polycentric regions, which are structured through a network of cities, have become complex territories. Cities and localities — which are functionally connected through business relations, the commuting of people, leisure and tourism, and even the electronic connections between firms — have seen the intensity of their relations increase, and this has strengthened the consistency of the network of cities (Green, 2007).

Among the cities and localities in the polycentric regions, there exist complementarities rooted in economic specialization that have been historically generated. Therefore, exchange of commodities, labor and capital flows, and investments are taking place, which condition the economic and social dynamic of a region. The exchange of goods within a region depends on the regional division of labor, the productive specialization of each locality and urban center, the articulation of the local production systems, and the multiple demands between cities and urban settlements. The integration of spaces through the new systems of transport and communications facilitates the flow and exchange of raw materials, agricultural products and manufactured goods, consumer and commercial services, financial services and business services, and particularly those services associated with the activities of construction and residential housing as well as leisure and tourism.

Furthermore, during the last few decades, trade and commercial exchange of commodities between the localities of every region with those of other regions have increased because of market integration, as occurs with regions and cities in the European Union. In addition, the reorganization of multinational corporations — specifically, the relocation of phases of the productive process to other countries — has enabled the development of international networks of suppliers and clients and global chains; this has led to an increase in international trade and commercial flows between cities and regions, to which the back-office activities of multinational corporations should sometimes be added (Minian, 2007). Lastly, the relocation of production plants from traditional industrial districts and clusters to countries with lower wages and lower costs has enlarged global relations and, therefore, the exchange between the regions and cities of advanced, emerging, and developing countries.

Yet, perhaps, the relations between the localities of the polycentric regions can be appreciated more clearly when observing the increasing population and labor flows within the interior of the polycentric region. All localities of a region are increasingly affected by flows coming from more distant localities, associated with the location of firms, farms, and private and public services. Noticeable changes in population flows are taking place within a region, as the relocation and outsourcing of segments of the productive activity are undertaken, people are changing residence, and transport and communication infrastructures are improved.

The increasing integration of the economy generates strong human resource flows between internationalized regions. The cities and regions of late developed countries of the European Union have experienced a strong migratory inflow, mostly from those countries which have recently entered the European Union, but also from Asia, Africa, and Latin America (Canullo and Vázquez-Barquero, 2007). In Ireland, 8% of employment was taken up by foreigners in 2005; in Greece, it is estimated that immigrants made up 10% of the population in 2004; in Spain, the foreign population reached more than 5.5 million people in 2009, accounting for 12% of the total population; and in Italy, immigrants represented close to 7.5% of the total population at the end of 2008. Such strong migratory flows have affected cities and regions in different ways, depending on their increasingly decentralized economic dynamic.

Finally, investments and capital flows have conditioned the economic dynamic within the polycentric regions of the advanced economies since the 1950s and 1960s, and in the emerging and developing economies since the beginning of the 1980s. During the last 50 years, investments in the construction of housing in the surroundings of the most dynamic cities and in other localities of the regions, as well as the location of industrial plants and services in the metropolitan areas of big cities and in medium-sized cities and small localities of the region and other regions, have contributed towards creating an economic dynamic that has affected, to different degrees, the different cities and regions, especially in Europe and the United States; it has also affected the population in general as well as the workers of those territories. The logic of the location pattern is not clear insofar as large parts of the territory and all kinds of localities and cities have been affected by the relocation of plants and the de-concentration of employment and residence.

Peter Hall (1993) has explained the dynamics of the European urban system since the 1970s up to the present time. He states that in the early stage, in addition to the construction of housing and residential buildings within the outskirts of the cities at the edge of public transport routes, the de-concentration of employment began. First, routine assembly manufacturing firms seeking spacious premises were located close to the highway system; next, R&D centers and high-technology firms moved to high-amenity locations, attracted by leisure services, and frequently chose places close to airports; and then back offices that carried out routine activities were displaced towards suburban centers and other locations in the region where, besides land, they could find the skilled labor supply required. This relocation of industrial activities towards different localities within a region was accompanied by the establishment of service activities such as shops and stores, as well as public and private services such as schools and health care centers. Finally, as happened in Madrid with the location of the Banco de Santander in Boadilla del Monte, in the late 1980s began the relocation of office headquarters towards suburban locations.

The network of cities gives a polycentric character to the region, whose model of spatial organization is articulated and structured by the system of transport and communications. The infrastructural endowment contributes to the functioning of the urban system by means of three mechanisms. In the first place, it facilitates the economic relations between firms, encouraging economic flows and the import and export of goods, as reflected in the companies' competitiveness. Secondly, it enhances the organization and physical structure of the territory, favoring those connections that link the most important centers, thus improving the efficiency of the productive system. Thirdly, it stimulates the agglomeration of the population and the productive activity within the region, the relations and exchange between firms, and, all in all, the external economies generated by the concentration of firms and urbanization.

The transport and communication infrastructure plays a strategic role in the development of the new industrial and service space. In the case of local production systems, the emergence and development of the productive activity normally takes place in locations that are well communicated (such as Aranda de Duero, the communication node between Castile and the Basque Country and between Levante and Western Spain; or Elda, in the Vinalopó valley, which has connected the Mediterranean sea to Castile since the time of the Romans), and their development calls for their continuous improvement and adaptation to today's constantly changing needs and demands. In the case of global cities or city-regions, high-quality transport and communication infrastructures, such as a good highway network and a big airport, are a necessary condition, among others, in order for a productive system to emerge and develop. The endowment of quality infrastructures, in any case, effectively constitutes a basic factor for the attraction of firms, as pointed out above.

The high-concentration networks, such as highways, frequently exercise a strong spillover effect on the industrial and service activities. Roads and highways play a singular role in the exchange of certain services that are very spread out in the territory, such as tourist services in regions with a low population density, and consumer services (commercial or social) that are more and more reliant on the accessibility and flexibility introduced by the widespread use of cars.

Highway and high-speed train networks have the capacity to create their own demand and to broaden organizational structures and markets. High-speed trains, for instance, in an early phase serve those service activities which are focused in big cities such as Madrid, Paris, London, Brussels, or Cologne; but this does not necessarily imply a weakening of the productive activity of localities, medium-sized cities, or other regions that are far away from big consumer centers. On the contrary, as the development of business services (especially the consulting firms) in the city of Lyon, France, shows, it may be a mode of transport that leads to a diversification of services and gives incentives to those who favor competitiveness. Therefore, cities such as Valladolid, Barcelona, or Seville, in Spain, will be able to develop new activities in modern services once they are connected to the European high-speed train network.

Furthermore, in an economy where business services (both national and international) require personal contacts and where tourist and cultural activities are spread throughout the territory, the demand for air transport — and, therefore, a bigger and better infrastructural endowment — grows progressively. The airplane has become a widely used mode of transport in tourist activities, whose services are already mass consumption goods. The continued expansion of national and international exchange of business services is also generating an increased demand for air transport in order to facilitate face-to-face contacts and relations. Therefore, the demand for air transport infrastructure requires increasing public and private investments that fulfill the firms' and citizens' demand for goods and services produced in cities and regions.

The new communication system, in turn, contributes towards improving the productivity of local industries and plays an important strategic role in the development of services, since many service activities can only be competitive on the basis of electronic communication. Cost reduction in telecommunications and the new technological developments may not reduce the competitive advantages of leading regions; nevertheless, they do allow emerging regions, localities, and medium-sized cities to be more dynamic, and to strengthen both business and consumer services.

Finally, the urban transport infrastructure and the regeneration of urban spaces play a strategic role in the competitiveness of cities and urban regions. The intra-metropolitan infrastructures such as highways, metro systems, or trains — i.e. economic and social overhead capital — and the infrastructures that link the nodes in a polycentric region facilitate access within a region, facilitate the supply of services, and increase exchange within the internal networks of the polycentric region.

Consequently, the actions taken for urban regeneration, with a high symbolic value and external projection, that the new urban strategies put forward stimulate the competitiveness of cities. Through projects such as eco-quarters, technology parks, or digital cities, new forms of urban land use are explored in order to attract enterprises and workers towards places and regions. Furthermore, the construction of cultural equipment (like the Guggenheim Museum in Bilbao) or the celebration of great sports events (like the 2008 Olympic Games in Beijing or the hosting of the 1998 Universal Exposition in Lisbon) stimulates important physical transformations in cities, and at the same time offers greater international projection and attraction for investing and living.

Productive Diversity in Low-Density Regions

The new dynamic of the productive system has created a new map of economic development in all types of territories, as a result of the growing integration of the economy and the market. Rural regions are experiencing strong productive change due to the increased market competition, the introduction of innovations in the production of goods and services, and the reduction in distance and transport costs. These transformations, aided by increased income during recent decades, have expanded the demand for the goods and services produced in rural regions.

Saraceno (2000, 2006) points out that new forms of exchange between rural localities and regions and distant regions and countries have developed in the European regions, as a result of improved accessibility as well as changes in the demand associated with increased income. Thus, the variety of leisure activities related to vacation time, such as the attractions of nature or the historical and cultural heritage, has witnessed a growing demand among certain social groups of city dwellers. Some urban residents may also desire a second home in rural areas, whether they are retired and seek a different lifestyle or professionals with flexible urban jobs. Furthermore, when the improved transport and communications infrastructures greatly reduce the distance between one's workplace and home, and when jobs carried out from the home are viable in professional activities, the residence in rural regions appears to be a viable alternative. When this phenomenon appears repeatedly, it has an attraction effect for administrative, health, educational, entertainment, and retail commercial services towards rural localities and regions.

Even though an improved transport infrastructure has been one of the factors contributing towards the accessibility of firms and people to the markets, as well as towards changes in the spatial organization of production, the effect has not been homogeneous in all rural regions. Low-population-density areas vary widely from each other. A wide variety exists, related partly to the location and accessibility, partly to the availability of natural and environmental resources, and partly to the economic history and the productive and technological knowledge accumulated within the territory over generations. Because of this, faced with the challenges posed by increased market competition, the responses have been very different.

Therefore, rural regions are characterized as having a diversified productive system. Traditionally, rural regions provided cities with agricultural products in order to provide food for the population, and these natural products and resources were traded in international markets in exchange for merchandise sought after by firms and people in general. In the 19th century, however, rural regions contributed in an outstanding manner to the industrialization processes. In England, Germany, and the U.S., the Industrial Revolution was based on the development of the chemical, iron, and steel industries, whose firms were located in rural regions. Likewise, in late developed countries like Spain and Italy, the textile, garment, ceramics, and shoe activities were located in rural areas. More to the point, in recent decades there has been a progressive reinforcement of public and private services in rural regions in the European Union countries and the U.S.

Porter *et al.* (2004) argue that in advanced economies like the U.S., agricultural activities are not the most important in rural regions in terms of income and employment; rather, industrial activities and services are becoming more and more important. The relative importance of agriculture today is seen, as Quigley (2002) points out, by the fact that farms use less than 7% of rural employment and that the income generated in farms is below 2% of the rural income. Moreover, since the 1980s, a change towards service activities has occurred and the participation of the manufacturing industry in total rural employment has diminished (from 29% in the late 1960s to 16% in 1995), due to advances in technology and more recently by having increased delocalization of manufacturing activities to China and Southeast Asian countries.

This phenomenon can be seen in late developed countries such as Spain. According to Regidor and Troitiño (2008), the economy of rural regions in the country is becoming increasingly diversified, with agriculture losing its hold and the majority of activities being linked to industry and services in most territories. Agriculture is no longer the principal source of wealth in the rural areas of Spain; activities linked to certain consumer goods (such as agribusiness products, textiles, and furniture) and activities related to the construction sector are now located in rural municipalities, along with new tourist activities as well as leisure and health services.

The research conducted by Porter *et al.* (2004) is conclusive when it analyzes the diversity of production in rural regions with respect to urban regions. On the one hand, the study points out that the percentage of jobs in industry and firm clusters producing goods and services for local markets (such as bottles for beverages, construction, retail sales, newspapers, health, and public services) is practically the same in both rural and urban regions in the U.S. (64.2% and 67.8%, respectively, in 2001); the same occurs in activities (such as airplane motors, motor parts, film, video, and car assembly) whose products are sold in other regions and countries (32.6% and 32.5%, respectively), although after the early 1990s the percentage tended to rise in urban regions. The difference lies in that the makeup of the activities is different. The productive structure of metropolitan areas is more concentrated in the production of knowledge-intensive goods and services as well as business services; whereas in rural areas, productive activities that depend on local resources (e.g. traditional products and tourism) are dominant.

The productive dynamic of rural regions in the last decade has varied widely from one territory to another, as shown by the case of Spain:

• Employment and income have decreased in territories specializing in the production of dairy products and grain, but have increased in those activities characterized as having potential. These include the wine clusters of Ribeiro, Valdeorras, and Rías Baixas in Galicia and of Ribera del Duero in Castilla-León as well as the flower cluster in Almería, which produce goods with a growing demand in national and international markets.
• The textile and footwear activity has decreased in the rural areas of Barcelona and Alicante, as a result of increased competition in

markets with products from China, Southeast Asia, and North Africa, and the ensuing delocalization of the activities of local firms towards other territories. At the same time, however, the ceramics cluster in the province of Castellón is stronger due to the increased domestic demand, the local firms' competitive advantage associated with the adoption of new technologies, the internationalization of its more dynamic firms to Latin America and Asia, and the development of strong commercial networks.

• Public and private services have risen continuously in the past 30 years, as a result of the development of the welfare state and the increased demand for business services by industrial firms and farms. Yet, construction activities and tourist services have grown spectacularly in rural areas.

In an ever-more integrated and competitive world, the appeal of rural regions rises when firms and farms are capable of using their competitive advantages. Clusters, like that of wine or ceramics in Spain, have improved their productivity as a result of introducing innovations in product and production processes, strengthening their commercial and information networks among firms and thus reducing transaction costs, spreading innovations within the productive fabric, and stimulating the start-up and development of innovative firms.

Also, the improved accessibility of rural regions opens up their markets and stimulates local firms' competitiveness in national and international markets. Increased competition stimulates firms to differentiate their production so that their products will find a way into the ever-more globalized markets. This is making the rural regions increase their production of manufactured goods, diversify their production, and, therefore, increase employment and local income.

Last of all, low-population-density territories are not always ideal for generating and potentiating all types of externalities between firms and farms, which is undoubtedly a weak point for the firms' and territories' competitiveness. However, this weakness becomes a strength for the development of certain types of activities, such as tourism and other activities where environmental quality is a necessary factor for the productive activity. In this sense, the good environmental conditions of rural regions may be an attraction for locating a business, besides being a quality standard-of-living factor for the people of these rural areas.

The Mechanisms of Polycentric Development

As previously pointed out, urbanization and development are two phenomena that interact. Therefore, one of the central questions that allows us to assess the relevance of the forms of organization of the territory is to ask how and to what extent they contribute to the economic and social development of cities and regions. In the case of polycentric regions, the mechanisms through which the spatial organization conditions the behavior of productivity and the competitiveness of firms and territories, and thus contributes to the economic and social progress of the population, should be analyzed.

As discussed above, the concept of economic development evolves as the economic and social actors make investment decisions and implement solutions to new problems. Development refers to a process of growth and structural change, generated by the diffusion of innovations and knowledge within the economic and social organizations. Even though the diversification of production is what satisfies the demand for goods and services by the population, the relevant point — in terms of development — is the increase in productivity, to which cost reduction, economies of scale, and economies of diversification contribute.

The concept of the polycentric region refers to different types of spaces that are associated with specific spatial and economic characteristics which contribute to an increase in productivity and the development of a region. Networks of cities which structure the territory are spaces that are characterized by their density and exploit the effects of the concentration of people, firms, and productive activities, thus favoring economies of agglomeration. Furthermore, there exist places with low population density that possess specific resources that become increasingly attractive for the location of productive activity of goods and services, which contributes to an increasing diversification of their productive system and, in turn, stimulates economies of diversification that have positive effects on territorial development. Finally, polycentric regions are a form of spatial organization of the territory that activate the mechanisms of capital accumulation through the stimuli that they give to the organization of production, institutional change, and the diffusion of innovations.

As Meijers (2005) points out, what is at stake here is to identify the mechanisms through which economies of agglomeration can develop in polycentric regions. The answer emerges when it is considered that networks, which articulate polycentric regions, are formed by cities that function as nodes of the regional grid within which exchange and flows take place, as discussed above. Every city is, in turn, a net whereby the different actors (enterprises, social and professional associations, centers of training and research, and public administrations) interact through economic, technological, informational, and cultural flows that lead to a structured order, generating mutual influence between the local actors.

Hence, a polycentric region can be understood as a network of local actors whose relations shape the production system in which economic, social, and political agents are organized in a specific way and share a common culture; and their relational dynamic allows them to exchange products, knowledge, and information. The relations and contacts established between them over time form a net of connections and links that drives the cooperation between public and private decision-makers as well as the interdependence between firms and organizations. Therefore, one can argue that, in polycentric regions, the relations and networks stimulate the appearance of economies of scale based on the cooperation among actors and the complementary role of firms and organizations within the productive system (Camagni and Salone, 1993).

Thus, cities and settlements of an urban network as well as the actors who make public and private investments form a group that shares interests and objectives, which is why establishing cooperation between them is possible. In some cases, these are cities and localities where the same type of productive activity is carried out, as in the case of the cities of Vigo and Coruña in Galicia, Spain, with activities related to portuary services and clothes manufacturing. In other cases, similar problems are faced, such as the necessity to improve the transport and communications system or to respond to the effect of economic integration on firms and the local productive system, as in the case of the cities and localities in Galicia. Under such circumstances, the conditions exist for the cities of the network to establish mechanisms of cooperation that enable the emergence of economies of scale.

When the grid of connections and links formed between cities and towns of a polycentric region helps to establish a differentiated and complementary production system, it produces a synergetic effect by itself that stimulates the formation of externalities and economies of agglomeration. When the region's productive system is organized through a value chain that links, even if only partially, the activities of different cities and localities, interactions that drive the appearance of external economies are generated.

In turn, the network of cities and regions can be organized into different product and service activities. For example, within the Randstad (Meijers, 2005), Amsterdam shows a specialization within the network in commercial, financial, and cultural activities, as well as in tourism and leisure; Rotterdam stands out for its position in the manufacturing and transport industries; The Hague is the city in which administrative services and government departments are focused; and Utrecht is a commercial city that provides training and educational services. The specialization in differentiated and complementary products generates a favorable situation for exchange and interaction between the actors of the polycentric region, resulting in the creation of economies of scale. When a differentiation in the production of goods and services develops, the conditions are then created for the market to expand and for the demand (of enterprises, citizens, visitors, and tourists) to choose among the products of companies from different places and cities in the region, which increases the supply available and stimulates economies of scale.

Beyond the generation of externalities and economies of agglomeration, associated with the interaction between different actors, a relevant point to consider is the effect and incidence of the diversification of production on the improvement in productivity and the dynamics of the regional production system. This is a question that affects, as we have just seen, not only the urban spaces, but also the rural regions and low-population-density territories in general. As Saraceno (2006) points out, during recent decades, the rural economy has diversified as a consequence of the relocation of industrial activities and services, and the emergence of new manufacturing and service activities (such as tourism) promoted by local actors. These processes of diversification and differentiation of agricultural, industrial, and service production are embedded, as explained above, in the dynamics of economic development and the increased productivity of polycentric regions. The strength of these processes is associated with the integration of productive activities, modern as well as traditional, in national and international markets for goods and services. The interaction between internal diversification and external integration generates a synergy that opens up new opportunities for those spaces to improve their competitiveness within the markets.

Therefore, the diversification of economic activities in rural areas and the multiplication of forms of external integration contribute in a singular way to the differentiated development of places and territories, and allow polycentric regions to develop a renewed dynamism by contributing towards increased productivity and competitiveness. The strength of these processes of development resides not so much in the economies of scale of agricultural farms, but rather in the increase of economies of diversification when the differentiation of agricultural businesses is combined with the development of industrial and service activities. The diversification of the rural economy and the combination of different types of activities improve the results in areas with a low population density and with farms and small firms, widely dispersed in the territory; this is particularly so when local economies are embedded within the region, are well integrated within the regional productive system, and are well connected to the transport and communications network that facilitates flows and exchange within the region.

In short, polycentric regions are a form of spatial organization of the territory that facilitate greater productivity in the local economies. When the mechanisms and the forces that determine the processes of capital accumulation are analyzed, one notices that the polycentric region characteristics and factors stimulate the formation of flexible production systems, institutional change, and the diffusion of innovations within the local productive system. Therefore, they reinforce the mechanisms responsible for greater productivity and, also, for economic and social progress.

Polycentric regions are the physical space in which firm networks settle and local production systems are formed, as the regions provide the resources, goods, and services necessary for them to function. In cities and towns, including the spaces where agriculture is the dominant activity, an innovative and entrepreneurial atmosphere is maintained, technological knowledge spreads, and meeting centers for entrepreneurs spring up. When productive systems are structured and organized through networks, the trade and exchange among firms, the diffusion of innovations and knowledge, the flows of information, and the interaction between enterprises and other local actors lead to the emergence of economies of scale and scope as well as a reduction in firm production costs.

As far as the institutions are concerned, they adopt specific forms in each territory owing to differences in the technological and economic history, cultural differences, and differences among the actors and the forms of association. Regions and cities have turned into places where modes of development, knowledge and technology, and patterns of behavior and culture have historically emerged and developed, all of which condition the evolution and the dynamic of institutions. Polycentric regions facilitate the formation of networks of actors whose interactions and exchange have established codes of conduct and a set of rules based on trust. To the extent that the behavior of the actors becomes strategic, agreements tend to be formal and relations are increasingly subject to rules that are explicitly agreed upon, thus reducing transaction costs. Finally, the dynamics and transformation of polycentric regions create needs and requirements for new rules and institutions that will contribute towards the stability of the network of actors, and that will regulate, formally and informally, the relations (even international relations) between regions and city networks.

Last of all, polycentric regions have become a space in which the different actors interact and, by approaching projects jointly, generate learning processes that allow innovations to emerge as well as processes that spread knowledge and technology. Polycentric regions favor the concentration and proximity of firms and actors, because this creates a favorable environment that is necessary for the emergence and diffusion of innovations and knowledge. The concentration and agglomeration of companies and actors stimulate the appearance of economies of scale, which are necessary for the development of creativity and new projects; while the proximity of local actors and companies stimulates competitiveness and facilitates the diffusion of ideas. Therefore, polycentric regions favor the creation of an adequate environment for the appearance of new products, processes, and forms of organization of companies, which contribute directly towards the improved productivity of firms and organizations and the increased competitiveness of territories.

Chapter 6

Creativity and Diffusion of Innovation

Put simply, economic progress takes place as a result of the application of knowledge and energy to the transformation of resources in a territory. Hence, the concept of economic development is associated with the accumulation of knowledge through learning and the diffusion of technological innovation throughout the economic and social fabric of a territory.

Creativity and diffusion of innovation and knowledge, changes in the spatial organization of production, and institutional change are the main forces in the process of economic development. Therefore, it could be said that economic development is not only a question of macroeconomics and policies that favor macroeconomic equilibrium; nor is it only a question of microeconomics, no matter how decisive firm investment and location strategies may be. It is also a systemic process in which the productive system, the institutional system, and the system of innovation co-evolve.

How does innovation emerge and diffuse within new forms of organization of production? What is the relation between innovation and polycentric development? Is technological innovation an interactive process among local actors? What are the sources of innovation and creativity? How is innovation diffused within a high-tech global value chain? Is the regional system of innovation useful for the creation and diffusion of innovation?

Innovation and Economic Development

It is generally recognized that the economic development of cities, regions, and countries comes about as a result of technological progress. According to Schumpeter (1934), innovation is the causal factor of the spatial organization of production and economic development, since innovation is the driving force behind the appearance of new products, processes, forms of industrial organization, markets, and sources of raw materials. Economic growth is the result of capital accumulation, which in turn embodies technological progress. Therefore, it can be said that economic growth is the outcome of the accumulation of technology.

Firms introduce innovation into the productive system through investment decisions. Thus, the content and the effect of innovation depend on the way production is organized, the strategies used by firms to maintain and increase their output and their market share, and the existence of required services to introduce technical progress into the productive organizations. When firms need external support for adopting and adapting innovation, they must resort to private and public external services.

In recent decades, important changes have taken place in how the production and regulation of capital are organized. The crisis of Fordism has favored the development of flexible organizational structures, at times through the formation and consolidation of local production systems, and at others through more flexible forms of organization within large firms. However, these structures have always been strongly rooted and integrated in the territory. Changes in organizational modes of production have been accompanied by changes in the approach, institutions, and regulations, so that the focus has gradually moved from linear innovation systems to interactive models (Asheim and Isaksen, 1997). Linear models of innovation hold that scientific advances occur and are transmitted sequentially; they emerge within the scientific institutions and centers, and are progressively transferred to the economic sector. On the contrary, interactive models consider that innovation emerges as a result of interaction between firms, technological and scientific centers, and government offices, as well as through contacts between local and regional actors within the system of innovation.

The evolutionary model, as Freeman (1988) points out, considers that innovation occurs when ideas about products, production methods, and marketing or organizational strategies go beyond the point of mere discovery to be implemented within the productive reality. Firms apply, through investment, new technological knowledge to the production process and the marketing of their products, which allows them to become more efficient. Thus, innovation is primarily an economic activity because it requires the use of financial resources to obtain better returns and profits.

Since it is the firms themselves who decide to invest in new products, processes, organizations, and markets, they are the strategic agents for technological evolution. Nelson and Winter (1974, 1982) indicate that companies are organizations, each with its own distinctive characteristics and level of profitability. In any case, they should be considered the true incubators of innovation. Firms "transport" technologies and all those practices that determine what is produced and how it is produced. That is, they are the carriers of what Nelson and Winter have conceived as "routines" (a concept analogous to the gene in biology, with firms representing living organisms).

In an increasingly competitive environment where firms deploy their strategies in order to preserve their market share and improve or maintain profitability, the process of selecting innovations (and, therefore, firms) depends on market results, which determine winning and losing technologies. However, it is not luck alone that makes a technology successful (i.e. adopted by the group of firms competing in a given market); it must be accompanied by improvements in the company itself and its environment, which are decisive in the struggle to compete with rival innovations.

The transformation of organizations and institutions participating in the process of innovative evolution is complex, since there are usually significant repercussions in the social environment. As Pérez (1986) points out, the diffusion of innovation requires that organizations and institutions adapt to the new situation and act as mediators of technological change. Increased flexibility during adaptation favors technological and structural change and, therefore, economic development.

Innovation is a learning process that takes place as a result of the evolution of the productive and entrepreneurial capacities, and of those that arise through the use of the goods and services produced. The social and territorial dimensions of innovation mean that an increase in knowledge will transcend the individuality of the firms and agents to become a collective learning process. From this perspective, one can speak of interactive learning among the actors within the environment in which firms make decisions to invest and locate.

Thus, we are dealing with a learning process, rooted in society and the territory, in which knowledge, embedded in capital goods as well as non-embedded, is exchanged. This knowledge is external to the firms and actors but internal to the network, and is introduced because of the relations between actors. In other words, innovative processes are interactive and not linear.

In fact, there are few leading firms that decide to incorporate innovations, whether radical or incremental. These are competitive firms, well endowed with quality resources and capable of relating to their environment, with an internal organization that facilitates information flow from one department to another.

As held by Kaufmann and Tödtling (2003), size is not necessarily a strategic factor, but the industrial context is. As Dosi (1988) points out, there are great differences in opportunities, incentives, investments in R&D, and innovative procedures from one industry to another. Pavitt (1984) identified four large groups of manufacturing activities, each displaying a different behavior toward innovation: supply-dominated sectors (agriculture, textiles, clothing, leather, printing and publishing, wood products, and simple metal products); specialized sectors (mechanical and instrumental engineering); sectors intensive in scale economies (transportation, durable electrical consumer goods, metal products, food products, glass, and cement); and science-based sectors (electronics, most of the organic chemical industries, drugs, and bioengineering).

The question of size in an enterprise seems secondary since, as maintained by the evolutionary approach, the relevant factor is the ability to compete, and the market is the selective mechanism. As Kaufmann and Tödtling (2003) state, small firms suffer from problems associated with the type of activity, making innovation difficult. However, innovative firms may actually be small, since their ability to compete may be the result of being part of an innovative milieu, of participating in a network of subcontracting firms with vertical ties through which technical knowledge is diffused, or of having competitive advantages because they carry out innovative activities in a modern and innovative field.

Firms adopt strategies — in particular, technological strategies — with respect to the industrial context, that is, the way production is organized within the territory. Strategy follows organization; thus, it is possible to extend the foregoing thesis and include the system of relations in the territory and, ultimately, the territorial display of the firm's offices and production plants. When firms are part of local productive systems, each and every one of them becomes more competitive because the system of internal relations favors the diffusion of innovations within the district (Grabher, 1993; Becattini, 1997). Trade and exchange, labor mobility, and personal contacts are some of the mechanisms that favor the diffusion of technical knowledge in clusters and industrial districts.

The connection of the network of firms with local institutions and organizations expands the interaction among the actors within the milieu, thus facilitating learning processes that promote the development of innovation within the district. Multiple exchanges, an industrial atmosphere, and a system of informal relations are proactive factors within the district. Moreover, as Ottati (1994) points out, mutual knowledge and trust among the actors strengthen the articulation of the system and reduce transaction costs. Both factors facilitate the introduction and diffusion of innovations within the district (Asheim, 1994).

Hence, innovation is an interactive process led by firms that decide to invest, supported by a network of political and institutional actors and by educational and research institutions. As pointed out by Aydalot (1986), the creation and diffusion of innovations depend on the organization of the territory, the interaction of the actors, learning mechanisms, and, therefore, local history itself. Cooperation among local actors in carrying out technological and innovation activities conditions the evolution of the process.

Learning and Innovation

Learning is undoubtedly a mechanism that facilitates both technical and technological change. Vegara (1989) relates that, during World War II, it was possible to massively construct transport equipment (such as ships or the fuselage of airplanes), due to the fact that technicians and specialized workers introduced changes in the production methods as a consequence of the learning processes undergone in their jobs. But, beyond the learning that results from practice, there is the phenomenon of learning through use (as happens with software in informatics). In order for this to be possible, it is necessary that the users experiment and learn so as to transmit their experiences and knowledge to the producers. Even through reverse engineering, which consists of disassembling and reassembling products (an activity that is very common in the microprocessor industry), learning can foster technological change.

In short, it is in the competitive struggle of companies where innovation emerges. According to the theory of evolution, innovations may be considered as *mutations* of existing technologies. They frequently tend to endanger the survival of existing technologies and they always alter the routines used up until then by the companies, who then adopt the new technology. Firms may decide whether or not to introduce a new technology, but it is the market, by indicating which companies are doing well and which are not, that decides on the adequacy of innovations. The profitability of a company is a good indicator of the suitability (*fitness*) of a technology and the good health (*fitness*) of the company.

The evolution of technology itself has to be analyzed as a function of the competitive strategies of companies. As Michael Porter reminds us in his book, *The Competitive Advantage of Nations* (1990), disadvantages of companies can be transformed into competitive advantages when they react creatively by introducing innovations, as is shown by the history of the car industry. At the beginning of the 20th century, Ford had a large quantity of migrant labor at his disposal, but with a low skill level, which presented a competitive disadvantage; this fact led him to the idea for the creation of the assembly line, which eventually became an innovation that changed the production methods in all manufacturing industries. Decades later, the Japanese car companies, along with some other industries, had to make do with limited space availability and high prices, which doubtlessly constituted an important restriction in such a globalized industry; this limitation became the stimulus to create "just-in-time" production techniques that aim at the delivery of raw materials and intermediate goods at just the right time, thus leading to a reduction in stocks and production costs.

The success of an innovation signifies a change in the process of evolution; however, this does not mean that the new technology which imposes itself is technologically superior to that replaced. For a technology to have success and to replace a rival technology, its introduction — besides needing luck — has to be accompanied by a number of improvements in the company and its environment, which are decisive in the competitive battle between rivaling innovations (think, for instance, of the competition between the Betamax and VHS video systems). To this end, firm routines must be improved by learning in such a way that they favor the diffusion of technology throughout the industry. The result, however, is conditioned by the effects of the investments that are implemented for the purpose of fostering the learning processes.

It is not a simple task to displace a technology installed in the production system because, once an innovation is consolidated, mechanisms are at work that allow it to maintain its dominance in the market. This can be seen in the case of the keyboard of traditional typewriters (QWERTY), whose innovation dates back to the end of the 19th century and is associated with the positioning of the letters in such a way so as not to produce "traffic jams" during their use by more experienced typists. Even though electric and electronic machines have allowed for these difficulties to be overcome, the traditional keyboard remains in use because the cost/benefit relation for using the old technology — instead of the new, technically superior technology — makes technological change unviable, as it would be too costly.

The selection principle works in all cases. A successful technological innovation generates profits for a firm in the long run, which provides an impulse to investment in equipment goods, which favors the use of human resources that are more qualified for the new tasks, which increases the productivity of the company, which permits an increase in wages and profits. Given that companies who use the most profitable technologies tend to grow, rival companies will feel pressure to imitate them and will adopt those technologies that have proven profitable, abandoning less efficient ones. In this way, the selection process introduces diffusion and growth mechanisms in the production system.

The diffusion of innovations is not an automatic phenomenon, but rather is conditioned by the internal functioning of companies and by the relationships that firms maintain with their environment. Therefore, companies' investment in physical capital and in improved human resource skills may have the effect of supporting the spread of innovations throughout the production system, as a result of the exchange and relations between firms and their suppliers and customers, as well as the relationship between firms and their immediate institutional environment.

The use of new equipment, as Arrow (1962) pointed out, transforms the environment within which the company produces and exchanges goods and services, generates knowledge among the workers, and increases the technological knowledge in the economy as a whole. Under these circumstances, knowledge can be considered a public good that, once used by the innovative firm, is accessible and available to all companies. Therefore, an increase in investment and capital stock signifies an increase in technological knowledge, which in turn spreads throughout the production system.

An improvement in the skill level of the labor force would also spread throughout the economy, similar to how learning processes accompany investment in physical capital. Lucas (1988) argues that education and training increase human capital, augment the abilities and knowledge of the individuals who participate in the production activities, and transform the environment in which companies are immersed. In this way, human resources acquire a higher production capacity and improve their returns, thus helping to sustain the productivity growth and competitiveness of firms. Knowledge, in its role as an endogenously produced public good, is transmitted from one company to another by the individuals who incorporate it into their work.

The creation and diffusion of innovations are part of the same process in which continuous interaction between the companies, organizations, and institutions that form the innovation network takes place. Firms do not innovate in an isolated manner based on their own sources of knowledge. They do so through their relations with their environment and through the mechanisms of learning that are generated as a consequence of the interactions with their suppliers and customers, as well as the interactions with the public and private institutions whose activities are part of the creation and diffusion of innovation. Innovation, therefore, emerges and is spread within a given economic, social, and institutional system that is subject to continuous transformations and change — hence, a "national system of innovation" (Nelson, 1993).

Freeman and Soete (1997) point out the influence of the development and strengthening of national systems of innovation on the performance of countries, as shown in the comparison of the economic dynamics and the progress in knowledge in Latin America and the "Four Tigers" of East Asia. According to the statistical information provided by the World Bank, the GDP growth rate maintained its level in East Asian countries during the 1980s (from 7.5% per year in 1965–1980 to 7.9% per year in 1980–1989), whereas in Latin America it fell significantly (from 5.8% to 1.6%). Among the factors contributing to this disparity in economic outcomes between East Asia and Latin American countries, the radical social changes in the former (such as land reform and universal education) should be emphasized; the profound technical transformations that took place within these countries' productive and social systems should also be pointed out (Table 6.1).

Table 6.1   Differences in National Innovation Systems in the 1980s.

East Asia	Latin America
Expansion of the system of universal education, including an increasing proportion of engineering and science graduates	Deteriorating educational system, with a low proportion of engineering and science graduates
Imports of technology, combined with an increasing participation of local companies in technological change	Much transfer of technology, with a weak participation of local companies in R&D
Industrial R&D with a share of more than 50% of total R&D	Industrial R&D with a share of less than 25% of total R&D
Development of important science and technology infrastructure, with later connections to industrial R&D	Weakening of science and technology infrastructure, and weak connections to industry
High levels of investment and major inflow of Japanese investment and technology; influence of Japanese models of management and networking organization	Decline in foreign investment (mainly U.S.) and generally low levels of investment; low participation in technology networks
Heavy investments in advanced telecommunications infrastructure	Slow development of modern telecommunications infrastructure
Fast and strong growing electronics industry with high exports	Weak electronics industry with low exports

Source: Freeman and Soete (1997).

Therefore, the diffusion process is conditioned by the behavior of the organizations and institutions with which the innovative firms exchange goods and services. These include research centers, universities, governmental offices, unions, and employer associations. The diffusion of innovation requires that institutions adapt continuously to the needs and demands of firms, and act in order to facilitate technological change. The higher the degree of flexibility shown in the adaptability of institutions, the more pronounced the effects of technological change will be in the economic development process.

Sources of Innovation: Networks and Value Chains

Innovation and change in the spatial organization of production are processes that co-evolve with economic progress in countries, regions, and cities. Recent literature on economic development (Scott and Garofoli, 2007) argues that economic growth and structural change are due to technological externalities and the associated increasing returns generated within the productive system and within industrial clusters located in specific territories. When productive systems are organized as firm networks, the labor market is large and diversified, knowledge flows among firms and workers, and the interaction among local actors leads to increasing returns.

In territories where the model of organization of production has changed, and large companies accept the importance of specialization through outsourcing and modularization of production, the diffusion of innovation acquires a special force in its dynamic. Knowledge and information, incorporated into goods and services, are diffused through the exchange between firms within the productive system. The introduction and diffusion of innovation leads to a greater and improved stock of technological knowledge in the productive system, which in turn creates external economies from which the firm network benefits.

The objective of innovative companies' strategies is to increase their productivity and competitiveness, as well as to improve their positioning in markets. In order to achieve this, the introduction of incremental innovations helps them reduce production costs, increase the quality of products, adjust their products to the customers' demands, and make the production processes more profitable, thus increasing their economic results in the short and long term. Innovations arise, basically, from inside enterprises and within the local environment, even though on occasion clients and suppliers from outside the productive system can be catalysts in the process of innovation.

Lester and Piore (2004) argue that this view of innovative firm strategy could hide capacities which are, in fact, what constitute the source of creativity and innovation in the productive activity. These include the capacity to integrate teams and ideas that come from different organizational, cultural, and intellectual areas; the capacity to transform reality; and the capacity to experiment with new products in order to satisfy the clients' needs.

In their excellent book, *Innovation — The Missing Dimension*, Lester and Piore (2004) point out that the main point is to identify the sources of innovation. For this, they use a set of case studies on cellular telephones, blue jeans, and medical devices, in whose design and development hundreds of people (e.g. designers, manufacturing specialists, accountants, and marketing and financial experts) participate. For the purpose of understanding how the integration of knowledge so disparate in the design and development of new products is achieved, they interviewed innovative firms in each of these activities. The production of mobile phones is a high-technology activity that integrates radio and telephone technology; fashion jeans combine traditional work clothes with hotel and hospital laundry technology; and medical devices are based on the basic life sciences and clinical practice.

The main lesson that emerges from these case studies is that in order to make new products, improve old products, or produce existing products more efficiently, two basic processes — which Lester and Piore (2004) call "analytical" and "interpretive" — can be followed. The analytical process works better when the possible results are already known and their differences are well defined; whereas the interpretive process is more appropriate when the possible results are unknown and it is still necessary to establish what their properties are. These two ways of generating innovations and knowledge require human resources with different skills, different ways of working together with experts and specialists, different forms of management and control, and even different ways of thinking about the development of economic and productive activities.

The analytical approach tries to solve the problem of designing a new product starting from the information gathered through market research on the needs and demands of the clients. Once the problem to be solved is established, the human, financial, and technical resources available to the firm are identified, and what is missing is also highlighted. The problem is divided into parts, and the technicians and specialists are requested to answer each of the questions put forth; the solution is found once each solution given by the experts is joined together. The purpose, therefore, is an approach whose objective is to improve the productivity and competitive advantage of the company, in accordance with the management theories and scientific and engineering research techniques.

The design and development of new products, however, often follows a different innovation process whereby the solution to the problem is clearly unknown, as occurred in the case of cellular telephones. This is a creative process in which new suggestions on behalf of the client begin to appear, along with new ideas about the product and new ways to produce it. The innovation process becomes an interpretive process in which technical staff, specialists, and managers need to share a new language — a new way of understanding the productive activity — that will allow them to identify a range of alternatives, from which the best one (from a business point of view) is chosen.

Lester and Piore (2004) add that, during the last 20 years, the innovation process has weakened in advanced economies because increased competition in the markets has conditioned the innovation processes of the firms, whose priorities were geared towards strengthening and widening their competitive advantage. Systematically, the fact that creativity in production and in the economy must necessarily reinforce the search for new products and processes and the improvement of goods and services, which is only possible when creativity in the productive and social fabric is stimulated, has been ignored. The analytical and interpretive processes are actually two complementary approaches to product design and development, in which the analytical view is dominated by industrial management and engineering practices, while the interpretive view is more creative and uncertain and evolves as different alternatives within the range of products and solutions arise.

During the last two decades, increased competition in the markets — as a result of globalization, technological change, and deregulation — has led to the changed conditions through which innovation and creativity within firms during the 1960s and 1970s were stimulated. For example, the leading firms in cellular telephone technology, such as AT&T, Motorola, and Nokia, have reorganized their firms in such a way that the laboratory shelters, where new products were developed outside the competitive pressure of the firm, have disappeared. As Lester and Piore (2004, p. 178) point out, "[T]hey are no longer in a position to support the kind of long-term development processes that sustained the earlier cellular industry."

Yet, as a result of the rising changes in today's economic dynamic, a new space for the design and development of new products and processes has opened up in advanced economies. Because of the decline of mass production and the increased production of goods tailored to the client's demand, innovation is recovering its protagonism in production. Reduced production costs, as a result of the adoption of more flexible organizational production models, permit greater adjustment to the client's taste and introduce innovations into the productive process. Moreover, the advances in information technology favor the differentiation of production, and so enable the necessary conditions for introducing more product and process innovations. Last of all, the tendency to blur the boundaries between productive activities has made those firms devoted to these activities (such as telecommunications, information technology, office equipment, and photography) compete among themselves, thus creating new products and processes.

This phenomenon is enforced by the development of "public spaces" in which the tension created between the two models seeking innovation is reduced. In the fashion industry, for example, creativity is most important in the design of new products, for which one contribution is the new developments of culture and their diffusion through the media. Besides this, university research centers are areas where firms can find the necessary cooperation, both for solving new problems in production and for participating in activities where advanced ideas are developed. Flexible forms of organization, such as the industrial districts, have created internal organization structures that stimulate the start-up and diffusion of innovations throughout the productive fabric.

The technological strategies of companies and the very process of innovation of local production systems are conditioned by their sectoral context (Pavitt, 1984). As Dosi (1988) maintains, great differences exist in the opportunities, incentives, R&D investments, and innovative procedures between different industries; this explains why, depending on the type of production activity, the characteristics of the innovation process change. Furthermore, every production activity has a different value chain, which determines its internal organization and the relations with other activities; this in turn conditions the type of innovation introduced into the principal chain and into the components of the value chain, the hierarchy of innovation, and the transfer of technology.

The literature on industrial districts explains that the design and development of new products and production processes are activated thanks to the technological externalities generated among the firms shaping the cluster. In an industrial district, a large variety of jobs are related to specific trades having to do with the predominant productive activities, and worker skills improve as the district develops. The accumulation of knowledge helps improve worker skills, which is one of the more relevant specific resources of the district. Knowledge, therefore, circulates among the firms, but it is not a public good; rather, as Rabellotti *et al.* (2009, p. 31) assert, "tacit knowledge is personal and specific" and is not talked about throughout the industrial district, but circulates between a small number of firms.

A large variety of capabilities for innovation and creativity exist in the industrial districts that Belussi and Pilotti (2002) classify with respect to the different learning systems:

* *Weak learning systems.* These are districts specializing in traditional activities, such as textiles or ceramics, that use an unskilled labor force and have few opportunities for innovation. They are characteristic of low-cost-labor economies and are shaped by groups of firms with activities and products that use artisan methods, as

occurs with textile production in Lima, Peru, or ceramics in the
metropolitan area of Hanoi, Vietnam.

- *Both artisan and scientific knowledge systems.* These are districts in
  which firms combine artisan know-how and scientific knowledge
  in the productive processes, with a skilled labor force. They combine internal knowledge with the adoption of technologies from
  outside the district. The technological strategy varies from one
  company to another, but in general is focused towards incremental innovations. Sometimes, they adopt production processes and
  methods by installing new equipment and new information systems that guarantee better quality and lower costs. Occasionally,
  they introduce innovations through the start-up of a new line
  of products for expanding markets. A good example is the toy
  industry in Ibi, Spain, which has diversified its production by manufacturing plastic toboggans and swings, and has widened its
  activity by constructing play equipment for kindergardens, parks,
  and backyards.
- *Dynamic evolutionary systems.* These are districts organized around
  innovative firms that have highly skilled human resources and produce for national and international markets. Examples include
  districts devoted to ceramics such as Sassuolo, Italy, and Castellón,
  Spain; those of Toulouse, France, and Madrid, Spain, in the aeronautics industry; that created by Nokia for the production of
  mobile phones in Beijing, China; and the electronics industry
  clusters in Silicon Valley, U.S., and in Penang, Malaysia.

The variety of capabilities for innovation and creativity has grown
as a result of the modification of the nature of economic innovation
(Maillat, 2008; Dunning, 2001). The increasing contribution of services to GDP is giving a strategic role to intangible assets within the
productive system; and innovation is expanding as a result of the
adoption of innovation in business services, health and educational
activities, and cultural arts industries. Therefore, technological innovation is losing its relative dominance insofar as social, institutional,
and cultural innovations are becoming increasingly important for
markets and for the development of places and territories. This

change is affecting the dynamics of development. The flow of capital, labor, and knowledge is creating a multi-local productive system by linking places from different polycentric regions, including those specializing in service activities.

Diffusion of Innovation Within High-Tech Clusters

In those districts where dominant activities are normally described as high-technology activities (e.g. electronic industry, biotechnology, pharmaceutical industry, aeronautical and aerospace activities), the process of innovation is linked to scientific advancement (Box 6.1). Investments in product innovation are relatively high, and the search for new discoveries and innovations is central to the strategy of companies (Saxenian, 1994).

Box 6.1

The Jura Innovative Milieu

The Jura region is traditionally known for its specialization in the production of watches, owing to the secular industrial tradition of its cantons. During the last 20 years, however, it has diversified its production system significantly through the introduction of high-technology activities, and has become one of Europe's most dynamic innovative milieus.

The economy of the region, consisting of the cantons Neuchâtel and Jura, the north of Vaudois and the Joux valley (Vaud canton), the Bernese Jura (Bern canton), and the Soleurois Jura (Soleure canton), has developed on the basis of activities that are related to the production of watches. Currently, its productive fabric is also based on activities such as precision mechanics and microtechnology, to which activities such as microelectronics and new materials have recently been added.

(Continued)

(*Continued*)

A dense network of companies (small- and medium-sized as well as big companies) constitutes the industrial organization and maintains cooperative/competitive relations between them. The region offers great industrial potential, a highly qualified labor pool, and traditional know-how associated with the activities carried out in the production processes. The production system of the Swiss Jura consists of 95% small- and medium-sized companies and is characterized by the vertical disintegration of production, which implies not only intense scientific and technical cooperation that is needed for maintaining the technological level of products and processes, but also economic cooperation between the companies.

The production of watches favored the emergence and development of industrial activities, such as the production of tools, instruments, and even machinery. Even though the industrial development was initially linked to the needs of the traditional industry, these activities have progressively acquired a higher degree of autonomy and a specific dynamic, including numerous applications in a wide range of products such as telephones, instruments for measurement and control, office machines, and peripheral computer equipment. The know-how from the watch-making activities was enriched by the knowledge from activities such as microelectronics, optics, and new materials, giving an impulse to the development of new activities such as microtechnologies, thus creating a link between traditional and new activities.

Historically, the region has been a beneficiary of its know-how in elementary microtechnology, essentially mechanics and electromechanics (e.g. grammophones, typewriters, telecommunication sets, micro-tools, radios). Its genesis dates back to the end of the 1960s and the beginning of the 1970s when the quartz watch was developed, in whose production a combination of micromechanics and microelectronics appeared for the first time. Modern microtechniques are

(*Continued*)

(Continued)

derived from a combination of precision mechanics, microelectronics, new materials, and, in some cases, optics and electro-optics.

Innovation in the industry of microtechnical combinations implies, in part, the creation and development of networks for the cooperation between companies and research and training centers. Because of their size, smaller companies do not always have the means and capacities that are indispensable for carrying out product or process innovations, given that this type of activity requires a significant effort in research and training. Therefore, a strong regional system of innovation in which the industrial sphere can interact has emerged. The fusion and reconversion of the old laboratories of the Swiss Center of Electronics and Microtechnology (SCEM), the creation of research and training university institutes in the field of microtechnology, the setting up of specific programs for microtechnological engineering in the higher technical schools of the region, and the participation in international cooperation programs (e.g. European R&D projects and cross-border collaborations) have thus undeniably contributed to the recovery of the local economy's dynamic.

The innovation process implies the combination of a number of functions (research, development, building of prototypes, industrial investments, and trade) that demand different resources (know-how, information, physical and financial capital), and thus is inevitably multi-sectoral and has a multi-locational character. Nevertheless, it is very open to the outside (such as in the participation of its research institutions like the SCEM in European R&D projects) for the purpose of enriching its resource and information potential. This environment is relatively homogeneous, and is based on a common technological culture and common values that are shared by all actors who are willing to participate in the innovation process.

Source: Maillat *et al.* (1995).

Innovations are produced throughout all segments of the value chain of an industry. In the case of the computer industry, for instance, innovations occur in microchips, software applications, disks, screens, and network-building instruments. Therefore, a single company cannot innovate in all components of the value chain; it has to seek support from firms specializing in complementary activities, and cooperate as a participant in a network of innovative firms. Each company tends to specialize in what it is capable of doing, and buys the rest from the other companies in the local production system. This not only reduces the development costs and the production time of new technologies, but also stimulates the development of innovations that are interesting for the entire network of firms.

However, the process of innovation is more complex when the value chain is internationalized, as seen in the field of aeronautics. The construction of an airplane requires a process of learning and the circulation of knowledge and know-how in order to make the aeronautical cluster become innovative. Negotiation between clients and suppliers plays a central role in the diffusion of innovations, since accumulated knowledge is transmitted in contract specifications as well as in the manufacturing of the airplane. The following discussion on the aeronautical cluster of Madrid shows how innovation is diffused within a high-technology cluster (Alfonso-Gil and Vázquez-Barquero, 2010).

Organization and relations in the aeronautical cluster of Madrid

The aeronautical cluster of Madrid — still in the process of formation — is a hub-and-spoke type of system, since the firms in the cluster that provide goods and services for building aircraft parts designed by EADS-CASA are established around the EADS group of firms. The aeronautical cluster of Madrid is a spatial concentration of very diverse yet interrelated firms that specialize in the production of specific parts of the product, marketed by EADS-CASA and Airbus España. At the center of the cluster in Madrid is the consortium EADS represented by its two subsidiaries, EADS-CASA and Airbus España.

Around this central nucleus, there is a group of firms that work not only with the EADS group, but also with Boeing and other firms and organizations in other aeronautical, aerospace, and industrial activities. These firms include Indra, Gamesa, Sener, and Tecnobit. Also present is another group of firms specializing in the production of goods and services for the aeronautics industry, such as CESA, TEGRAF, GARC, and Aerlyper. Yet another significant part of the firms in the cluster manufacture products and provide services for other industrial activities. Some of these have emerged from industries that have undergone acute restructuring, as is the case with TAM, APRIM, and RANEM, which were previously producers for the automobile industry.

The formation of the cluster and the consolidation of relations among the firms in the network are based on agreements or alliance contracts. Thus, firms obtain scale economies in the production, research, and development of products and processes, while reducing the production costs and the costs of diffusion of innovations and knowledge within the network. Relations between suppliers and clients are based on certifications which guarantee that firms in the cluster have sufficient knowledge, know-how, and equipment to manufacture the product or provide the service.

Subcontracting is widespread among firms in the sector, but its significance depends on the firm's position in the value chain of the final product. Gamesa, for example, sources about 60% of its production from other firms located in the Basque Country, Madrid, Andalusia, and the South of France. Between 2002 and 2003, CESA subcontracted to other firms a total volume of €7 million, representing approximately 50% of its production. This type of relation is most often established with local firms (the city, metropolitan area, and region of Madrid) or national firms, although some are from the European Union (4%) and 1% are from other countries. The subcontractor usually specifies the characteristics that the products on order should fulfill, indicates the processes that should be used, and supplies the raw materials; sometimes, the subcontractor will supply engineering and quality support or even transfer technology. The subcontractor selects its suppliers carefully to assure that they will be capable of fulfilling the technical and marketing requirements of the first-tier client. Both suppliers and clients carry out quality controls for the product.

The Madrid cluster is also part of a network of centers and clusters located in various European territories, as both manufacturing and technology transfer in aircraft production (civil and military) have become internationalized. EADS is an international consortium that manufactures its products, components, and structures in several countries and territories where its network of suppliers is located, and its sales and client policies are also international. The Airbus A380 construction program, for example, assigned work not only to the EADS network of local suppliers, but also to suppliers from other countries such as Japan, Korea, Malaysia, and Australia. In addition, suppliers and firms subcontracted by EADS are linked to other international networks. Indra, for instance, operates in more than 40 countries in five continents, with its main clients in Europe and the U.S; it also has subsidiaries in the U.S., China, Portugal, and Brazil.

The diffusion of innovation in the aeronautical cluster

Aeronautical and aerospace activities maintain a high-tech profile not only because of the constant flow of knowledge, but also because of never-ending quality controls in the manufacture of products, components, and structures.

The manner in which aeronautical-aerospace production is organized conditions the process of innovation in firms and in the cluster of firms, as can be seen when analyzing the flow of knowledge involved in the building of an aircraft. EADS is enriched by the knowledge of its own highly qualified human resources, placing it on the global technological frontier, and by the cutting-edge technology provided by a relatively small number of firms that are independent of the leading firm. These major suppliers have special relations with the leading firm, such as a predisposition to assume risk in the production of their products and the sharing of knowledge strategies.

Along with these horizontal flows of knowledge, EADS channels vertical knowledge flows toward firms located on lower technological tiers that display varying levels of knowledge. These are the systems suppliers with relatively high levels of knowledge, and they in turn source part of their production from third- or fourth-tier firms. The latter are auxiliary firms which specialize in less complex tasks with less innovation content, and whose ability to act independently of the lead firm or major suppliers is very limited. These small firms, often family-owned, are the most numerous. They normally proceed according to blueprints provided by the leading firm or systems supplier, and their activity usually involves a low level of incremental knowledge. In recent years, some small firms that were originally mere receptors of the blueprint-based subcontract have come to participate in the actual design of the subcontracted parts.

The key component in the process of innovation is the very act of sharing the knowledge accumulated in each of the firms in the cluster as a result of the learning acquired during the process of manufacturing each component. The flow of tacit knowledge impregnates the entire productive fabric, and so each one of the firms reduces the costs of developing innovation as well as the time employed in the production and application of new techniques and technologies. The flow also facilitates the diffusion of knowledge within the network by means of commercial transactions and the circulation of ideas and knowledge.

Therefore, innovation is a learning process that takes place as a result of the exercise of productive and entrepreneurial capabilities. Diffusion of innovations in the case of the aeronautical industry comes about through a learning process that arises from the interaction between firms in the cluster. Although the original design, features, and quality aspects of the production of an aircraft depend on the specifications of the leading firm, the technical participation of engineering firms and suppliers — particularly those within the major top-tier groups — is becoming increasingly decisive. Most of the engineering involved in the development of the main components of the aircraft (above and beyond the basic concept and blueprints) is the result of collaboration between engineers of the leading supplier firms.

Commercial, professional, and technical relations within the aeronautics cluster facilitate the diffusion of knowledge between the most innovative firms and the less dynamic firms. Firms that carry out the easier tasks have a low-intensity innovative capacity, and body parts specifications are usually dictated by the client. But when there is a long-lasting, continued relationship between clients and suppliers, the supplier often manufactures the parts according to knowledge accumulated in the firm and in human resources. In this way, a proactive relation takes place at all levels of the network through the effects of two kinds of knowledge: one resulting from the productive experience in firms and workers, and the other a product of interaction between firms and workers.

Regional System of Innovation

As mentioned in previous chapters, the development of a country, region, or city is the result of the accumulation of capital and knowledge, which favors increased productivity in those factors that affect production systems. Thus, in the development processes, a vital role is played by the systems of innovation, as shown by the fact that since the beginning of the Industrial Revolution the regional system of innovations has been the base on which growth and structural change, and hence the economic and social progress of economies, are built (Arcangeli, 1993).

However, not all regions and cities of a country have the specific resources or the capacity necessary to innovate and introduce knowledge in the productive activity. The reason for the existence of different regional and urban responses is that the appearance and application of knowledge involves territorial actors with different backgrounds, strategies, and objectives. As Vence (2007) points out, the development of a territory depends on the ability of its innovation system to facilitate the co-evolution of firms, technologies, and institutions.

The system of innovation is composed of a set of actors and a set of relations established between them for the purpose of producing, diffusing, and using knowledge (Lundvall, 1992). Therefore, actors form a network in which, according to the case, the innovative impulse can be found in private firms, in the training and research centers, or in the government. But, as Nelson (1993) points out, at the heart of the systems of innovation are the firms. When what is being analyzed is the region, the territorial dimension acquires a central role. Thus, it is necessary to argue in terms of the firm clusters that characterize the region's productive system, the network of research and training centers, and the institutional development produced in the political sphere through the local and regional governments (Cooke, 2001).

It can thus be pointed out, as Etzkowitz and Leydesdorff (1997) suggest, that the interaction between the actors of a region is the mechanism through which the technological base changes and is transformed. Hence, the network factor explains the economic dynamics of the region as well as the regional disparities. In this sense, the institutional question is key, given that the rules of the game within a territory condition the development of the ties between the actors, as well as the set of relations required for the development of scientific and technological knowledge and for the diffusion of innovations within the productive fabric.

A regional system of innovation is shaped by a set of actors, whose ties and relationships reinforce the learning process and facilitate the production and accumulation of innovation and knowledge. The firms, farms, and clusters produce goods and services and make the investment decisions that are necessary in the capital accumulation and development processes, and therefore condition the creation and diffusion of innovations. The training and research centers as well as the technological development centers stimulate learning and the capacities of human resources, focus the direction of research and participate in technological developments, and make the social and cultural resources that facilitate development available to the firms. Lastly, the public administrations design the policies, decide on public investments, and carry out the government's actions.

Learning and the diffusion of knowledge require that cooperation and coordination stimulate the interaction among actors. In order for this to take place, the cluster of firms and productive activities is not enough; what is also needed is that the actors shape the system of innovation, share interests and objectives, and have a common language and trustworthy relations. These are, according to Camagni (1991), precisely the characteristics that stimulate the collective learning processes and the diffusion of both tacit and codified knowledge among the local actors.

Knowledge flows through the existing ties among the actors, based on the norms and rules — the region's social capital — which enhance the relations within the territory. When the productive system is articulated through a network of firms, the ties between them may be formal (as in the case of agreements and technological alliances) or informal (based on personal relations between the members of the firms). The agreements and alliances among research and training centers stimulate academic collaboration, both within the local system as well as with external organizations, and also help in the exchange of researchers and students. At the same time, exchange of knowledge among firms and research centers is very important for the diffusion of knowledge because it allows for the transfer of tacit knowledge. Moreover, the ties with the government and its offices help achieve a trusting atmosphere between the local actors, the implementation of public policies, and the coordination between actors.

Vence (2007) stresses two important issues while discussing the systems of innovation: the demarcation of territorial boundaries in the innovation processes, and the change in innovation policies. The relations between the local actors go beyond regional and national boundaries as the value chain is internationalized, the relations between clusters of different countries increase, and science and technology spread worldwide. Hence, one could argue that the national and international innovation systems are the most efficient. Yet, Lundvall (1992) maintains that the core of the system of innovation tends to be organized around the region, given that in the innovation and learning processes the interaction among actors is made easier when they share the same culture and the same norms and institutions. Furthermore, in this way, the possible conflicts that could arise between actors in fulfilling their needs and demands within different national and international systems, as occurs in the European Union, are kept to a minimum.

Proximity makes the regional systems of innovation more efficient, since it helps both the appearance of economies associated with the specialization of the actors in different tasks and the reduction of transaction costs. Some firms and technological research and development centers devote particular attention to the creation and development of innovations. The leading enterprises store knowledge and information and, through inter-industrial relations, stimulate the diffusion of innovation and knowledge within the regional productive fabric. Other actors play a special role in defining the language and approach that must be shared among firms, managers, and researchers in order to stimulate creativity and the diffusion of knowledge.

Yet, the government and public administrations tend, out of necessity, to change the direction of their actions, given that firm results depend on how the system of innovation in which they are immersed is organized and on their dynamics (Vence, 2007). In the production process, firms learn to produce, innovate, organize themselves, and export, which explains why the variety of learning methods (learning by doing, learning by using, and learning by interacting) are so important in the innovation process. Thus, as Freeman and Soete (1997) indicate, government actions in the promotion of strategic industries, the coordination and implementation of long-term industrial and economic policies, and the proactive role played by the government are very important, so as to create the conditions that will strengthen the interaction between the actors in the regional system of innovation. In this sense, governmental initiatives that enable institutional change are particularly important.

Undoubtedly, the strength of a regional system of innovation lies in the knowledge accumulated within the firms and organizations of the region, in the skills of its human resources, and in the organization of the system of actors. The continuous creation of incremental innovations, as Lundvall (1993) points out, is only possible thanks to both the cultural and geographic proximity among the principal users and the tacit knowledge accumulated in the local human resources. In the case of radical innovations, the learning and knowledge capacity located within the territory, the availability of specific resources (cultural, human, and technological), and institutional changes — which form the basis of a firm's competitive advantage — are even more crucial. Therefore, it is the regional system of innovation that provides local firms with the necessary factors in order to maintain and improve their competitive position within the global markets.

Creativity generates very diverse innovative and technological capacities, and so makes the territories widely diverse with respect to the level of knowledge and innovation. Innovative spaces, as Camagni (1991) points out, are characterized by a system of technological externalities that diffuse knowledge and innovation, by a system of economic and social relations that constitute the relational capital, and by a governmental system shaped by the local actors; whereas peripheral and less innovative spaces must adopt and adapt innovations as well as reinforce their productive, technological, institutional, and governmental systems. In both cases, it is necessary for the industrial policy to change direction and combine actions that are focused on individual firms with actions that try to improve the organization and functioning of the regional system of innovation.

Chapter 7

Local Development Policies

The high unemployment and poverty rates experienced by many developing countries in the 1980s and 1990s called for a profound change in their development policies. In order to respond to globalization, increased competition, and changes in market conditions, these countries needed to restructure their productive systems. The local development policy represents a spontaneous response on behalf of local communities for the purpose of neutralizing the negative effects of globalization and productive adjustment on employment and the population's standard of living.

Faced with the limitations of the macroeconomic policies in reaching the goals of the eradication of poverty, job creation, and improved social welfare, the local and regional actors attempted to manage the adjustment process. Through their actions, they tried to increase the productivity of the farms and the industrial and service firms, and to improve competitiveness in the national and international markets of firms located within their territories. However, the economic, political, and institutional environment in which local initiatives were implemented has changed since mid-2007, when developed and emerging economies found themselves affected by the financial crisis that has spilled over into the real economy.

How have local development policies responded to global challenges? Do they help create the conditions for sustainable development? Are local policy tools making the productive system more competitive and creating jobs? Which are the most efficient policy tools? How are local initiatives designed and implemented? What is the role played by local actors and civil society? What lessons can be learned in order to respond to the global crisis? How can local policy tools foster economic recovery?

Local Response to Global Challenge

The facts previously discussed — such as increased competition due to the increasing integration of the economies, the extent of existing poverty (especially in the developing countries), and the rise in unemployment resulting from the processes of adjustment and restructuring of the production systems, together with the diversity of the territories — present a picture that calls for a complex and broad interpretation of the processes of development. In any case, the approach should go beyond the neoclassical approach and take into account what the new facts indicate: that the growth rate in poor countries is not necessarily higher than that in rich countries; that innovation is an entrepreneurial and economic phenomenon which is key to the growth process; that institutional change is a central force for sustainable development; and that economies adopt very diverse development strategies, leading to different results, as Lasuén and Aranzadi (2002) argue.

Furthermore, during the last two decades, a radical change in the economic policies of market economies has taken place. At the same time that industrial and regional policies were abandoned, because of the acceptance of economic policy recommendations formulated in the Washington Consensus of 1989 (an informal agreement between the World Bank, the International Monetary Fund, the Inter-American Development Bank, and key U.S. government agencies for developing policies that reflect the free market approach to development), new development policies emerged in late developed and developing countries during the 1990s. These new policies were based on the initiatives designed and implemented by the local private and public actors and the civil society.

Since the time when President Ronald Reagan of the U.S. and Prime Minister Margaret Thatcher of the U.K. drove liberal policies forward, governments have continued to focus their policies on maintaining a stable macroeconomic framework through their fiscal and monetary policies, in order to create the most favorable conditions for the economic agents to implement their investment decisions. For over two decades, the governments of poor and rich countries have encouraged the reduction of the presence of the state in economic activity; the privatization of public firms and public economic activities; the reduction of the role of redistributive, industrial, and regional policies; and the control of the public deficit. These measures have, more frequently than hoped (such as in the case of Argentina), brought negative effects for income growth and employment as well as allowed corruption to thrive.

The high unemployment and poverty rates attained in the early 1980s served as a stimulus for profound change in development policies. Local and regional actors began to implement policy actions that were directed towards having an impact on the growth processes of their local and regional economies. The new development policy began with the purpose of counteracting the negative effects of productive adjustment on employment and the standard of living of the population (Figure 7.1).

Since then, cities and regions in Asia and Latin America have found themselves facing the need to restructure their productive systems in order to respond to the challenges of increasing competition and changes in market conditions. They have launched initiatives to pave the way for changes or improvements in the organization of production, the diffusion of innovation, the channels used to commercialize products, and the access to product and factor markets — in short, to increase the competitiveness of firms and territories. Macroeconomic policies were insufficient to achieve social goals associated with the adjustment processes, job creation, and the improvement in social well-being; thus, local and regional actors have spontaneously designed and implemented the new strategy through actions that are ultimately aimed at increasing productivity in farms and in industrial- and service-sector firms, and at increasing the competitiveness of the firms located in their territory in national and international markets.

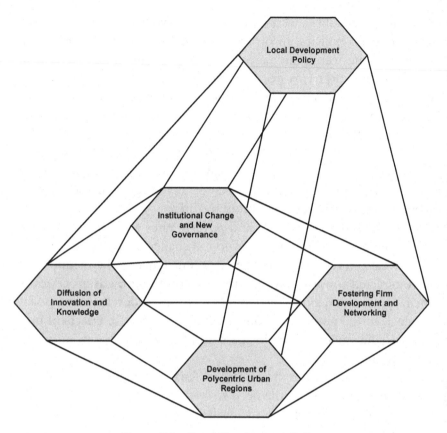

Figure 7.1   Local Development Policy.

Fostering firm development and networking

Local initiatives are very diverse in nature. Yet, the basic characteristic of the new development policy is that an important part of the local initiatives is designed to spur on the forces and mechanisms that are decisive factors in the capital accumulation process. One of the objectives of local initiatives is the start-up and development of firms and the formation of firm networks. In Rafaela, Argentina, an industrial district under productive restructuring (Ferraro and Costamagna, 2000) — the Centre for Entrepreneurial Development — was created in 1996, financed by the Inter-American Development Bank (IDB) as well as by local firms and the municipality. The Centre gives technical and financial assistance to local and regional firms in order to help them improve their production and have a greater presence in the markets, thus increasing the internationalization of small firms.

Similarly, in the Sierra de los Cuchumatanes, in Guatemala, on the border with Chiapas (Cifuentes, 2000), cooperatives and associations (e.g. the Formal Organization of Agricultural Producers) were revived in the 1990s and began to acquire full legal capacity. These organizations also recovered the experience and knowledge of self-management that existed within the local population and was lost during the civil war. Moreover, more informally structured organizations or interest groups were encouraged, and this brought people with common productive and commercial interests together.

In Marikina, the Philippines, one of the objectives of the group of shoe manufacturers is to improve the cooperative base of the shoe production cluster (Scott, 2005). The Marikina Footwear and Leather Goods Manufacturers Cooperative, for example, provides financial services to members of the cooperative; these services include "the right to take out loans, to purchase raw materials at a reduced price, and to discount letters of credit". The cooperative has a footwear brand (B&G) that its members may use when manufacturing their shoes. The cooperative also provides distribution and marketing services to its members.

The government of Penang, in Malaysia, created the Penang Development Corporation (PDC), whose main objective is to promote socioeconomic development, including the attraction of export-oriented multinational corporations (MNCs). The PDC played an important role in the creation of the electronic cluster in Penang, with an important presence of MNCs (e.g. Clarion, National Semiconductor, Intel, Motorola, Hewlett-Packard, AMD, and Hitachi) during the 1970s and of consumer electronic firms (e.g. Sony, Toshiba, Pensangko, Komag, and Seagate) during the 1980s and 1990s. The PDC has helped to stimulate the formation of firm networks as well as differentiate and diversify the productive fabric, particularly after the late 1980s. A productive fabric was created in which the domestic small- and medium-sized enterprises have established ties among themselves and with the MNCs. However, the lack of coordination between the government of Penang and the Federal Government of Malaysia has restricted the development of local initiatives aimed at upgrading human resources and diffusing innovations within the local productive fabric (Rasiah, 2007).

Finally, over the last decade in Latin America, Asia, and Africa, various forms of microcredit and financial support to micro-firms and small businesses have appeared (Lacalle, 2002; Armendáriz de Aghion and Morduch, 2001). The Grameen Bank, created in 1974, is a story of success; in 1999, it had over 2.3 million clients (95% women) and a volume of loans of over US$2.715 billion, and it is estimated to have helped 12 million people in Bangladesh. In addition, International Action, founded in 1961, has a network of 19 credit offices in Latin America, with over 380,000 clients (57% women) and over US$335 million in loans.

There are many experiences in fulfilling the local firms' needs and demands for services in Latin America (Muñoz, 2001; Londoño, 2001). In 1992, the Municipal House of the Small Businessman (Casa Municipal del Pequeño Empresario) in the town of Rancagua, Chile, was established in order to promote qualification in business management and to render technical and financial assistance to micro-firms and small businesses. The Program for the Support of Small- and Medium-Sized Firms (Programa de Apoyo a la Pequeña y Mediana Empresa) in Antioquia, Colombia, aims to provide small textile and clothing industry entrepreneurs with knowledge of textile materials and design, and to provide technical consulting and export assistance through a strategic alliance with the Export and Fashion Institute.

Diffusion of innovation and knowledge

Another major axis of the new development policy is the diffusion of innovation and knowledge throughout the local productive fabric, as can be seen in the initiatives that work in territories with very different productive dynamics and levels of development. Thus, in Rafaela, the

Rafaela Regional Centre (Centro Regional de Rafaela) — which was created in 1997 as a part of the National Institute of Technology — provides services such as analysis and laboratory tests, research and development of products, technical assistance to local firms, and training to qualified workers.

A particularly interesting case is that of the Centro Tecnológico do Couro, Calçados e Afins (CTCCA) in Novo Hamburgo, Rio Grande do Sul, Brazil. A private, non-profit institution established in 1972, the CTCCA was founded for the purpose of helping the shoe wear firms at the beginning of their export activity, by providing services that would allow them to maintain the quality standards required in international markets. After 30 years, it has become an institution capable of stimulating research activities as well as product and process developments in the shoe industry of Brazil.

In Asia, both in developed as well as emerging countries, the technological policy is at the core of the development programs. In Japan, the policies in support of technology during the 1980s were focused on promoting structural change in less developed regions, through the support of high-technology activities in peripheral locations. In Beijing, China, the Zhongguancun Science and Technology Park has become, since 1999, an example of how to combine training, scientific research, and the creation and diffusion of innovations. In its central area are located 2,400 firms and public centers, a result of the investments of MNCs like IBM, Microsoft, HP, Oracle, Siemens, Motorola, NTT, Fujitsu, Panasonic, Samsung, and Mitsubishi, among others.

Last of all, in Malaysia, the Technology Park Malaysia — located within the "Multimedia Super Corridor", at the outskirts of Kuala Lumpur — was created in 1996 as an instrument for converting Malaysia into an economy focused on the production of high-technology, knowledge-intensive goods and services. This complex provides firms with services and infrastructures that stimulate the creation and diffusion of technological innovation and knowledge. It gives technical and financial services to entrepreneurial initiatives that wish to transform an innovative idea into a business; it helps in the implementation of research projects through its Biotechnology division (in the fields of molecular biology, biochemistry, pharmacology, and food sciences); it provides training services in the fields of engineering, biotechnology, and information technology; and it provides fully equipped floor space and services to firms that wish to locate in an environment focused towards a knowledge economy.

Building up infrastructures for sustainable development

Initiatives targeted at the buildup of infrastructures and social overhead capital are traditional instruments for urban and regional development. Investment in economic overhead capital is, at present, a long-term policy response to the challenges of globalization and competition between cities. In Asia, during the last 15 years important investments in infrastructure (such as international airports, ports, roads, underground systems, and high-speed railways) have taken place in leading cities like Bangkok, Kuala Lumpur, Seoul, Beijing, and Shanghai. The purpose is to make these global city-regions more attractive to inward investment and global capital, and as a result inter-city networks are taking shape (Scott *et al.*, 2001; Douglas, 2001).

Furthermore, in Latin America, practically all local development experiences involve improving accessibility, meeting the needs of economic and social overhead capital, and making cities more attractive places in which to live and produce. The Villa El Salvador initiative (located in Southern Lima, Peru) bases its strategy on the creation of an industrial park in order to provide industrial land, equipment, and the services required by micro-firms and small- and medium-sized firms (Benavides and Manrique, 2001). The Local Development Program of the Mayor's office in Medellín, Colombia, includes urban and metropolitan infrastructure projects, such as the construction of the Metro de Medellín railway.

The concern for sustainable development has led cities to develop imaginative projects. For example, in Curitiba, Brazil (Campbell, 2001), a project was launched in the late 1990s that tried to integrate urban infrastructure actions (e.g. construction of a road that connected 14 neighborhoods in the periphery of the city) with business initiatives based on community huts, in which micro-firms and small enterprises could be located with the support of the services available through professional and entrepreneurial training. The urban trans port system was transformed into a surface metro system, and it is now considered the main element of the urban development model. The innovations introduced in the urban transport of Curitiba were subsequently imitated in other cities of Latin America, such as the surface metro (TransMilenio) in Bogotá, Colombia.

An example of measures that act on the economic, social, and physical systems of a city as a whole is the remodeling of Puerto Madero, located in Buenos Aires between the Río de la Plata and the historic city center, which allowed the incorporation of the old port into the city. The initiative not only put a stop to the degradation of a space that had already met with its urban function, but also recycled it by enhancing leisure activities (e.g. cafes, restaurants, and bars) as well as locating educational and business service activities and quality housing. All of this served as an economic motor force for the city, at a time when the city's economy was very weak. The transformation of the old seaport into an urban area, housing key activities for economic development, was accompanied by the recuperation of its architectural heritage.

Some cities have launched urban development initiatives to neutralize the negative effects of social exclusion, such as the neighborhood restructuring in Caracas, Venezuela (Baldó and Villanueva, 1996; Villanueva, 1998). A good example is the Catuche Project of 1993, an initiative which relied on the Jesuit Fathers of the Pastora to provide this marginal neighborhood with the basic services and economic and social overhead capital needed to improve the environment and living conditions of the population. Some of the most important actions of this initiative were the environmental clean-up of the Catuche River, improved neighbor relations, the building and reconstruction of public services and new housing, and the promotion of micro-firms to carry out the construction work. The project was managed by the Consortium of the Quebrada de Catuche, made up of members from the Catuche community, representatives from the group of promoters, and professional participants. It was funded by the Caracas municipal government, the national government, and non-governmental organizations.

New governance for local development

At the center of new development policy are actions aimed at improving the organization of development in the cities and regions in order to give an efficient response to the problems and challenges ahead. The development of places and territories is organized by the investment decisions of the public and private actors. Frequently — as occurred in Bogotá, Rosario, and Quetzaltenango — in the early stages of the local development policy, local leaders stimulate the implementation of local initiatives, but they should count on explicit or tacit support from other local actors as well.

In Latin America, as in Asia, endogenous development policy is also based on initiatives whereby social and economic projects are coordinated through new forms of governance, such as partnerships among public and private actors, international agencies, or non-governmental organizations. In Villa El Salvador, the Autonomous Authority of the Cono Sur Industrial Park (Autoridad Autónoma del Parque Industrial del Cono Sur) brings together public and private agents working to develop the Industrial Park. In Jalisco, Mexico, local entrepreneurs (including managers of MNCs as well as public actors) participate in the creation of local networks of suppliers.

Endogenous Development Policy

As seen above, endogenous development policy has a relevant function in the economic development processes, for it acts as a catalyst of the development mechanisms through the local initiatives. It facilitates entrepreneurial development and the creation of firm networks, encourages the diffusion of innovation and knowledge, improves urban diversity, and stimulates institutional change. In other words, the new development policy tools favor the improvement of the functioning of each of the determining forces of capital accumulation and sustainable development.

One of the main objectives of the new development policy is to foster the continuous improvement of entrepreneurial resources. All of the local initiatives propose, as their main objective, to promote the start-up of new firms and the upgrading of the entrepreneurial and organizational capacity of economic agents. As mentioned above, firm incubators, business innovation centers, and initiatives that encourage the entrepreneurial capacity of social target groups (like young people and women) are some of the tools that are implemented in developing countries. Furthermore, in recent years, the firm attraction policy has reappeared. The "endogenization" of modern large firm activity within the territory has been aided by new forms of regulation, such as territorial agreements, that facilitate relations between external firms and the territory.

Additionally, the initiatives for the creation and diffusion of innovations also play a central role in the new development policy. For decades, one of the pillars of the restructuring and modernization of local economies has been to facilitate the adoption and adaptation of technology through instruments such as innovation centers, science parks, technology parks, and technology institutes. Among their objectives are to stimulate the transfer and diffusion of innovations within the productive fabric, favor the start-up and development of high-tech firms, and ultimately fulfill the firms' needs and demands for technological services, at a time when increased competition requires improvements in technology.

The urban development of the territory is one of the main features of the new development policy. On the one hand, the initiatives focused on making cities more attractive for living and producing include actions such as providing equipped land to firms, reinforcing the urban transport and communications system, improving the social capital of cities, reviving the historical and cultural heritage, and making the development processes more sustainable. On the other hand, the creation of services such as fairs or business centers, urban marketing through image campaigns, and the construction of emblematic buildings make the city more attractive, encourage inward investment, promote the demand for urban services, and activate the urbanization processes. In any case, the adaptation of norms and regulations to the needs and demands of firms and citizens, as well as improved public services, fosters city networks and favors the urban development of the territories.

From another point of view, the local development policy is based on a new form of regulations and relations between the economic, social, and political actors. It is a new form of governance that designs and carries out policies based on negotiation and specific agreements between public and private actors, non-governmental organizations, and international agencies. The implementation of the actions is made through specific intermediary agencies promoted and managed by the local actors. Lastly, partnership and networking among firms and organizations are the most common forms of cooperation. Transactions in partnerships are based on formal agreements among local actors, whereas networking is less diffused at this time.

The local development policy is also an instrument that tries to integrate the various types of actions in such a way that it is more closely adjusted to the needs of productive systems and to the demands of firms and citizens. Its objective is to act in a combined manner on all of the mechanisms and forces of development in an attempt to create and improve synergy, in such a way that the conditions for self-sustaining growth and structural change are created, and the sustainable development of cities and regions is stimulated.

In short, what gives an innovative character to endogenous development policy is, among others, the following set of features:

- It is an economic development policy (industrial, technological, training-oriented, and environmental) — designed and carried out by the municipal governments and regions within the general macroeconomic framework — that is financed by different areas of the state, non-governmental organizations, and international agencies.

- It is a policy that has emerged spontaneously and that has a direct effect on the development forces, as explained above; thus, it can be said to have economic rationality. Although the central administrations of many countries do not always consider this kind of policy relevant, international organizations (such as the UNDP,

ILO, IDB, and EU) are using it more and more often in the form of "decentralized aid" to development. This permits them to overcome the limitations of the "financial deficit" approach characteristic of the previous period, where market fundamentalism was the development model that inspired international aid policy.

- It is a development policy that seeks the creation of local wealth and employment, and not a redistributive policy — as was the case in the 1950s–1970s — which claims that the central administration is more effective in carrying out social and welfare policies as well as macroeconomic policies. It is, essentially, a policy directed towards fostering the start-up and development of firms in an ever-more integrated and competitive world. Thus, it is not a welfare policy, even though social goals (such as job creation, eradication of poverty, and improved income and well-being for the population) are kept in mind.

- It is a policy in which organized civil society designs and controls the development policy, through instruments like strategic planning and management. It is also a policy in which local actors participate in the management of the development tools; this occurs, for example, in the CTCCA of Novo Hamburgo, with the participation of entrepreneurs in the technical boards (of fashion, machinery, training, and environment).

Yet, what lessons can be learned from the results obtained with this type of policy? Which factors, if any, condition the final results? Why do some instruments work and others not? Why do some territories have better results than others?

It is difficult to answer these questions with a limited knowledge of the evolution of endogenous development policies and their instruments, as gleaned from occasional studies or specific technical visits. Nevertheless, there is an issue that affects the success of the policies and the results of the instruments used in a remarkable way: the actions and initiatives should obey a specific strategy and development policy in each city or region that define the main objectives and actions to be accomplished, because economic development is a result of the interaction of economic forces. When this is not the case, it is only by chance that the results can meet the expectations.

The success of the policy depends, therefore, on the adaptation of the actions to the economic and social conditions of each place or territory. Endogenous development policies take on different shapes in old industrialized regions, such as the Gran ABC in São Paulo, Brazil, which is currently experiencing strong industrial restructuring processes; in endogenous industrialization areas, such as Rafaela in Argentina, the State of Santa Catarina in Brazil, or Marikina in the Philippines, where production service activities are becoming more and more developed; and in rural areas with development potential, such as the region of the Sierra de los Cuchumatanes in Guatemala, which is now in the first stages of the agribusiness development process.

The success of the development instruments depends on the existence of a market for the services offered by the business centers, technological institutes, and development agencies, as well as for services that are not already covered by private firms or other organizations similar in nature to what the policy intends to create. Good practice recommends that every development tool should, from its inception, precisely define its target group, the needs to be covered, the objectives that the services should reach, and the necessary technical facilities that should be supplied to clients.

These types of considerations will, for example, lead us to accept the fact that science and technology parks are instruments for the diffusion of innovations in a specific entrepreneurial fabric. Assuming that an entrepreneurial fabric is created (as in the case of the Technology Park Malaysia or the Beijing Science Park) but the target group to which this action is directed is not sufficiently precise, the results — in terms of the creation and development of innovative firms — may be found lacking with respect to the project. For instance, the selection criteria for initiatives in the firm incubator of the Beijing Science Park are rather ambiguous. They mix aspects such as the technical and economic viability of the project and its innovative nature together with aspects related to the academic interest of the project, which is an issue outside the functioning of the instrument.

This may have a negative effect on the efficiency of the instrument and, thus, on the results that could be expected from the firm incubator.

The management of local initiatives and development tools seriously affects the results of the development policy. Policy success rests on the strength of the commitment to the project and the motivation of the promoters. In order to reach the objectives, the expressed and tacit support of those organizations and firms which are part of the top management of the city or region is necessary. Furthermore, the people responsible for the management of the agencies and service centers must necessarily have experience in managing intermediary organizations, as well as a strong ethical commitment to the values regulating the market system. Because of this, bad results of the development actions and faulty working of the instruments are often associated with management deficiencies. In this sense, it is advisable, as occurs in the Novo Hamburgo Technological Center, for those firms that use the services — the clients of the agency — to participate in the management councils of the center.

With respect to the financial aspects of the projects and the financial means of the services to be made available to the firms, they should be clearly established before the development initiatives and tools are set in motion. Thus, best practice recommends that the business centers, technological institutes, or training centers be created based on a firm's plan for the center that is clear, coherent, consistent, and realistic; the plan should identify the financial needs, the financial objectives, the firm's own resources devoted to the financing of the center, and the actions for attracting outside resources. A high degree of internal cohesion between the financing of the development strategy and the foreseeable results of the services supplied should exist from the start, although it would be convenient to adjust the development strategy to changes in the environment and to policy tool performance after having carried out the project. Local development agencies are usually non-profit organizations that try to cover their financial needs by charging for services rendered; this is often an unobtainable objective, but it does not mean that managers of the policy tools should not be focused in that direction.

Last of all, the state's central administration has an important role to play in the application of the endogenous development policy, on both technical and financial levels. To be sure, endogenous development policy cannot be understood as a state policy, given that it appeared spontaneously as a response on behalf of the cities and regions to the productive adjustment problems and to social exclusion. Nevertheless, good practice again recommends that the central administration should take the policy on as its own, since the policy is in line with its objectives of growth, increased productivity, and productive adjustment. This could be put forward as an action, as done by international organizations, financing the endogenous development actions and tools or specifying the requirements for local initiatives in order to be eligible for state financing.

International Organizations and Local Development

The definition, design, and promotion of local development initiatives and strategies have received strong support from international organizations such as the OECD, the European Commission, the United Nations Development Programme (UNDP), the International Labour Organization (ILO), and the World Bank. Even though their proposals have sometimes been branded as ambiguous, they have exercised an important influence on the change in employment policies, industrial policies, technological policies, and development policies.

During the 1980s, when Europe was under a marked process of productive adjustment and restructuring, the first initiatives for local development were brought underway. The OECD encouraged, from July 1982 onwards, a cooperation and action program directed at local employment initiatives. The program's purpose was to exchange experience and information regarding entrepreneurial development, job creation, and the delivery of technical assistance between the member states carrying out programs of productive adjustment and restructuring. The Local Economic and Employment Development Programme (LEED) has enlarged and reinforced this line of work since the mid-1990s, under the auspices of the OECD Territorial Development Service, providing services that stimulate the strengthening of entrepreneurship and job creation in the OECD countries.

The promotion of local employment initiatives in the European Union is more pragmatic and more efficient than that undertaken by the OECD. Its planning is focused towards actions for financing specific local economic development projects. To this end, part of the resources is contributed by two European Structural Funds, the European Regional Development Fund and the European Social Fund. Thus, in recent decades, the European Commission has supported the financing of initiatives such as the European Business and Innovation Centres, and other actions that favor the exchange of products among small- and medium-sized enterprises.

Since the early 1980s, an important change has been seen in the commitment of international agencies with an active presence in developing countries, and they have begun to adopt strategies and management criteria that are closer to this new approach towards economic development. The international institutions that work in Latin America have shown a growing interest in the local development approach, above all due to the fact that the decentralization and modernization of local governments have created the conditions to adopt a "development from below" approach as a strategy for the growth of cities and regions. For instance, the Economic Commission for Latin America and the Caribbean (ECLAC) tried to understand the relevance and significance of local initiatives in Latin America. With the support of the German Society for Technical Cooperation (*Deutsche Gesellschaft für Technische Zusammenarbeit* or GTZ), it sponsored the Local Economic Development and Decentralization Project in Latin America, which was overseen by the ECLAC Economic Development Division (Aghon *et al.*, 2001). The most important conclusion was that, during the 1990s, in all Latin American countries there was a proliferation of local development initiatives that adapted well to the economic, political, and social conditions in every country; these initiatives were financed by the IDB, different United Nations programs, the ILO, and non-governmental organizations.

It is from 1991 onwards that the new development policies have become an increasingly important line of action in the international organizations. Various agencies of the United Nations — frequently through joint programs (e.g. between the ILO and the UNDP) — propose the promotion and creation of Local Economic Development Agencies (LEDAs) in developing countries and transition economies, for the purpose of promoting economic activity and helping to improve the living standards of populations which are faced with economic and social problems (Box 7.1) (Canzanelli, 2007).

Box 7.1

The ILO Local Economic Development Agencies

Currently there are almost 60 LEDAs in Central America, the Balkans, Africa, and Asia operating with a high degree of autonomy, and they are gathered into the ILS LEDA network (see http://www.ilsleda.org). They are non-profit organizations, with mixed public and private capital, whose objective is to create and develop the environment for firms' start-up as well as to provide support for the economic development of the territory and for social inclusion. Thus, LEDAs support the formation and development of networks of local actors, thereby allowing a degree of local autonomy in development decisions and stimulating innovation processes.

These LEDAs integrate governance components (public–private partnership, local–national relations), strategic components (coordination between planning and action), human development components (social inclusion, instruments of support to the vulnerable groups, relation between the center and suburbs of the territory, environmental protection), components of territorial promotion (project financing, international marketing), and components of business services (technical assistance, professional training, marketing, loans).

Typical services of the LEDAs promoted by the United Nations ILS LEDA Program (as of 2006) include the following:

(Continued)

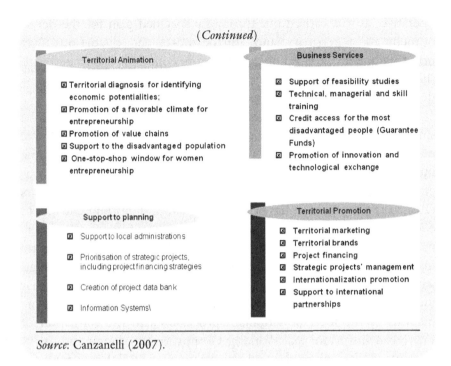

(*Continued*)

Territorial Animation

☒ Territorial diagnosis for identifying economic potentialities;
☒ Promotion of a favorable climate for entrepreneurship
☒ Promotion of value chains
☒ Support to the disadvantaged population
☒ One-stop-shop window for women entrepreneurship

Business Services

☒ Support of feasibility studies
☒ Technical, managerial and skill training
☒ Credit access for the most disadvantaged people (Guarantee Funds)
☒ Promotion of innovation and technological exchange

Support to planning

☒ Support to local administrations
☒ Prioritisation of strategic projects, including project financing strategies
☒ Creation of project data bank
☒ Information Systems\

Territorial Promotion

☒ Territorial marketing
☒ Territorial brands
☒ Project financing
☒ Strategic projects' management
☒ Internationalization promotion
☒ Support to international partnerships

Source: Canzanelli (2007).

The adoption of new development policies by multilateral organizations has served to reinforce new forms of aid to developing countries. Foreign aid has traditionally been tied to the donor countries; loans and grants may be spent on goods and services of the donor country, funds may be used for specific projects, or aid may be tied to imports of machinery and equipment from a firm in the donor country. At the same time, the recipient countries often use these funds for national strategic objectives (such as improvement in the balance of payments) or for private interests, as Easterly (2001) points out. During recent years, however, new forms of aid have been defined, such as decentralized aid, whereby the donor (which may be a city, a province, or an institution in a developed country) contributes directly to the implementation of a project that is undertaken in a specific territory in a less developed country through a multilateral agency such as the UNDP or the ILO. This kind of aid is much more operative, as it is carried out through a specified plan for the development of a territory and, furthermore, the distortions (i.e. non-fulfillment of the aid objectives) more commonly associated with the traditional mechanisms of aid from developed countries to less developed countries are avoided.

The Local Human Development Programme underway in Cuba since late 1998, supported by the UNDP and the ILO, is an example of the new form of international cooperation that has promoted the introduction of relevant innovations, particularly in the field of cooperation practices and in the implementation of development projects (Panico *et al.*, 2002). It has helped bring about important changes in cooperation through the articulation of resources from various international agencies, governments, and other public and private institutions. It has also enhanced decentralized cooperation, through which the efficiency of cooperation has improved and its impact has increased. Furthermore, it has encouraged innovation and transformations in the local development processes with the formation of Provincial and Municipal Working Groups for the design and carrying out of local initiatives; and the creation of FRIDEL (a fund for initiatives of local economic development), a tool for financing small- and medium-sized local firms.

Within this general framework, the Old Havana project is a good example of good practice with respect to development policies through multilateral finance, thanks to the stimulus given by the Office of the Historian of the City, which works as a development agency. Among the more important initiatives are the rehabilitation of the historic architectural heritage, the improvement of urban infrastructures, the support for tourist activities, the recovery of craftsmanship (such as the sisterhood of embroidery and weavers), and the improvement of social services (for the elderly and handicapped children).

Lessons for an Economic Recovery in 2010

The ongoing crisis has affected, in a combined manner, the financial system and the productive fabric of most of the dynamic regions and countries, and there is a strong interaction between the two crisis dimensions. As pointed out by Romer (2009), recovery of the financial system and recovery of the real economy are processes that are interacting. Therefore, the stabilization of the financial system depends on the recovery of the real economy, and vice versa. The recovery calls for a treatment that combines a number of measures which aim, on the one hand, at re-establishing trust in the financial system and extending bank credit and, on the other hand, at improving the productivity of firms and making economies more competitive.

The search for a response to the global crisis

A necessary condition for overcoming the economic crisis is to make the financial system of the advanced and emerging economies work again. The combined action of several countries has as its main objective to satisfy the needs for liquidity, if and when the banking system requires it, and to act decisively in cases of bankruptcy of financial firms and banks. Therefore, actions aimed at rescuing banks in difficulty vary from country to country: the nationalization of insolvent banks and firms, as in the U.K. and the U.S.; the injection of funds into solvent banks which are short of liquidity; the encouragement of mergers between financial entities; or the support of bank recapitalization through public and private funds, as in the case of the Federal Deposit Insurance Corporation in the U.S. (Tamames, 2009).

The task for banks to recover their role as financial intermediaries, as well as to activate the functioning of the markets through the credit system, is not an easy one. The adjustment of the nominal value of assets to their real value is a win-lose game, and countries are seeking a negotiated solution to the problem. In any case, changing the rules and norms of the financial system's functioning seems urgent, and this requires an agreement between the economic operators and the institutional agents. The purpose is to regain trust in the financial system so that the market can regain its role within the economic activity.

Economic recovery requires a number of stimuli to foster increased productivity and competitiveness. The International

Monetary Fund (IMF, 2009b) describes some structural policy measures that the G-20 countries have either adopted or plan to adopt. Among these, the following should be emphasized:

- A fiscal stimulus package is often employed to boost demand. Some G-20 countries have announced reductions in personal income taxes, indirect taxes, and corporate income taxes. They also plan to stimulate consumption through a line of credit to citizens with low income levels.
- Increased spending in transport and communications infrastructure, either through the central or local administrations, is an initiative that the majority of G-20 countries take into consideration.
- Policies for entrepreneurial development play a key role among the measures implemented by G-20 countries to neutralize the effects of the economic crisis. These policies include the provision of support to small- and medium-sized companies, the fostering of strategic activities (such as high technology or defense), and the development of renewable energies.
- Social policy measures can also be found among the initiatives proposed by G-20 countries in recent months. Some actions aim at improved health care (e.g. by affecting the endowment of hospitals and doctors) and education (by improving the skill of human resources through training and education programs). Other measures aim to support vulnerable groups such as the unemployed, the poor, and pensioners.

Local development: a response to the global crisis

Local development policy emerged and developed in poor and late developed countries as a response on behalf of places and territories to the challenges of poverty, productive restructuring, and increased competition. Could local development be a strategy for fostering entrepreneurial development in places that have been affected by the ongoing global crisis? Why are local development tools useful in times of crisis?

Local development and structural policies share the same objectives: increased productivity, improvement in social cohesion, and conservation of natural and cultural resources. But, their approach to economic recovery is different. While structural policies choose a functional approach, local development policies define their actions based on a territorial viewpoint that seems more effective in the process of structural change. The reason for this is that actions carried out in a particular territory must interact with the social, institutional, and cultural dimensions of the place. Therefore, measures are more efficient when they make use of local resources, and when projects and investments are implemented by the local actors.

Two aspects condition the results of policy actions: the development potential that exists within the territory, and the organizational capacity of the local actors. From this perspective, all localities and territories possess development potential. This is true for rural areas (such as the Cuchumatanes in Guatemala) as well as dynamic cities (such as Rosario in Argentina). At the local, regional, or national level, one can find a determined production structure, a labor market, a technical knowledge base, entrepreneurial capacity, natural resources, a social and political structure, and a tradition and culture, on which local initiatives are based. Also, the development of a place or territory requires public and private actors to carry out the investment programs in a coordinated manner. In Latin America, the local development projects are coordinated and managed through new forms of governance, in which public and private actors, international organizations, and non-governmental organizations participate (Alburquerque *et al.*, 2008).

It should be noted that the local development strategy differs from one case to another. This is because the demands of each territory are different; the capabilities of the people, companies, and local community change; and the priorities to be incorporated in the development policies differ from one local community to another. Territorial strategic planning has turned, therefore, into a valuable instrument for the rationalization of the decision-making process and management in cities and rural areas. There are multiple examples of this, such as in Rosario and Córdoba in Argentina, as well as other cities and regions in El Salvador, Guatemala, Honduras, the Dominican Republic, Ecuador, and Colombia, where the UNDP and the ILO encourage the creation of LEDAs on the basis of strategic plans.

Innovation: a strategic factor in productive adjustment

Understanding the crisis as an opportunity for transforming the production system, and for making the economy stronger and more competitive at the international level, should be at the core of the strategy for economic recovery. The key element is the introduction and diffusion of innovations throughout the productive fabric.

Local development policies address the question of the adjustment and restructuring of production systems in order to make firms more competitive in product and factor markets. Income growth and changes in demand have led to the diversification of production in cities as well as in rural areas. The development of tourist activity in the cities of Cartagena de Indias and Havana, as well as the strength of cultural tourism in Chiapas and in the Yucatán Peninsula, shows how changes in international demand stimulate the diversification of production and, thus, create the conditions for the continuous introduction of innovations that upgrade local resources and make them competitive.

When economic integration increases, firms try to develop their competitive advantage in local and international markets. In this way, production systems are always evolving and, frequently, the activation of change is carried out on the basis of a renovation of traditional know-how by introducing new knowledge during the structural change process. In the case of Cuchumatanes, for instance, reproduction and feeding techniques in ovine production have improved, and the technological package that led to the restructuring of natural coffee production into organic coffee was perfected and brought about increased output and quality. The adaptation and transfer of technology allowed the differentiation of production, which made local products more competitive in national and international markets.

In other places and territories, the question is not so much the differentiation of production or cost reduction, but rather the finding of new products for markets in which local companies may keep their competitive advantage. This was the case in Tapachula, in Mexico, for instance, where the local coffee producers had to react in the face of strong competition from Vietnam in their markets, with whom they could not compete over prices. The answer was to change their production activities and start cultivating tropical flowers for markets such as the U.S., for which the farmers had to adopt new production technologies from abroad, enter into new markets, and adapt their knowledge to the new productive and commercial reality.

Firms and territories can also opt for the production of new goods and services for which the demand in markets is increasing. These include products that incorporate high-tech components and for which a strong internal and international demand exists, as occurs in the electronics cluster in Jalisco, Mexico (Rasiah, 2007).

Local initiatives and increased productivity

It is through development actions that local initiatives can make an important contribution in overcoming the economic crisis. Their strength rests on the fact that the local policy tools used stimulate capital accumulation and, therefore, contribute to increased productivity and competitiveness, as discussed above.

One of the objectives of local initiatives is to foster entrepreneurship and the formation and development of firm networks. The start-up and development of firms is a necessary condition in the development process, as firms transform savings into investment through entrepreneurial projects. Furthermore, when the development of networks and clusters of firms is encouraged, it favors the appearance of external economies of scale and the reduction of transaction costs.

In addition, the diffusion of innovation and knowledge throughout the local productive fabric allows for the introduction of new products and the differentiation of existing ones, changes in production processes, and the opening of new markets. All of this contributes toward an increase in productivity and in the competitiveness of the companies.

Actions for the training of human resources are strategic instruments for local development, for it is through these measures that knowledge is incorporated into the production of goods and services and into the management of development strategy itself. When training activities are included in the development strategy, the improvement in the quality of human resources can help increase productivity, stimulate competitiveness, and even affect the cultural model in which the development process must seek support.

Finally, initiatives targeting the buildup and improvement of economic and social overhead capital are instruments frequently used for local and regional development. Firms prefer locations in accessible places that are well endowed with services which allow them to make good use of economies of agglomeration and to have good accessibility to product and factor markets. Furthermore, the improvement of infrastructure attracts industrial and service activities to rural and peripheral localities and regions, generating economies of diversity and favoring increased productivity.

Local response for economic recovery

Advanced and emerging countries are experiencing a process of important productive and social change due to the financial crisis and the bank credit crunch, which have had profound effects on the real economy. In order to solve these problems, it is helpful to combine measures that lead to the recuperation of trust in the financial institutions and to the expansion of bank credit with actions directed towards increasing productivity and competitiveness.

As previously mentioned, local development is a policy that could help to overcome the economic crisis. Its strength is inherent in its strategy, which focuses on the issue of productive adjustment according to a territorial perspective. This encourages the search for concrete solutions to the problems of specific territories, using precisely the territory's development potential which has not been utilized because of the crisis. Its merit lies in that local development is a strategy that stimulates increasing returns to investments and, therefore, helps to increase productivity and competitiveness.

Local development also seeks social progress and sustainable development. Development is a process in which economic growth and income distribution are two aspects of the same phenomenon, given that the public and private actors choose and carry out their investments for the purpose of increasing productivity and improving social well-being. Local development is, likewise, a strategy that is based on the continuous upgrading of available resources, particularly the natural, historical, and cultural resources; in this way, it contributes to increasing the sustainability of the territory.

Yet, local development is not a strategy whose results are guaranteed. Local development policy seeks economic and social progress and job creation by stimulating entrepreneurial development; however, an excess of foreign aid could reduce the creative capacity of entrepreneurs and local actors, and thus limit the results of local initiatives. Furthermore, it is a policy whose results depend on an efficient coordination of the measures and the actors in the territory; it would lose its effectiveness if actions were carried out in an isolated manner because the positive feedback effects from the interaction between development instruments would be neutralized. Finally, local development is a participatory policy in which the local actors design and control its implementation; therefore, its results would be affected if actions and/or objectives were imposed in a unilateral manner by local and external actors.

Chapter 8

The Quest for a
New Development Policy

Development economics emerged more than 50 years ago, as a discipline aiming to identify and solve the economic and social problems of developing countries and regions by analyzing their economic realities and proposing measures for economic policies. Since then, the societies and economies of countries and regions have changed, and new theories and interpretations of economic dynamics have appeared. Hence, these new conditions demand a new development policy.

This book began with a discussion on the process of economic integration, on persistent problems such as high poverty levels and inequality in some countries and regions, and on the current global financial crisis. Following this, some interpretations of economic dynamics that replaced old ideas associated with the neoclassical market fundamentalism were discussed. Changes in the forces of development have been analyzed; and new processes such as polycentric development, the formation of global value chains, and new patterns of creation and diffusion of innovation have been discussed.

These new facts, new processes, and new interpretations call for a new development policy. Why is a new development policy necessary? Should the actions of governments and markets be complementary? Are the territorial policies stimulating the efficiency and coordination of public and private actors and companies? What are the goals and actions for fostering sustainable development? How do social capital and institutional change facilitate the governance and implementation of the new development policy? Should the new development policy create the conditions for networking development?

Institutional Change and Development Policy

For decades, economists have held an open discussion about the relation between state and market, considering that market as well as governmental failures have had a negative effect on the efficiency of production systems and, therefore, on economic progress and social welfare. The new interpretations of development have transformed the discussion into one about the search for a response to the challenges caused by globalization, and suggest a combination of actions by governments and entrepreneurial initiatives for the purpose of achieving economic development and social progress in cities and regions.

Development economics has traditionally focused on analyzing and stimulating the production of goods and services, based on the assumption that GDP growth would reduce poverty and increase the living standards of a population because it was assumed that a strong correlation between economic and social variables existed. Following World War II, development economics supported strong governmental intervention, following the "big push" approach, through substantial investments in the industrial sector aimed at generating economies of scale as well as external economies. During the 1970s, the neoclassical approach re-emerged and was very critical of development planning; instead, it proposed that the mobilization and allocation of resources should rest on the price system in markets, thus minimizing the role of governments in the development process.

The new development economics that emerged in the 1980s introduced important changes in the analysis of economic dynamics, and argued that it is market failures which explain the lower income in developing and emerging economies (Stiglitz, 1986; Meier and Stiglitz, 2001). The formulations rest on different production functions, different ways of organizing the economy, and a different functioning of markets in advanced and developing countries. It is assumed that the economies of developing countries lack the capacity for using their development potential (including externalities and agglomeration and urbanization economies), as they face substantial market failures, especially in financial markets and in coordinating the decisions made by economic agents.

For the purpose of analyzing and adequately explaining the development of developing and emerging economies, the new development economics (Stiglitz, 1985, 1989; Hoff, 2000) proposes to overcome the neoclassical model and considers that relevant subjects for development such as poverty traps, multiple equilibria, institutions, and development paths should be included in the analyses. It offers a detailed analysis of some of the weaknesses of the functioning of markets in developing countries, and underlines that market imperfections in the transmission of information affect developing countries more than developed ones. A consequence is that a decentralized resource allocation is not possible, as it may make the economies of less developed countries less efficient and may even prevent market equilibria.

Furthermore, information failures explain the malfunctioning of financial markets in developing countries and generate uncertainty, risk, and high transaction costs, which in turn affect resource allocation as well as trade. As Prieto Pérez (2006) points out, without an active and efficient financial system, savings do not flow adequately and are not turned into productive investments, as the case of the Argentine financial system at the beginning of this decade proves. In order for a country to reach the level of financial depth necessary for fostering the economy, financial markets must support the growth of productive investments, through the issue and negotiation of financial products and the development of a market for public debt and a stock market. Therefore, the development of emerging and developing countries requires reforms and changes in the financial system that will stimulate the creation and diversification of financial institutions, improve the functioning of financial institutions, connect their financial market with those of other countries, and regulate and control financial institutions and markets.

Yet, coordination failures among economic agents are possibly the greatest weakness in developing countries. For a production system to function efficiently, it is necessary that complementary relations between the different activities and companies which form the value chain and clusters develop in such a way that a sufficient demand in internal markets for goods and services is generated.

The coordination of productive activities generates external economies of scale and reduces the transaction costs of companies, which improve productivity and favor economic development. In many developing countries, however, there exist deficiencies in the configuration of inter-industrial markets and in the coordination of the investments of individuals and economic agents, thus limiting social and economic progress.

Beyond market failures, it is appropriate to consider the changes that the globalization process has produced in the functioning of markets during the last two decades. Globalization has led to an increase in competition among firms and territories, due to the shorter distances between territories and the increased integration of markets for goods and services. This has resulted in very different scenarios in developing countries; in particular, in those economies without a well-developed institutional system, the increase of economic integration does not automatically lead to the entry of capital and labor from abroad that would utilize the existing development potential, but may instead lead to the discouragement and exit of local resources. In turn, the current financial crisis has generated, as pointed out above, a significant contraction of the real economy in both advanced and emerging countries, leading to the shutdown of companies and banks, reduced international trade, increased unemployment, and greater insecurity and risk in markets for goods and services.

Thus, market failures and the impact of the globalization process have substantial economic and social effects in developed and developing countries, which means that public policies must play an important role in supporting economic dynamics (Meier, 2005; Hoff, 2000). What is at stake in the developing countries and regions is to secure the transition of the economy from a low-level equilibrium to a high-level equilibrium using the development potential that exists within the territory. In situations where market forces push the economy to low levels of growth, breaking the vicious cycle of underdevelopment is only feasible through government actions or measures that neutralize market failures, that stimulate the private sector by internalizing potential external economies, and that increase returns to scale, which lead to increasing productivity in the economy.

Hence, as Meier contends, the new development policy redefines the relationship between the state and markets such that, "unlike the usual view that government intervention and market solutions are substitutes, there is a change in thinking of the state and market as complementary" (2005, p. 127). In this way, the new focus of development policies enables the actions of governments and market participants to be complementary and proactive, and to affect economic dynamics and social progress in a positive manner.

The development of institutions permits the transformation of government policy measures into economic and social progress. However, this approach to development is inefficient if it is a *spatially blind policy* — if it leads to coordination failures of economic agents and does not use all of the resources available within a territory — because it would maintain substantial information failures. Production, networks, and markets change and are transformed by the actions of public and private agents who are located in specific places and territories. A lack of visibility in the diversity of places and territories would limit the effects of public policy actions, invest-ments, and institutional change. Even though state intervention is also present in processes that appear naturally, territorial policies are more efficient when local actors participate in their design and implementation.

The institutional effects of globalization clearly show how the net-works of actors have become increasingly complex (Prats i Catala, 2003). The state's central administration is no longer the only decision-maker on public policy or the sole strategic agent in national economies; the rules, norms, and institutions that govern production and commerce have become globalized because of increased eco-nomic integration; and the local level has strengthened because the government is not capable of integrating all of the territory's interests. Thus, institutional change facilitates the appearance of new political actors and an increase in the complexity of economic institutions.

As previously mentioned, information and coordination failures can be overcome through the promotion and development of efficient economic institutions and development initiatives that support the functioning of markets and that allow cities and regions to use their development potential. Institutional coordination requires the coordination of agents and actors, and of cities and regions in which the processes of growth and structural change are developing; and when the participation and cooperation of the civil society in the design and implementation of projects is added to this, the new conditions capable of stimulating development are created. Given that not all places possess the institutional capacity for a democratic participation in the decision-making process, it becomes necessary to stimulate institutional change. However, as Barca argues, "the purpose is obviously not to import institutions from the outside, but to provide the prerequisites for them to develop" (2009, p. 22).

Territorial development policy goes beyond sectoral and national policies. It follows a bottom-up approach, thus making the policy more efficient as its actions are adapted to the needs and demands of specific places and territories, presenting solutions to specific problems and using the development potential of the territory. But, its effectiveness is conditioned above all by the participation of local actors and by the institutional arrangements which support governance at different levels of the state and society.

The Territorial Development Policy Rationale

Territorial policy is a policy with multiple objectives, with the final objectives being efficiency, equity, and an improved environment (Figure 8.1). Efficiency means improving the competitiveness of cities and regions by using the development potential of every place. Equity refers to the strengthening of social cohesion by eradicating poverty and increasing the welfare of the population. An improved environment is intended to conserve natural resources as well as the historical and cultural heritage, protecting the environment and strengthening the attractiveness of cities and regions. But, territorial policy is also a policy that, as we have seen, uses very different instruments for

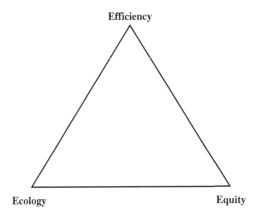

Figure 8.1   Territorial Development: Policy Goals.

strengthening the hardware, software, and orgware of development, and is applied to very diverse places and territories.

There are strong ties between goals and actions, given that territorial development is a systemic process in which the final objectives are mutually connected and in which the actions affecting the development process must be connected if a positive effect on the forces and mechanisms of development is desired. The multiplicity of goals makes territorial policies complex, as it is necessary to act in a combined manner so as to affect a number of goals, employing sets of actions that require keeping in mind the positive and negative effects of each measure. Furthermore, the efficiency of policies requires establishing priorities (the conservation of the environment, for instance), under the condition that a certain minimum level of other connected objectives (competitiveness and social cohesion) can be achieved.

The local development policies discussed above present a package of actions associated with the objectives of territorial development. From the actions aimed at improving the competitiveness of cities and regions, interesting lessons can be learned regarding how the results of each of the measures taken stimulate efficiency, increase productivity, and improve the competitiveness of cities and regions (Vázquez-Barquero, 1993). Among the measures that affect the hardware, software, and orgware of development, the following stand out:

- Public investments in transport and communication infrastructure stand out because they connect urban systems, reduce trade costs, and favor economic exchange.
- In the field of development policy, a strategic role is played by those policies that support the diffusion of innovations and knowledge between companies and that favor the formation of human resources, as they facilitate the introduction of new machines and fixed capital as well as the diversification of goods and services.
- Measures that introduce new forms of organization of companies improve relations within the production system and ease the flow of information within the production structures, strengthening social capital and reducing friction in the exchange processes between companies that comprise value chains and clusters.
- All those measures that improve the coordination between firms and public and private actors, raise the quality of institutions, and, therefore, favor institutional development are also crucial.

Harrod (1939) connected economic growth to the resource endowment of an economy; and maintained that the growth of income and the potential development of an economy depended on population growth (the size of the labor force), investment (the physical capital accumulated), technological improvements (the state of technological knowledge), and the endowment of natural resources. He understood this to mean that potential development (or, in his terminology, "natural growth") is associated with the potential production capacity. From the endogenous development perspective, the competitiveness of an economy depends on the efficient use of available resources in the production processes and the building up of territorial development capabilities, which are linked to "the quality of human resources, the organizational capacity of the economic agents, the quality of institutions, forms of cooperation and learning, and the coordination of economic and social policies, where external impulses are integrated into the territory" (Madoery, 2008, p. 28).

Therefore, public policies that aim at the improvement of efficiency and competitiveness in cities and regions propose measures to stimulate institutional development, encourage entrepreneurial capacities and changes in the organizational model of companies, foster the transformation of the territorial system, and support technological innovation. The point is for local initiatives to create the conditions for public and private investments to generate increasing returns. Thus, economies of scale, externalities, and a reduction in transaction costs should be fostered by way of territorial policies. The overarching objective is to increase the productivity and competitiveness of firms and places, which then leads to increased income and welfare improvements for the population.

Poverty and inequality have risen in very different places and territories in recent years, and occasionally problems of social exclusion emerge. Territorial development policies try to overcome these problems through measures whose objective is to meet the population's basic needs and contribute to the sustainable development of the local economy. Social exclusion and income inequality are concentrated and form pockets in rural areas and cities, both in more advanced as well as developing countries. As pointed out when discussing local development policies in the Cuchumatanes region in Guatemala, the priority objective is to increase the population's income for those who fall below the poverty line and to meet their basic needs.

The question of measuring poverty levels and planning development policies in places and territories with problems of inequality is a widely discussed subject (Ray, 1998). Poverty deprives the population of the chance to enjoy requisite nutritional levels and elementary education, as well as the possibility to satisfy their hopes and aspirations. In fact, the poor population finds itself in a vicious cycle that limits their access to markets: in the labor market, poverty provokes malnutrition and this implies less capacity for work, leading to further poverty; in the financial markets, poverty signifies a lack of resources and this impedes the access to credit that would allow them to engage in productive activities, thus preventing improvements in productivity and keeping income low; and in the market for land, the lack of resources among the poor limits their access to the land and reduces their activity to low-productivity tasks, thus keeping their living standards low. Consequently, the poor are frequently excluded from their societies.

The human development approach (Sen, 2001) proposes basing the strategy for the development of cities and regions with low income levels on the utilization of the capabilities of the population as the key factor in the processes of growth and structural change. Therefore, in order to use the development potential, it is necessary to break poverty traps, and so foster the expansion of the population's capabilities. In this way, local initiatives — besides supplying basic goods and services in food, shelter, clothing, health, and education — can promote the emergence and development of activities that make use of the local development potential.

Policy actions and measures are very diverse, and necessarily utilize the available human and natural resources. Through public investment in transport infrastructure and physical social capital, the links of places to the network are strengthened, which allows trade to expand. Local initiatives foster the development of local entrepreneurial capacities either through measures that stimulate the emergence and development of companies or through the social economy (by expanding the cooperation and formation of groups with similar interests). Local initiatives also encourage the diffusion of knowledge in the local production system, thus allowing improvements in productivity (as has happened with the introduction of new techniques of reproduction and fattening amongst the sheep farmers in Cuchumatanes) and the differentiation of production (e.g. varieties of organic coffee). Most importantly, local initiatives foster institutional development, creating organizations such as the development agencies, increasing the participation of citizens in the design and implementation of projects, and encouraging relations among the population and trade with other localities.

Barca (2009) raises the question of the compatibility of the objectives of equity and efficiency in territorial development policies and argues that the integration of social inclusion with the efficiency goal is a fallacy, since an increase in income and GDP may be achieved while at the same time income inequality in the population may increase. In any case, both objectives imply different measures and decisions; some objectives (e.g. social policy objectives) are focused on solving the basic needs of society, while others require measures that favor the self-sustaining growth and structural change of the economy. To combine equity and efficiency is, therefore, a challenge for the decision-makers and planners.

The conservation of natural resources and of the historical and cultural heritage is another strategic objective of development policy. The Brundtland report (United Nations, 1987) argues about the need for sustainability in development, and stresses that development is sustainable when it is capable of satisfying the necessities of the present generation without compromising the ability of future generations to develop and attend to their own needs. Alburquerque *et al.* define sustainable development as "a continuing process of change in which the use of resources, the orientation and evolution of technology, and the modification of institutions have to co-evolve according to current and future human needs" (2008, p. 107).

The current production model combines the labor force, natural resources, knowledge, and energy inefficiently, which instills doubts about the sustainability of development. The substitution of labor by capital is accompanied by increased energy and raw material consumption, which translates into an overexploitation of natural resources and environmental degradation. Therefore, a growing social demand about the necessary changes required in the growth model is being heard; among these changes are that the direct relation existing between economic growth and pollution should be broken, and that policies which favor a sustainable development process should be formulated and implemented.

Territorial development policies, in this sense, consider the environment as a resource for the development of cities and regions. Territories with good environmental conditions are attractive for the location of companies whose productive activities require environmental quality. It is, hence, a specific resource of a territory that improves the competitive capacity of companies in markets. Furthermore, it is a factor that contributes to the standard of living of the population and helps to attract those who seek to improve their welfare. It is possible, therefore, to formulate a strategy for sustainable development using the existing potential in places and territories.

Every territory needs a specific policy for its sustainable development with respect to its resources and capacities. What is at stake is the search for a system of production that is based on clean technology, a diversity of productive activities, and production processes that guarantee environmental quality. The policy should also contain the following measures that contribute towards the creation of capacities required for development: fostering the development of ecological networks; protecting the environment, landscape, and biodiversity; strengthening the quality of infrastructure; and implementing strategies and plans of spatial development for protected areas or fragile ecological areas that are subject to erosion. The solution to the conflicts that may emerge between the dual objectives of competitiveness and conservation necessitates an institutional development that is geared towards cooperation between public and private agents.

Social Capital and Development

In the preceding chapters, the discussion on the dynamics of local production systems, polycentric territorial systems and innovation systems, and the functioning of local development policies has invariably included norms, codes of conduct, rules, patterns of behavior, and agreements between economic agents in the analysis. This means that any discussion regarding the economic dynamics and social progress inevitably leads us to argue in terms of institutional development; and constitutes a group of institutions such as the market, the state, company networks, economic and social organizations, and communities of local actors. All of the institutional actors make decisions and behave according to norms accepted by their social peers shaping the institutional arrangements, thus creating the institutional environment (Reis, 2007).

Therefore, development is a systemic process that depends not only on the accumulation of capital, the adoption of innovations, the dynamics of organizations, and the forms of organizing the territory;

it also depends on the institutional environment and the stimuli this offers to the actors. In developing countries, the institutional environment influences the formation and development of the production structure, as the institutional framework provides incentives for the creation of firms and the attraction of foreign companies. Only when property rights are guaranteed, contracts are honored, the justice system works, and no barriers exist in markets do companies decide to carry out investments that allow them to maximize their objectives. Institutional development also facilitates the functioning of public policies that create the conditions for macroeconomic and financial stability, productive development, and economic and social progress (Prats i Catala, 2003).

There are two clearly distinct viewpoints among the authors who analyze economic and social progress within an institutional context: the original institutionalism, known through the works of Veblen (1899), Commons (1934), and Mitchell (1967); and the new institutionalism, based on the works of Coase (1937), North (1990), Simon (1982), and Williamson (1985). According to traditional institutional thought, economic activities are carried out by organizations within an institutional and cultural context that is co-evolving with society and the economy. Mainstream institutionalism considers the economic system as "an evolving process that is being impelled along the path of industrialization by rapid and extensive technological change" (Gruchy, 1987). It argues that technologies (Veblen), institutions (Commons), and the hierarchical organization of political and economic organizations determine the economic performance of countries.

The new institutional approach, on the other hand, holds that a mutual relationship between economic growth and institutions exists, which causes the gradual change of institutions. North (1990, 1994) and Williamson (1985) argue that the connections between institutions and economic growth lie in the economy of transaction costs. The exchange and transactions between economic agents always involve a cost. In the ideal world of neoclassical models, there is no friction and no cost; the reality, however, is more complex, and the exchange of goods and services generates commercial and non-commercial costs.

Despite its advances, the new institutional economics presents a view that is just as limited as the other approaches. It analyzes institutions from the point of view of the exchange of goods and property rights and transaction costs, but it does not conceptualize transaction costs in a satisfactory way. In some cases, these costs are vaguely characterized by using Arrow's (1962) definition, i.e. "the costs of running the economic system"; in other cases, a functional taxonomy of the different transaction costs is used that is too meticulous and detailed, listing types of activities such as the search for information regarding prices, the implementation and follow-up of contracts, and the protection of property rights. In addition, the new approach uses a restrictive concept of exchange as it only considers economic and commercial transactions, and tends to ignore the fact that exchange also includes interpersonal transactions which have nothing to do with the exchange of property rights.

From this perspective, economic development is a process of growth and structural change in which the economic and social actors and organizations make investment decisions, exchange goods and services, and reach agreements and contracts. All of these decisions are supported by institutions that are created to facilitate transactions among actors and organizations, and to reduce the uncertainty and the associated costs that arise when carrying out exchange.

Thus, there are mechanisms between institutions and growth that affect the functioning and the results of productive activity. Exchange is carried out efficiently when transaction costs are low. The interactions among companies and organizations that arise as a result of the implementation of their strategies generate external economies through their formal and informal exchange of goods, information, and knowledge. The reduction in production and transaction costs and the external economies improve productivity, which leads to increasing returns to production factors.

The processes of economic growth change the environment in which the production systems are immersed and create new opportunities for economic, social, and political actors. When the existing institutions become a constraint to the functioning of productive and commercial activities and, therefore, to the processes of growth and structural change, the actors and organizations that lead the processes of accumulation introduce institutional changes in order to facilitate the process of capital and knowledge accumulation.

Economic development is ultimately institutional development, as the economic agents and actors make their decisions within the institutional and cultural context in which the economy is immersed. The very economic rationality under which companies and organizations make their investment decisions is embedded within the institutional and cultural context of every place and every territory (Tomassini, 2000).

In developing countries, therefore, the limited economic success achieved during the last decade is associated with the weakness of institutions and the uncertainty this generates for companies (Prats i Catala, 2003). The situation is aggravated because, as happens in Latin America, the elites in these countries are not conscious of the fact that the economic institutions are not sufficiently developed. Thus, companies do not find a favorable environment for carrying out their investments; in particular, foreign investors consider the risk too high, given the prevailing institutional and legal insecurity.

Institutional security is key in development processes, since it has a positive impact on productivity and economic growth. Above all, it limits economic risk and reduces companies' uncertainty, creating the basis for investment by local companies as well as for the attraction of foreign capital. This in turn generates an increase in economic exchange and leads to a widening of markets, thus creating the conditions for an enhanced specialization of companies and a differentiation of products. As a result, companies are able to increase their production, favoring the creation of economies of scale; and at the same time the development of clusters and value chains in the economy is encouraged, which produces an increase in inter-firm relations. In this way, positive externalities are generated that benefit the functioning of companies, since production costs tend to be reduced because of the reduction in transaction costs.

Therefore, in order to push forward economic and social progress in developing countries, it is necessary to foster institutional reforms within the development strategy of cities and regions.

As Prats i Catala (2003) points out, in many developing countries, formal institutions of the state (and economic institutions in particular) are very fragile, which explains why the system of internal and external relations seeks support in external institutions and cultural patterns. Hence, what is at stake is how to let the institutions evolve and how to transform the institutional system in order to improve competitiveness and social progress.

Governance and Development Policy

Territorial development policies are complex policies whose design and implementation are carried out at different levels of government with the participation of private actors and civil society. Therefore, a central aspect is the coordination of economic, political, and social agents, i.e. the coordination of the collective action of all actors in order to achieve the development of a territory such that all of the participants optimize the results of their management.

According to Reis (2007), the mechanisms that allow for the coordination of actors are not simple ones, as the market or the hierarchical organization of an administration may be. The difficulty derives, on the one hand, from the fact that the actors are part of a network in which the very relations that shape the economic, social, and political fabric are interdependent; and, on the other hand, from the fact that the actors are consciously aware of their decisions. Therefore, the first task of governance is precisely to coordinate the diversity of actors and their actions and incentives.

Governance can be defined as the "rules and institutions that set the limits and the incentives for the constitution and functioning of networks of territorial actors, government, the private sector, and civil society" (Prats i Catala, 2003. p. 76). The reference here is to the institutional framework that facilitates the coordination of private and public actors' behavior. It differs from governing which, following Kooiman (1993), refers to the actions by private and public agents who interact within a socio-institutional system; in this case, governance constitutes the specific system of the rules of the game in which the actors make their decisions to further their own interests.

Hence, governance is a broad concept. On the one hand, it includes the institutional rules that regulate the exchange carried out by private and public actors within the economic system (Hollingsworth *et al.*, 1994). On the other hand, it refers to the actions of actors that change and improve norms and relations between actors for the purpose of improving their collective action potential, which requires a change in the power relations between interest groups that set out together in order to improve the social and economic situation in cities and regions (Osborne and Gaebler, 1992). Finally, it also entails the very idea of interaction and mutual influence among actors.

Change in institutions occurs when actors who participate in governance find that new institutional arrangements offer them higher benefits. Restructuring entails a change in the formal rules as well as the informal norms, and encounters support from organizations whose interests can be foreseen to benefit from this change. When actors perceive that institutional change is strategic for reaching a group's objectives, they create organizations that take on the responsibility of negotiating the changes in the rules of the game and in the norms.

In developing countries, such as those of Latin America, the process of institutional change so necessary for effectively influencing the development process is difficult and slow. There are many public actors, organizations, and interest groups that must agree in order to build up the intermediate organizations and to negotiate objectives and strategies. The issue becomes more complicated when the focus is on economic institutions through which power structures are changed (Haggard and Kaufman, 1994).

The interactive mode of governance employs those initiatives where collective action is more efficient relative to the hierarchical, administrative mode of governing to forge its own path. As pointed out above, local development policies and instruments such as strategic planning are based on the idea that the actors in cities and regions interact and organize by forming networks. Therefore, in the design and implementation of local initiatives, the participation of different levels of government, social and entrepreneurial organizations, and civil society is ensured through intermediate organizations. In this way, the mode of interactive governance is added to the traditional hierarchical, administrative governance mode, leading to a new equilibrium of the governance models within the territory (Prats i Catala, 2003).

Hence, a central question in the discussion is how responsibilities are assigned to actors in places and territories where a great variety of actors are present (Barca, 2009). In the European Union, decisions are structured through multi-level networks of public and private actors, in accordance with the agreements and institutional arrangements that allow sharing responsibilities in the production and provision of goods and services. The subsidiarity principle establishes, as a criterion, that it is more efficient to assign specific tasks to each actor instead of assigning a certain number of services to each of them; in this way, actors are only engaged in tasks that cannot be carried out at a lower level of organization.

From the perspective of actions aimed at territorial development, the responsibility for their design and implementation is shared by different levels of the state's organization, private actors, and intermediate organizations that have interests and competences in the territory. In an interactive governance model, local organizations play a strategic role in the supply of services. Local actors have direct contact with the population of each place, and so they are in a better position to identify the needs of the local citizens, which the actions should satisfy; thus, their participation in the design of projects is of utmost importance in order to tailor the projects to the local context. Furthermore, their participation in supplying services through intermediate organizations (such as development agencies, firm incubators, technology institutes, or science parks) facilitates the effectiveness and control of territorial development initiatives. In addition, local organizations are an instrument on which the coordination of collective actions of administrations, social and economic agents, and the civil society in the implementation of projects in specific places and territories rests.

Multi-level governance solves some of the failures in the provision of goods and services, because it is through local intermediate organizations that access to information on the preferences and needs of local actors and citizens is favored, development potential is utilized, and interaction among local actors is activated. However, local organizations also have their deficiencies and flaws. First of all, they are organizations whose actors may be incapable of creating adequate economic tools to tackle the problems that the development process presents for places and territories. Furthermore, elites who administer projects may use public resources for their own benefit and disentangle themselves from the implementation of projects. The solution to these potential problems revolves around the control that other interested actors (including the administration and foreign actors) may exercise in the implementation of projects, and the citizens who are committed to the development of their territory.

Development of Places and Territories

Territorial policy is a development policy that responds to a model of analysis which considers development as an endogenous process in which public and private agents decide to invest progressively, subject to norms and culture which co-evolve with the changing economy and society. Territorial policy, thus, intends to foster economic and social change in cities and regions gradually through initiatives that optimize the use of specific local resources and the development potential. It represents a policy that is tailored to the conditions of each place, so that its own path of growth and structural change is pursued.

Furthermore, territorial policy is a policy of multiple objectives that attempts to improve the competitiveness of firms and territories as well as increase the welfare of the population in a sustainable manner, through projects in which public and private actors with a specific interest in the territory participate. The implementation of policies is carried out through organizations that allow for the coordination of collective action by the local actors. It is a policy that aims at the development of cities and regions that are part of territorial networks, which change and transform as a result of the increase in economic integration and the development of transport and communication infrastructures.

The emergence of the territorial policy is associated with the changes that have spontaneously arisen in the models of organization of production and territorial systems. The effect of the increasing economic integration, the organizational restructuring of enterprises, technological change, and institutional development on the territorial processes is leading to new spatial structures and new forms of organization of cities and regions. Therefore, these transformations call for a new approach to the development policies of places and territories.

The territorial policy is a development policy of cities and regions. As Batty (2001) argues, radical changes in technology cause cities and regions to adopt new forms of organization, enterprises to adopt new strategies for choosing their locations, and citizens to change their residential habits and routines. The traditional model of spatial organization has been affected, in a singular manner, by the fact that the application of new technologies to transport and communications systems has not only reduced the costs of transportation and exchange of products, but also improved accessibility and changed the perception of proximity, thus changing spatial organization in a significant way.

As Parr (1979, 2004) points out, the processes behind the economic dynamics of recent years are key to understanding the changes in regional spatial structures. In this sense, the new industrial and service companies (including multinational corporations) have decided to locate their production plants and offices in urban centers, cities, and localities of polycentric regions whose factors and attractions offer them competitive advantages. The infrastructures, labor supply, and occasionally commercial networks have exercised a strong attraction on new activities, and this has produced a positive effect on the formation and development of polycentric regions. Development processes are based on the existence of a strong interrelation between the process of growth and structural change, on the one hand, and the form of organizing the territory, on the other; more specifically, technological, productive, social, and political changes are produced within the territory, which is why they depend on the organization of the urban systems while simultaneously conditioning their change and transformation.

This phenomenon has appeared in all technological revolutions that drove industrial development forward. During the Industrial Revolution in the second half of the 18th century, urban industry consolidated itself and this favored the appearance of a constellation of small industrial cities. As a result of the electrical revolution, between 1870 and 1914, the development of big enterprises located in big cities was strengthened and this triggered the development of monocentric cities. With the current information revolution, polycentric regions appear as the new spatial structure.

Throughout recent history, the economic dynamic has generated specific forms of spatial organization of production that follow one another during a process of continuous restructuring, making previous forms obsolete and re-adapting them to changes propelled by the processes of accumulation of capital and knowledge. Therefore, a progressive re-adaptation of the forms of urban organization is taking place in every type of city and urban system, making them more flexible and compatible with the organization of firms and with the priorities of local citizens. This new reality has led to the appearance of a more complex territory in which cities and regions with development potential are present; their firms adopt product, process, and organizational innovations; goods and services of rural and more distant localities and regions enjoy a better-priced access to markets; and institutional change allows citizens and local organizations to participate in the decision-making process for the development of places and territories.

These transformations do not respond to traditional policies that obey a core-periphery approach, or to other views which argue that the objective is to achieve what was traditionally known as "balanced growth". The new reality demands policies that stimulate the use of resources and capacities existing in every territory, especially those capacities that constitute the territory's distinctive strengths. It is also about overcoming interpretations that analyze development in static terms, and considering that the use of local development potential is the main element of the new policies in order to achieve improvement in global competitiveness. The approach to development should adopt a dynamic interpretation in which the strategic advantage is the territory's development capacities. Therefore, the strategy and actions should be focused toward continuous transformation of the local potential as well as the upgrading of factors and resources in every city or region; furthermore, the economic and financial resources should be invested in those mechanisms and development forces that allow for the appearance of increasing returns.

From the perspective of territorial development, redistributive policies have given way to a new approach in which localities and cities continue to play a strategic role, but not as mere spaces in an increasingly globalized world where cities and regions are connected through more or less efficient infrastructures. Rather, localities and cities constitute spaces of polycentric regions in which the different nodes are well integrated in order to make places and territories more competitive. Complex relations are established among these spaces as a function of the productive specialization of every city and every region, and of the competitiveness of their firms and organizations.

This interpretation of the development of cities and regions requires the adoption of a territorial approach for the definition of the strategies and policies, and not a functional approach. As Priemus and Zonneveld (2004) suggest, the traditional public policies, in which firms and productive organizations were the target of initiatives and actions, should be abandoned. The territorial approach is focused towards fostering the dynamics of production networks, technological networks, and urban networks, which form the framework that facilitates the functioning of polycentric regions. From this perspective, the important thing is not so much to favor the dynamics of the individual enterprises, but rather to create the conditions for the strengthening of the production systems and to make enterprises and territories more competitive. Therefore, the purpose should be to create the conditions for the development of firm networks and organizations so as to help develop the territory.

This kind of development policy strengthens those processes that shape new territorial organization models, in which the hierarchical structures are softened and new geographies emerge that replace the old models of urban centrality. Hence, the approach is about policies for territories whose organization is changing, giving way to polycentric regions, and whose local networks of firms and organizations are being integrated into global networks. This transformation is possible due to the increased exchange of goods and services, the increased mobility of capital, and the appearance of new rules and norms that facilitate market functioning.

Chapter 9

Territorial Policy

The previous discussion on the new development policy concluded that the territorial approach is an adequate response to the current challenges. What is at stake is how to design and implement a strategy that stimulates endogenous development through physical planning, policy tools for entrepreneurial development, and innovation policy. The new reality calls for a strategy that fosters synergies between spatial, economic, and innovation policies in order to make them more efficient.

Policies for the development of a territory should be anchored in the institutional development of recent decades, in which local actors play an increasingly important role, through bottom-up policies that are defined and implemented as a result of negotiations and agreements between local actors. Moreover, the new reality — besides demanding the joint action of public and private actors with competences in the territory — requires that institutional development continue and that the competences of the actors be progressively redefined in the new scenario opened up by the crisis and recovery within globalization.

In sum, the answer to the challenges raised by the new forces of development requires measures that will stimulate the physical and entrepreneurial development of places and territories, the creation and transformation of institutions, and the diffusion of innovations between firms and organizations which form local networks and clusters. The issue is not the reinvention of development policies that seek balanced growth, but rather the definition and implementation of development initiatives that use and stimulate the capacities and potential of the territory, and that foster the economic progress and social welfare of its citizens.

A New Institutional Environment for Territorial Policy

Territorial development policy arises within a relatively new institutional context that emerged in, and has expanded since, the mid-1970s. The pronounced restructuring of production stimulated by the spread of new technologies, the process of economic integration following the fall of the Berlin Wall, and the economic and political deregulation which favors organizational change in firms and in states all steer institutional change and create new conditions for the governance of the economy and society (Brenner, 1999).

First of all, an important modification of the institutional system as well as a new definition of the relation between state and society are taking place (Governa and Salone, 2005). In European countries, the process of the devolution of competences to regions and municipalities has strengthened the regional and local levels in state organization, while some significant powers are transferred to supranational organizations like the European Union. The main innovation here, according to Bobbio (2002), is the reduction of internal hierarchies within countries, which characterized the dominant core-periphery model during a large part of the 20th century. This reduction of hierarchies allows for greater participation in the decision-making processes on behalf of civil society, the proliferation of associations between public and private organizations in decision-making processes, and the development of agreements between institutions at different levels. As local actors acquire a leading role in economic and territorial policies, local and regional governance changes, as do the strategy, implementation, and management of actions for territorial development.

This transformation of the governance pattern coincides with the spontaneous emergence of new forms of territorial organization of production, as a result of the adoption of flexible forms of organization of companies at both local and international levels. The transition from mass production to flexible production shows the complexity of the territory, with its networks of firms and actors that spur the spread of innovations and favor increased competition in markets. The process of globalization fosters the formation of international firm networks to the extent that international value chains, which link clusters and enterprises located in cities and regions of different countries, take shape. Horizontal forms of spontaneous governance thus emerge among firms and clusters at the international level, favoring the strategic coordination of enterprises and organizations and directly connecting cities and regions of different countries.

Finally, the formation of polycentric regions creates the conditions for the appearance of new forms of regulation of relations between local actors in cities and localities who are called upon to define and implement the policies of territorial development. The new economic spaces ask for a change in sectoral policies and also in physical planning, as shown by some European experiences: the promotion of urban regions in the Ruhr Valley in Germany, the new Dutch policies for transforming the Randstad into a motor force for national economic progress, and the new initiatives for shaping the development of Scotland on the basis of a polycentric urban region in central Scotland (the Edinburgh-Glasgow region). In all of these cases, the lack of governance structures called for a reform in the administrative organization and for institutional change in the governance of territories, with new roles to be played by different administrative actors.

Hall and Pain (2006) summarize the specific policy responses to the planning challenges of the eight polycentric urban regions studied in their EU research project. According to them,

> [T]here is no support in the policy-making structures or in public finance for an integrated MCR [megacity region] administration: in all eight regions, decision-making is fragmented, competition between cities is rife (though felt to be counterproductive), and nowhere does a territorial definition of MCR exist. There is a mismatch between the political pace (short and sometimes medium term) and the tangible results of any decision in the field of spatial planning (medium and especially long term). [Hall and Pain, 2006, p. 207]

Therefore, at the center of the policies of territorial development, new forms of governance that allow for the design and implementation of policies of economic development and physical planning are needed. Given the diversity of actors with decision-making competences regarding public and private investments, governance affects the different administration tiers of a country. Thus, the question of how to achieve the cooperation of public and private actors so as to permit the coordination of the initiatives and investments carried out in the territory arises.

Projects that are carried out as a result of policies for territorial development are often projects that demand important investments; this can be seen in policies of infrastructure, housing, and transport, and other measures to promote economic development (Parr, 2004; Priemus and Zonneveld, 2004). Their implementation requires the involved actors' agreement and commitment to sharing the financing of the projects and, in this way, the multiplicity of individual efforts for achieving these objectives is avoided. The definition and fulfillment of these objectives are only possible when cooperation between the actors is strengthened.

The cooperation between actors is based on the construction of alliances and agreements among actors in cities and regions to channel existing public and private resources, coordinate the implementation of projects, and define strategies for the new regions. Cooperation and agreements between actors are facilitated when the society's institutional environment creates the conditions through which a strengthening of trust between organizations is fostered; and when local citizens share a culture, a history, and institutions which contribute specifically to this end. In cases where the institutional environment undergoes a change process and there are no norms or rules to define the role of the actors in the new territorial development policies, then projects can only be carried out if results and benefits are distributed among the actors based on their contribution to the financing of a project. Hence, trust and the system of payments condition the cooperation processes.

In a world that is increasingly competitive and globalized, the new economic spaces need governance organizations that coordinate the efforts of coalition members and regional actors in order to be efficient. In the process of the formation of polycentric regions, governance is needed to lead initiatives and steer the coordination of local organizations and actors, to foster the initiatives through technical instruments (such as strategic planning and management), and to stimulate the cooperation of actors in those projects that serve the common interest. Therefore, questions often revolve around finding mechanisms that cover up failures in administrative coordination, and there is nothing better than those mechanisms facilitating strategic cooperation between actors in cities and regions. But, the project implementation depends on the institutional context and the administrative structures, which should be adapted to the needs of the territorial development policy.

In the case of the Randstad, for example, calls were often made for the establishment of a regional authority that could play a decisive role in stimulating cooperation between localities and cities, and among local actors, with legal capacity and autonomy to carry out the projects (Lambregts *et al.*, 2006). Traditionally, a solution to the failure of the governance structures was found through the adoption of different forms of cooperation by local and regional actors. The Dutch national administration opted recently for a decentralization of management and coordination of the spatial strategy for the Randstad — called the Nota Ruimte — to lower levels (the so-called North Wing, South Wing, and Green Heart); and it appears that coordination between the local and regional levels has improved, albeit not without problems.

The need for new forms of policy organization and management has generated a new approach to economic and physical planning, based on negotiation, consent, and commitment among those actors with competences in the territory. Changes in the institutional system have been progressively adopted since the early 1990s, although not without tension among central, local, and regional administrations. Instruments for negotiated programming between economic, social, and political actors have appeared, such as the territorial pact, at the same time that the need to establish agreements in planning processes with the firms and organizations from other regions and territories has appeared.

A territorial pact is a planning instrument that facilitates an agreement between public and private actors, and that identifies the different kinds of actions and measures necessary to promote urban and regional development. Hence, it is an instrument that allows the coordinated implementation of actions by different actors, each with their own competences, interests, and financing. Territorial pacts are an expression of the capacity of association among the local actors of a territory; and can be designed and promoted by the local public administration, chambers of commerce, representatives of entrepreneurs, workers, and local society in general.

As Governa and Salone (2005) indicate, territorial pacts make an innovative contribution to economic planning. They give a strategic role to networks of actors in designing policies and promoting local economic initiatives. They also introduce a contractual logic among actors that is used in the allocation of resources to favor those projects which show a greater possibility of success. Moreover, they define the political space as a function of the interests of those actors who contribute to the construction of a new geography of development, and so favor inter-territorial relations.

At any rate, territorial development requires specific agencies and organizations for planning and management, and they must be capable of implementing the actions and projects agreed upon. In order to reach the objectives and goals that the actors have set, it is not sufficient to merely design a lucky strategy and initiate the most adequate actions; management of the projects is also a necessary condition, as are the financial and human resources. Just as important as initiating and implementing the strategy of territorial development is the efficient management of each of the projects through which the action of the actors in the territory is carried out.

The optimization of the actions and project results requires an answer to the strategic and operative needs of the territorial development policy. This calls for an organization capable of assuming the responsibilities for designing and implementing policies that aim at setting up territorial development, and an instrument capable of coordinating actions in the territory implemented by distinct actors.

Territorial development needs an integrated policy that combines physical planning, policy tools for entrepreneurial development, and innovation policy. Therefore, territorial development agencies should be able to establish mechanisms that allow for production restructuring and self-sustaining growth, which are necessary for strengthening economic competitiveness. These agencies should foster and coordinate investments in matters of transport and communications that help to overcome situations like those of peripheral regions, which are scarcely connected to markets and to national and international decision-making centers; and they should promote joint activities by different actors who are interested in operations that require multiple financing resources.

Physical Planning and Territorial Development

The application of physical planning to the development of places and regions takes place at a time in which important changes in the development policy have occurred. The functional approach has been replaced by the territorial approach, whereby the territorial interests and actors enjoy greater strength; development policies have abandoned their focus on the redistribution of income and employment, and have instead directed it towards increasing economic progress and improving the well-being of the population by increasing the competitiveness of places and territories; and the regions have recovered their leading position in territorial development policies, but as polycentric regions in which the system of cities, the transport networks, and the production systems connect the territory. Therefore, the efficiency of territorial development policies requires the combined effort of physical planning and economic development policies.

Physical planning has been transformed during the last 20 years in such a way that policies dealing with land use have ceased to be the central element of territorial development. At present, cities, localities, and regions are the support for firm networks, transport networks, and the environmental system. They are progressively integrated into a world that is organized and governed by internationalized production systems, with transport systems that reduce the

distances and transport costs of goods and people, and with new technologies that strengthen production systems and communication and
transport networks. Territorial development needs a policy that stimulates the functioning of networks and systems which link and
organize the territory. Therefore, as Priemus and Zonneveld (2004)
recommend, it is advisable to support territorial development with
spatial policies that have an effect on city networks, transport and
communication systems and networks, and environmental systems.

Networks of cities and, hence, the cities themselves are at the center of spatial policies insofar as they provide public services for citizens
(such as housing, commercial service zones, and recreational spaces),
promote new locations for productive activities and businesses in
cities and regions, and create services in those locations that become
communication and traffic nodes in polycentric regions. But especially, as the European Union report (CEC, 1999) indicates, the
growing competition between firms and territories advises strengthening relations and cooperation among cities and localities —
specifically among those that form polycentric regions — to make
them more attractive for the location of enterprises and residential
areas.

The purpose of physical planning is not only to strengthen decentralization and favor the development of metropolitan regions, but
also to find methods that increase the relations and cooperation
between cities and regions, thus creating interregional and international city networks. In particular, the integration of polycentric
regions requires the establishment of connections between rural localities and urban centers, creating a network of flows and exchange that
are connected to other regions and territories.

The path for achieving this passes through the implementation of
policies that stimulate the integration of production systems of cities
and places in polycentric regions, initiatives that define industrial
zones and residential spaces, and actions that create transportation
and communication infrastructures. The strengthening of polycentric
regions will also strengthen the cooperation with other regions and
territories in different countries, as local firms and clusters will have
productive and commercial relations with external firms due to the

process of de-location, the internationalization of production, and the emergence of global value chains.

The territories of polycentric regions and urban systems are linked and connected to the international system via the communication and transport networks. An ideal transport and communications system requires the development of roads, tracks, maritime routes, and air travel systems, as well as the development of places of modal and intermodal connection such as transport transfer hubs, train stations, ports, and airports. The smooth functioning of territories, and the consequent improvement in the competitiveness of cities and regions, requires a network of infrastructures that connects places in the territory and also connects them to other spaces and regions. To achieve this, specific actions must be taken in each territory that will combine the construction of modern, high-capacity infrastructures with the improvement of secondary infrastructures of transport networks, in such a way that the territory is well linked and well served, and that international accessibility is guaranteed with good time-cost efficiency (CEC, 1999).

The strengthening of secondary transportation networks and their connection to international networks is, hence, a priority, given that the efficiency and density of secondary networks are decisive for the integration of regional and urban economies and, thus, for the improvement of the competitiveness of their enterprises in international markets. This implies the modernization of regional transportation services, always bearing in mind the adequacy of different modes of transport to the local and regional conditions (be they conventional railroad networks, a system of inter-urban public transport, or regional airports). The development of the secondary network allows for local flows to be channeled through modern, high-capacity networks, and also to reach the necessary critical mass for long-distance connections.

In today's globalized world, the competitiveness of regions and cities is only possible when accessibility at the international level is guaranteed. At present, great differences exist between regions in relation to the networks and communication nodes (ports, airports) available, and the quality of services provided by maritime firms and airline companies that operate from cities and regions according to the logic of the market. The development of cities and regions needs the connections with international traffic hubs to be strengthened, and thus it is necessary to develop and connect the maritime and air transport subsystems in such a way that the needs and demands of all cities and regions are met efficiently.

In order to improve the efficiency of transport networks, it is necessary to strengthen intermodal connections so that transport transfer hubs and freight loading centers serve the entire territory, and to accelerate the modernization of railroads and regional air transport. In any case, it is necessary to create the conditions for the different transport systems to operate jointly in an efficient way, and to improve logistics in general. A key element in the operative transformation of the transport systems is the coordination of policies so that those responsible for the ports, airports, railroads, and principal corridors of road networks, as well as the operators of the different networks, implement this coordination within the framework of an integrated multi-modal system. Thus, cooperation between the various offices responsible for the management of national, regional, and local transport policies is necessary when the objective is for an efficient connection between the different levels of the networks. Furthermore, the transport system must improve its services through the development of intermodal transport, the strengthening of inter-urban transport, and an improved supply of urban transport services within the cities and regions (Hooghe and Marks, 2001).

Development Policy for Cities and Regions

Nevertheless, physical planning alone is not sufficient for stimulating processes of territorial development (Davoudi, 2003). Too much trust has perhaps been put on the role that infrastructure policies and physical planning play in development processes, especially by those who advocate a polycentric development. In fact, the development of a territory is a complex process in which different mechanisms interact to affect different dimensions of development: the organization of production model, the functioning of the institutional system and sociocultural processes, the creation and diffusion of innovations within the productive fabric, and the networks of actors in the territory. In practice, as Albrechts (2001) indicates, spatial planning is only efficient if it is embedded in the economic dynamics and the processes of transformation of cities and regions.

Therefore, policies and measures to promote endogenous development play a relevant role in the processes of territorial development, as the different approaches to endogenous development show. For the self-development approach, the purpose of local initiatives is to mobilize the development potential that exists in localities and territories, and to use it in projects that are designed and managed by the citizens themselves and by local organizations. For the human development approach, local development initiatives are efficient when they use the capabilities of the population, especially their creative and entrepreneurial capacity, to transform the economic system and society. As for the evolutionary development approach, local initiatives obtain good results when they affect the development forces that have a multiplier effect on investment insofar as they generate increasing returns and stimulate the processes of territorial development.

As Madoery (2008) argues, it is convenient to introduce an important nuance when speaking about local development policies. According to him, economic and social progress does not depend on the availability and use of the development potential, but rather on the upgrading and broadening of the resources and capabilities for the development of the territory. Development is the result of the capacities that are endogenously generated, bound to the organization of firms and actors, to the skill of human resources, to the introduction of innovations and knowledge in public and private organizations, and to the flexibility of institutions that facilitate investment and generate progress and social welfare.

Endogenous development policy, which emerged as a result of the local communities' learning processes, attempts to improve the responses of local productive systems to the challenges represented by increased market competition and changes in demand. Even though the response of cities and regions varies greatly from one territory to another, the key question is how to make their firms, clusters, and production systems more competitive — namely, how to improve the integration of the local economies within the international economy. Territorial development calls for a structural change of the production system, based on the strengths of the territory as well as on the adjustment of the institutional, cultural, and social model of each territory, in order to enable firms to make good use of the opportunities that emerge in the markets as a result of environmental changes and increasing competition. Local development experiences show that the path to follow must include the definition and implementation of a strategy of entrepreneurial development, through actions focused towards self-sustaining growth and social progress.

The challenge for the new development strategy is to achieve a process of sustainable development of territories embedded in a competitive environment, with high levels of competition and uncertainty. Hence, it is about favoring the emergence and development of firms and increasing flexibility in the production system, facilitating access to financial and specific resources, strengthening and fostering the diffusion of innovations and knowledge within the productive fabric and networks, fostering the polycentric urban development of the territory and making cities and regions more attractive, and transforming the institutional environment into a system that favors the emergence and development of entrepreneurial initiatives.

One of the main objectives of endogenous development is to continuously support the process of improving the entrepreneurial and organizational capacity of the territory. In part, all local initiatives propose to generate the start-up of new firms and improve the entrepreneurial and organizational capacities of their economic agents as a priority. In accordance with this objective, firm incubators and business innovation centers have appeared in recent decades, as have initiatives that foster the entrepreneurial capacity of social target groups such as women and youngsters. Furthermore, during recent years, a revitalization of policies aiming to attract external firms which are willing to endogenize their activities within the territory has begun, by means of new regulations (such as territorial pacts) that facilitate the relations between external firms and the territory.

Those who defend the self-development approach argue that the social economy is an expression of the learning capacity of a society in response to the challenges raised by economic development and social change in an increasingly integrated world. Society responds to social exclusion through initiatives focused towards improved citizen welfare, often using instruments (such as cooperatives and non-profit institutions) where decisions are made democratically by their members.

In turn, for the purpose of improving the competitiveness of local firms and clusters and favoring their integration into the international economic system, regional governments and central administrations stimulate the cooperation among local firms and the reinforcement of value chains that create, strengthen, and maintain competitive advantages in the long term. In this sense, it should be pointed out that the formation of well-connected clusters and local production systems is a key mechanism for strengthening the competitiveness of local firms. This is because it improves the productivity of firms through productive specialization and the circulation of information and knowledge, which increases external economies of scale and reduces transaction costs; it stimulates the emergence and diffusion of innovations and the upgrading of human resources, which in turn encourages firms to respond to opportunities in the market; and it stimulates economies of agglomeration, making the territory more attractive to local and external firms, including firms providing business and financial services as well as firms in the leisure and cultural-product industries.

These spontaneous processes are facilitated by initiatives focused towards the creation and diffusion of innovations within the productive fabric, and international value chains. For decades, one of the axes of the restructuring and modernization of local economies was to facilitate processes of adoption and adaptation of technologies within the production system through instruments such as innovation centers, science parks, technology parks, and technology institutes. Among their goals was to stimulate the transfer and diffusion of innovations within the production system, and the technological response by the local enterprises. New policy tools for innovation are needed today in order to foster the flow of knowledge and innovation within international networks.

Polycentric urban development is one of the main axes of the local development policy. Initiatives that reinforce urban transport and communication infrastructures, improve access to cities and localities while containing their expansion, provide developed real estate to firms, improve the quality of the urban social capital, and conserve the historical and cultural heritage, among others, constitute activities that try to make cities more attractive for living and for producing. At the present time, functional polycentricity has also become a policy objective; therefore, development policy actions should foster complementary functions and specializations of different cities and localities of the territories and regions, and strengthen their interaction, in order to improve economic competitiveness.

Also among the instruments for achieving a greater attraction for cities and territories are those initiatives directed towards improving social and environmental sustainability. The fight against poverty and social exclusion allows for a better use of urban resources and development potential, and increases the attractiveness of cities and regions. In addition, the promotion and good management of urban resources — including an integrated treatment of natural resources, energy, and waste — reduce the consumption of non-renewable resources, reduce air, ground and water pollution, and improve the environment.

Moreover, through the creation of services such as exhibition and business centers as well as urban marketing through image campaigns and the construction of emblematic buildings, urban regions become an attractive space for the location of investments, the demand for urban services increases, and urbanization processes are developed. In any case, the adaptation of regulations and norms to the needs and demands of the firms and citizens as well as the improvement of public services reinforce the city's attractiveness, favoring the urban development of territories.

Finally, the new development policies are based on a new form of understanding of the relations between economic, social, and political actors that tend to be less hierarchical and more participatory. This is a new form of governance that designs and implements policy actions based on negotiation and specific agreements by the actors and, in polycentric regions, on cooperation between cities and localities. The management of local development policies, in turn, tends to be more decentralized and becomes operative through intermediary organizations that provide real services, such as development agencies, in the management of which clients and local actors participate. Furthermore, the emergence of associations and the creation of networks of local actors give a more participatory character to decision-making and development management. At the polycentric-region scale, however, governance structures should be created in order to promote the horizontal and vertical coordination of policy-makers and economic and social actors.

Development policies are, in short, an instrument that tries to integrate different types of actions in order to satisfy the needs of the production system and the demands made by firms. The purpose is to jointly influence all the mechanisms and forces of development in order to create and improve synergetic effects between them. Hence, the sustained growth in competitiveness of local firms fosters the self-sustaining development of places and territories, and economic and social progress.

New Policy Tools for Innovation

Innovation policy plays a key role in the economic development of countries, regions, and cities. In an increasingly integrated world in which firms are organized into international networks, initiatives to support the creation and diffusion of knowledge have responded by basing their policy on a system of innovation centers to stimulate the flow of knowledge among networks and clusters and to make firms and territories more competitive. Given the diversity of actors existing in cities and regions, the coordination of actors and institutional governance are strategic for territorial development.

Integration, networks, and innovation policy

Regional and national technological policy can only be efficient if its concept and design are based on how knowledge emerges and circulates within firm networks. For this reason, in global value chains, the impact of policies is greater when initiatives acquire an international dimension.

As seen above when analyzing the Madrid aeronautical cluster (see Chapter 6), Spanish and European firm networks are located in European Union territories and elsewhere. Therefore, aeronautical (and other) activities are deeply integrated into international markets. Clusters in Spain and other EU countries exchange products, services, and knowledge, thus forming a network of relations on which the productive activity is based. In turn, the globalization process has stimulated firm networks to develop global value chains and productive systems have integrated at an international level. So, global networks require rules and norms of a global nature as well as innovation policies that apply to firms in global networks.

As a result, technological innovation policies will be more efficient if they are based on a strategy that targets global networks of firms and if local, national, and international organizations and actors adopt a common strategy. Policies will also be more efficient if goals and tools are shared and if proactive policies are defined that influence the creation and diffusion of knowledge.

National and regional innovation systems are at the root of the functioning of productive systems because the goal of productive organizations is to produce knowledge. As Soete and Weel (1999) point out, knowledge is created when and where the various actors who cooperate in the production of knowledge are in close proximity. Clusters and large firms are unique actors (along with universities, research centers and laboratories, centers of global competition, and other instruments created by technological innovation policies) in the process of the creation and diffusion of innovation and knowledge.

From this point of view, innovation policy aims to further the creation and diffusion of knowledge within firm networks and productive systems. Thus, initiatives are designed to promote R&D; support and maintain laboratories, research centers, and science parks; and, in sum, promote the creative capability of the actors in scientific and technological systems. The objectives of innovation policy vary, depending on the territory where firm networks are located, on the organization of firm clusters, on the characteristics of regional and national innovation systems, and on the culture of production and innovation existing in the territory.

Therefore, the definition of innovation policy must necessarily be based on the resources, institutions, and incentives of the innovation processes (Metcalfe, 1995; Fonfría Mesa, 1999). Resources refer to the human resources and their skill, the physical capital in equipment goods and centers that promote the flow of knowledge and innovation, and the funding of the policy. Regional and national institutions refer to all actors who participate in the management, production, and distribution of innovation, and to the norms and rules that condition their activities and decisions. Finally, incentives for innovative processes refer to the conditions under which the results of innovation are appropriated, particularly those concerning the protection of property rights.

Centers for global competition

Centers for global competition are innovation policy tools designed to make knowledge accumulated in the network available for use by firms in clusters, that is, to facilitate and promote the flow of knowledge among the firms and networks (see Figure 9.1).

Significant changes have taken place in innovation policy since the 1990s (Asheim *et al.*, 2003). Firms continue to demand services offered by first-generation technology policy tools, such as quality control, technical certification, material resistance testing, and on-the-job training. At the same time, however, economic integration and increased competition have created new demands to help firms react faster with an increasingly competitive response. Firms, then, express the need for new services that will help them form competitive networks at a global level and show them how to learn to innovate and improve their innovative processes.

The new, increasingly widespread centers for global competition are aimed at the learning processes both within and between firms, and extend this process to the rest of the actors that make up the territorial innovation system. One of the strategic lines of action is to

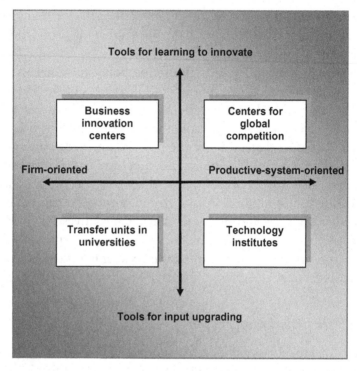

Figure 9.1 Policy Tools for Innovation (adapted from Asheim *et al.* (2003)).

improve human resources in firms and transfer tacit knowledge required to stimulate innovation. Moreover, to foster mechanisms for the creation and diffusion of innovation, the centers provide support to the formation of networks and cooperation between research centers and firms, so that creative interaction between institutions and firms takes place and learning processes are generated within the firms and organizations in each territory. Cooperation among the actors in a territory is often the foundation for the success of innovation policies. The formation of high-tech clusters, the diffusion of innovation through the exchange of knowledge among centers for global competition, or the financing of in-house innovation projects requires that actors in a territory come together to cooperate on projects.

When firms and firm networks belong to international or global chains, it is essential that the public and private research centers that support the global firm networks also build their own networks. Research centers that have emerged spontaneously to provide support to firms and firm networks improve their efficiency when they themselves operate in networks because innovation and knowledge flow more efficiently within international networks as network economies appear.

As occurs with firm networks, the optimal functioning of a network of innovation centers requires that ideas and knowledge flow freely among managers, technicians, and scientists when local labor markets are connected. As Soete and Weel (1999) argue, innovation and technology policy should deal with all barriers, such as the lack of labor mobility within global clusters, and it should promote the movement of scientists and technicians from research center to research center and from firm to firm, thus facilitating the flow of ideas and knowledge within firm and research center networks.

Finally, as Fonfría Mesa (1999) maintains, cooperation among local actors is necessary in order to finance public and private research centers that are attempting to create knowledge in firm networks and promote joint ventures for specific innovation projects. At a time when public funding is normally considered to be exclusive, Fonfría Mesa argues that co-financing of an innovative effort by several actors (public and private) is an adequate mechanism to create and develop innovative firms.

Governance and coordination

The existence and development of global chains of firms, as in the case of the European aeronautics sector, presupposes the existence of multiple public and private actors whose actions are relevant at local, national, and international levels of the system of relations. As seen above, commercial, productive, and technological links among firms tend to be mirrored among research centers. However, codes, norms, and rules only operate at a local or national level; rules at the international level are lacking. If they did exist, there would be reduced transaction and production costs for firms, and greater efficiency of innovation policies would be generated.

In the EU, an innovation system is only now being contemplated that will facilitate the diffusion of innovation and knowledge through firm networks and clusters of all kinds. At present, European firm networks lack global institutions to promote creative and innovative capability in firms and to assist innovation and knowledge transfer within global firm networks. However, as previously mentioned when analyzing the Madrid aeronautics cluster, innovative clusters have constructed their own rules, norms, and codes that favor the continuous injection of knowledge into product manufacturing and quality control.

Both EU and regional and national innovation policies targeting firm networks are currently basing their actions on existing research systems, whether they are associated with large firms or local firm systems. Regional and national policies support research centers and activities for large, often multinational, firms and clusters in high-tech activities. In this way, policy takes advantage of network economies existing in global value chains and multiplies the effectiveness of the public policies.

Innovation policies also concentrate on developing technological centers that facilitate and provide services to local firms. But, the efficiency of these centers is limited by the fact that they only meet the needs of small- and medium-sized enterprises, and not new demands for global services. In an attempt to overcome this limitation, an international network of innovation centers that promotes cooperation and the diffusion of innovation and knowledge should be created in order to improve the global competitiveness of firms and territories in the EU (Asheim *et al.*, 2003).

Development Policy for Low-Density Regions

The endogenous development approach gives an integrated interpretation of the dynamics of the territory. There is a great diversity of places and territories in terms of the population density, the productive activities carried out, and the position they occupy within the international division of labor. Yet, the relevant fact is the capacity of this approach for arguing in favor of a better use of the local development potential, self-sustaining growth and structural change, job creation, and the improvement of the firms' competitiveness in national and international markets.

Historically, territories with low population density in which agricultural activities were dominant were submitted to a certain kind of discrimination in sectoral policies. They were treated as low-productivity territories, where it was understood that increased welfare would only be possible through social and welfare policies, their farms and production were supported by subsidies, and their historical and cultural heritage was protected by the state. The basic reason was that public decision-makers intended to foster the industrial development of national and regional economies, and attract the location of firms into cities (frequently the big cities), through public policies. The result, over time, is that rural regions have often developed grave structural problems since their farms and agribusiness firms tend to operate at low productivity levels, their products compete poorly in markets, their connectivity to markets is limited, and they lack sufficient infrastructures as well as quality social services.

From the perspective of endogenous development, the economic development of rural regions can also be understood as the development of territories with their own resources and development potential, on which a strategy and policies for local development should be built. The objectives are the improvement of the local firms' and farms' competitiveness in the markets, and the economic progress and enhanced well-being of the population. This territorial approach requires the joint action of public and private actors in order to stimulate the local entrepreneurial capacity, which will enable them to exploit economic opportunities when they appear in national and international markets.

Therefore, for rural localities and regions integrated into polycentric regions, their participation in the network of flows and exchange with other localities and regions (both close by and far away), their secondary transport networks, and their connection to interregional and international networks should be strengthened. The transport network eases the accessibility of local firms and farms to markets under good cost conditions, and also fulfills the role of structuring the territory, connecting small cities, villages, and localities with the cities and urban regions of the polycentric region. Improvement in the connectivity of rural regions requires the strengthening of telecommunication infrastructures, placing the new information and communication technologies at the disposal of local firms and organizations.

The existence of a system of small- and medium-sized cities connected by an efficient transport and communications system creates strengths for the process of rural economic development. When localities, villages, and small cities in rural regions are endowed with financial and commercial services, and possess a transport and communication infrastructure that connects them to product and factor markets, then it becomes possible to adopt a development strategy based on the use of the development potential and on the upgrading and enlargement of the development capacities in rural regions.

Rural economic development policies can be implemented through initiatives that direct the diversification of production systems. As pointed out, the relative weight of agricultural production tends to diminish in emerging and late developed countries, as specialized activities are gaining in strength for agricultural products with expanding markets (e.g. fruit, vegetables, and flowers), agro-industrial products, traditional manufactures, and public, tourist and leisure services. Therefore, it seems strategically correct to support the spontaneous structural changes of the production system based on the returns and profits of productive activities in rural regions.

The diversification of economic activities in rural areas and the multiplication of forms of external integration have become a singular characteristic of the development of rural localities and regions. The strength of rural development is based not so much on the scale economies of farms as on the economies of diversity, especially when the diversification of agricultural activities is combined with the development of industrial and service activities. The diversification of the rural economy and the combination with different activities strengthen the production model and reinforce the competitiveness of rural localities and regions. Therefore, it seems reasonable to limit subsidies to agricultural production, and also to promote entrepreneurial initiatives in all those activities (industrial and service) that improve the competitiveness of localities and regions.

Productive diversity and the production of high-value added goods are priorities for rural economic development policies that should be jointly fostered with stimuli for the formation and promotion of clusters and local firm systems in agricultural and industrial products. Flexible forms of organization of production have traditionally characterized productive activities in rural areas, as occurred in Spain in the case of shoe, timber, and ceramics clusters, and at present with the wine and olive oil clusters. This kind of organization of production generates a network of productive, technological, and commercial exchange; and this allows for external economies of scale, economies of diversity, and a reduction in transaction costs, which favor increased competitiveness in firms and territories. The effect of policy measures, always in the long term, is favored when there are good-quality agricultural resources and raw materials demanded by the market, when a local entrepreneurial capacity exists, and when the local demand for final products exists.

Furthermore, increased competitiveness in rural regions calls for initiatives that foster the start-up of firms, the diffusion of knowledge among firms and organizations, and the improvement of the economic and financial framework. The training of human resources for specific tasks where local demand exists, stimuli for the emergence and formation of local entrepreneurs (including those in the social economy, such as cooperatives), and the building up of centers for the diffusion of innovations that satisfy the needs and demands of local firms and farms are strategic initiatives. When they are adequately implemented, the positioning of firms in markets is reinforced, and this fosters the competitiveness of rural regions. Finally, the continuous improvement of the economic environment, with the provision of real and financial services that satisfy the demands of enterprises and citizens, fosters the competitiveness of rural localities and regions.

References

Abramovitz, M. (1952). Economics of growth. In B. F. Haley (ed.), *A Survey of Contemporary Economics*. Homewood, IL: Richard D. Irwin.

Aghon, G., Alburquerque, F. and Cortés, P. (2001). *Desarrollo Económico Local y Descentralización en América Latina: Un Análisis Comparativo*. Santiago de Chile: CEPAL/GTZ.

Albrechts, L. (2001). How to proceed from image and discourse to action: as applied to the Flemish Diamond. *Urban Studies*, 38: 733–745.

Alburquerque, F. (2001). Evaluación y reflexiones sobre las iniciativas de desarrollo económico local en América Latina. Mimeograph. Madrid: Consejo de Investigaciones Científicas.

Alburquerque, F., Costamagna, P. and Ferraro, C. (2008). *Desarrollo Económico Local, Descentralización y Democracia*. Buenos Aires: UNSAM EDITA.

Alfonso-Gil, J. and Vázquez-Barquero, A. (2010). Networking and innovation: lessons from the aeronautical cluster of Madrid. *International Journal of Technology Management*, 50: 337–355.

Alonso, J. A. (2006). Cambios en la doctrina del desarrollo: el legado de Sen. In V. Martínez Guzmán and S. París Albert (eds.), *Amartya K. Sen y la Globalización*. Castellón: Universitat Jaume I.

Altenburg, T. and Meyer-Stamer, J. (1999). How to promote clusters: policy experiences from Latin America. *World Development*, 27: 1693–1713.

Amin, A. and Thrift, N. (1993). Globalization, institutional thickness and local prospects. *Revue d'Economie Regionale et Urbaine*, 3: 405–427.

Arcangeli, F. (1993). Local and global features of the learning process. In M. Humbert. (ed.), *The Impact of Globalisation on Europe's Firms and Industries*. London: Pinter.

Armendáriz de Aghion, B. and Morduch, J. (2001). *The Economics of Microfinance*. Cambridge, MA: The MIT Press.

Arocena, J. (1995). *El Desarrollo Local: Un Desafío Contemporáneo*. Caracas: Nueva Sociedad.

Arrow, K. J. (1962). The economic implications of learning by doing. *Review of Economic Studies*, 29: 155–173.

Asheim, B. T. (1994). Industrial districts, inter-firm cooperation and endogenous technological development: the experience of developed countries. In G. Garofoli and A. Vázquez-Barquero (eds.), *Organization of Production and Territory: Local Models of Development*. Pavia: Gianni Iuculano Editore.

Asheim, B. T. and Isaksen, A. (1997). Location, agglomeration and innovation: towards regional innovation systems in Norway. *European Planning Studies*, 5: 299–330.

Asheim, B. T., Isaksen, A., Nauwelaers, C. and Tödtling, F. (eds.) (2003). *Regional Innovation Policy for Small-Medium Enterprises*. Cheltenham: Edward Elgar.

Athukorala, P. (2007). *Multinational Enterprises in Asian Development*. Cheltenham: Edward Elgar.

Aydalot, P. (1985). *Economie Régionale et Urbaine*. Paris: Economica.

——— (1986). *Milieux Innovateurs en Europe*. Paris: Economica.

Baldó, J. and Villanueva, F. (1996). Plan de reestructuración de los barrios de la estructura urbana. In H. Garnica (ed.), *Los Barrios no Tienen Quien les Escriba*. Diario El Universal (Venezuela), December 9: 1–4.

Barca, F. (2009). An agenda for a reformed cohesion policy: a place-based approach to meeting European Union challenges and expectations. Independent Report. Brussels: European Union.

Barro, J. R. and Sala-i-Martin, X. (1995). *Economic Growth*. New York: McGraw-Hill, Inc.

Batten, D. F. (1995). Network cities: creative urban agglomeration for the 21st century. *Urban Studies*, 32: 313–327.

Batty, M. (2001). Polynucleated urban landscapes. *Urban Studies*, 39: 635–655.

Becattini, G. (1979). Dal settore industriale al distretto industriale: alcune considerazione sull'unita di indagine dell'economia industriale. *Rivista di Economia e Politica Industriale*, 1: 7–21.

——— (1990). The Marshallian industrial district as a socio-economic notion. In F. Pyke, G. Becattini and W. Sengerberger (eds.), *Industrial Districts and Inter-Firm Cooperation in Italy*. Geneva: International Institute for Labour Studies.

——— (1997). Totalità e cambiamento: il paradigma dei distretti industriali. *Sviluppo Locale*, 4(6): 5–24.

——— (2001). *The Caterpillar and the Butterfly*. Firenze: Felice le Monnier.

Becker, G. (1996). Preferences and values. In G. Becker (ed.), *Accounting for Tastes*. Cambridge, MA: Harvard University Press.

Bellandi, M. (2001). Local development and embedded large firms. *Entrepreneurship & Regional Development*, 13: 189–210.

Belussi, F. and Pilotti, L. (2002). Knowledge creation, learning and innovation in Italian industrial districts. *Geografiska Annaler*, 84B(2): 125–139.

Benavides, M. and Manrique, G. (2001). La experiencia de desarrollo económico local del distrito de Villa El Salvador. In G. Aghon, F. Alburquerque and P. Cortés (eds.), *Desarrollo Económico Local y Descentralización en América Latina: Un Análisis Comparativo*. Santiago de Chile: CEPAL/GTZ.

Bernabé Maestre, J. M. (1983). Industrialización difusa en la provincia de Alicante. Mimeograph. Valencia: Facultad de Geografía de la Universidad de Valencia.

Best, M. (1990). *The New Competition: Institutions of Industrial Restructuring.* Cambridge, MA: Harvard University Press.

Bobbio, L. (2002). *I Goberni Locali Nelle Democrazie Contenporanee.* Roma-Bari: Laterza.

Boisier, S. (2003). *El Desarrollo en su Lugar.* Santiago: Universidad Católica de Chile.

Boone, P. (1996). Politics and the effectiveness of foreign aid. *European Economic Review*, 40: 289–329.

Bordo, D. M. (2008). An historical perspective on the crisis of 2007–2009. Working Paper No. 14569. Cambridge, MA: National Bureau of Economic Research.

Bramanti, A. and Senn, L. (1993). Entrepreneurs, firm, "milieu": three different specifications of networking activities. In D. Maillat, M. Quevit and L. Senn (eds.), *Réseaux d'Innovation et Milieux Innovateurs: Un Pari Pour le Développement Régional.* Neuchâtel: Gremi-Edes.

Brenner, N. (1999). Globalisation as reterritorialisation: the re-scaling of urban governance in the European Union. *Urban Studies*, 36: 431–451.

Brusco, S. (1982). The Emilian model: productive decentralization and social integration. *Cambridge Journal of Economics*, 6: 167–184.

Camagni, R. (1991). Local "milieu", uncertainty and innovation networks: towards a new dynamic theory of economic space. In R. Camagni (ed.), *Innovation Networks: Spatial Perspectives.* London: Belhaven Press.

——— (1992). Organisation économique et réseaux des villes. In P. H. Derycke (ed.), *Espace et Dynamiques Territoriales.* Paris: Economica.

Camagni, R. and Maillat, D. (eds.) (2006). *Milieux Innovateurs: Theorie et Politiques.* Paris: Economica.

Camagni, R. and Salone, C. (1993). Network urban structures in Northern Italy: elements for a theoretical framework. *Urban Studies*, 30: 1053–1064.

Campbell, T. (2001). Innovation and risk-taking: urban governance in Latin America. In A. J. Scott (ed.), *Global City-Regions: Trends, Theory, Policy.* Oxford: Oxford University Press.

Canullo, G. and Vázquez-Barquero, A. (2007). Sviluppo economico e transformazione nei pàesi dell' Europa Mediterranea. *Economia Marche — Review of Regional Studies*, 26(1): 63–96.

Canzanelli, G. (2007). Strategie di sviluppo economico territoriale nei programmi di sviluppo umano delle Nazioni Unite: la valorizzazione del potenziale endogeno e le agenzie di sviluppo economico locale. In N. Leotta (ed.), *La Cooperazione Decentrata.* Milano: Franco Angeli Editore.

Cardoso, F. H. (1972). Dependency and development in Latin America. *New Left Review*, 74: 83–95.

Carpi, T., Banyuls Llopis, J., Cano Cano, E., Contreras Navarro, J. L., Gallego Bono, J. R., Picher Campos, J. V., Such Juan, J. and Torrejón Velardiez, M. (1999).

Dinámica Industrial e Innovación en la Comunidad Valenciana: Análisis de los Distritios Industriales del Calzado, Cerámica, Mueble y Téxtil. Valencia: IMPIVA, Generalitat Valenciana.

Casanova, L. (2009). *Global Latinas: Latin America's Multinationals.* Houndmills, Hampshire: Palgrave Macmillan.

Castells, M. (1996). *The Information Age: Economy, Society and Culture. Volume I: The Rise of the Network Society.* Cambridge, MA: Blackwell Publishers.

CEC (1999). *European Spatial Development Perspective: Towards Balanced and Sustainable Development of the Territory of the EU.* Luxemburg: European Union Publications.

Chandler, A. D. (1990). *The Dynamics of Industrial Capitalism.* Boston: Harvard University Press.

Chen, S. and Ravallion, M. (2008). The developing world is poorer than we thought, but no less successful in the fight against poverty. Policy Research Working Paper No. 4703. Washington: The World Bank.

Christaller, W. (1933). *The Central Places in Southern Germany.* Englewood Cliffs, NJ: Prentice Hall (2nd ed., 1966).

Ciccone, A. and Hall, R. E. (1996). Productivity and the density of economic activity. *American Economic Review*, 86: 54–70.

Cifuentes, I. (2000). Proyecto Cuchumatanes: transferencia de servicios técnicos a las organizaciones de productores. Mimeograph. Huehuetenango, Guatemala: Ministerio de Agricultura, Ganadería y Alimentación.

Coase, R. (1937). The nature of the firm. *Economica*, 4: 386–405.

Commons, J. (1934). *Institutional Economics.* Madison, WI: University of Wisconsin Press.

Cooke, P. (2001). Regional innovation systems, clusters and the knowledge economy. *Industrial and Corporate Change*, 10(4): 945–974.

——— (2002). *Knowledge Economies: Clusters, Learning, and Cooperative Advantage.* London and New York: Routledge.

Cooke, P. and Morgan, K. (1998). *The Associational Economy: Firms, Regions, and Innovation.* Oxford: Oxford University Press.

Copus, A. K. (2001). From core-periphery to polycentric development: concepts of spatial and aspatial peripherality. *European Planning Studies*, 9: 539–552.

Courlet, C. (2008). *L'Economie Territoriale.* Grenoble: Presses Universitaires de Grenoble.

Davoudi, S. (2003). Polycentricity in European spatial planning: from an analytical tool to a normative agenda. *European Planning Studies*, 11: 979–999.

Dematteis, G. (ed.) (1991). *Il Fenomeno Urbano in Italia: Interpretazioni, Prospettive, Politiche.* Milano: Franco Angeli.

Domar, E. (1946). Capital expansion, rate of growth, and employment. *Econometrica*, 14(April): 137–147.

Dosi, G. (1988). Sources, procedures and microeconomic effects of innovation. *Journal of Economic Literature*, 36: 1126–1171.

Douglas, M. (2001). Intercity competition and the question of economic resilience: globalization and crisis in Asia. In A. J. Scott (ed.), *Global City-Regions: Trends, Theory, Policy.* Oxford: Oxford University Press.

Dunning, J. (1998). Location and the multinational enterprise: a neglected factor? *Journal of International Business Studies*, 29: 45–66.

——— (1999). Globalization and the theory of MNE activity. In N. Hood and S. Young (eds.), *The Globalization of Multinational Enterprise Activity and Economic Development.* London: Macmillan.

——— (2001). Regions, globalization, and the knowledge economy. In J. H. Dunning (ed.), *Global Capitalism at Bay?* London and New York: Routledge.

Easterly, W. (2001). *The Elusive Quest for Growth: Economists' Adventures and Misadventures in the Tropics.* Cambridge, MA: The MIT Press.

ECLAC (2002). *Globalization and Development.* Santiago de Chile: Economic Commission for Latin America and the Caribbean.

Eichengreen, B. (2000). *La Globalización del Capital: Historia del Sistema Monetario Internacional.* Barcelona: Antoni Bosch Editor.

Etzkowitz, H. and Leydesdorff, L. (1997). *Universities in the Global Knowledge Economy.* London: Pinter.

Fei, J. and Ranis, G. (1997). *Growth and Development from an Evolutionary Perspective.* Oxford: Blackwell Publishers Ltd.

Feldman, M. and Audretsch, D. (1999). Innovation in cities: science-based diversity, specialization and localized competition. *European Economic Review*, 43: 409–429.

Ferraro, C. and Costamagna, P. (2000). *Entorno Institucional y Desarrollo Productivo Local. La Importancia del Ambiente y las Instituciones Para el Desarrollo Empresarial. El Caso de Rafaela.* Buenos Aires: CEPAL.

Ferrer, A. (1996). *Historia de la Globalización.* Buenos Aires: Fondo de Cultura Económica.

Florida, R. (1995). Towards the learning region. *Futures*, 27: 527–536.

Fonfría Mesa, A. (1999). Patrones de innovación y política tecnológica. Mimeograph. Madrid: Facultad de Ciencias Económicas de la Universidad Complutense.

Frank, A. G. (1966). The development of underdevelopment. *Monthly Review*, 17: 17–31.

Freeman, C. (1988). Diffusion: the spread of new technology to firms, sectors and nations. In A. Heertje (ed.), *Innovation, Technology and Finance.* London: Frances Pinter.

Freeman, C. and Soete, L. (1997). *The Economics of Industrial Innovation.* Cambridge, MA: The MIT Press.

Friedmann, J. (1973). *Urbanization, Planning and National Development*. Beverly Hills: Sage.

———— (1986). The world city hypothesis. *Development and Change*, 17(1): 69–84.

Friedmann, J. and Douglas, M. J. (1978). Agropolitan development: toward a new strategy for regional planning in Asia. In F. Lo and K. Salih (eds.), *Growth Pole Strategy and Regional Development Policy*. Oxford: Pergamon.

Friedmann, J. and Weaver, C. (1979). *Territory and Function*. London: Edward Arnold.

Fuá, G. (1983). L'industrializzazione nel nord est e nel centro. In G. Fuá and C. Zachia (eds.), *Industrializzazione Senza Fratture*. Bologna: Il Mulino.

———— (1988). Small-scale industry in rural areas: the Italian experience. In K. J. Arrow (ed.), *The Balance Between Industry and Agriculture in Economic Development*. London: Macmillan.

———— (1994). *Economic Growth: A Discussion on Figures*. Ancona: ISTAO.

Fujita, M., Krugman, P. and Venables, A. J. (1999). *The Spatial Economy: Cities, Regions and International Trade*. Cambridge, MA: The MIT Press.

Fukuyama, F. (1995). *Trust: The Social Virtues and the Creation of Prosperity*. London: Penguin Books.

Furtado, C. (1964). *Development and Underdevelopment*. Berkeley, CA: University of California Press.

Garofoli, G. (1983). Le aree sistema in Italia. *Politica ed Economia*, 11: 7–34.

———— (1992). *Endogenous Development and Southern Europe*. Aldershot: Avebury.

Gereffi, G. (1994). The organization of buyer-driven global commodity chains: how US retailers shape overseas production networks. In G. Gereffi and M. Korzeniewicz (eds.), *Commodity Chains and Global Capitalism*. Westport: Greenwood Press.

———— (1999). International trade and industrial upgrading in the apparel commodity chain. *Journal of International Economics*, 48: 37–70.

Gibbon, P. (2001). Upgrading primary production: a global commodity chain approach. *World Development*, 29(2): 345–363.

Gilly, J. P. and Torre, A. (2000). Introduction générale. In J. P. Gilly and A. Torre (eds.), *Dynamiques de Proximité*. Paris: L'Harmattan.

Giordani, J. (2004). *Hacia una Venezuela Productiva*. Caracas: Ministerio de Planificación y Desarrollo.

Gordon, I. R. and McCann, P. (2000). Industrial clusters: complexes, agglomeration and/or social networks? *Urban Studies*, 37: 513–532.

Gore, C. (1984). *Regions in Question: Space, Development Theory and Regional Policy*. London and New York: Methuen.

Governa, F. and Salone, C. (2005). Italy and European spatial policies: polycentrism, urban networks and local innovation practices. *European Planning Studies*, 13(2): 266–283.

Grabher, G. (1993). Rediscovering the social in the economics of interfirm relations. In G. Grabher (ed.), *The Embedded Firm: On the Socioeconomics of Industrial Networks*. London: Routledge.

Green, N. (2007). Functional polycentricity: a formal definition in terms of social network analysis. *Urban Studies*, 44: 2077–2103.

Grossman, G. M. and Helpman, E. (1994). Endogenous innovation in the theory of growth. *Journal of Economic Perspectives*, 8: 23–44.

Gruchy, A. (1987). *The Reconstruction of Economics: An Analysis of the Fundamentals of Institutional Economics*. New York: Greenwood.

Guelpa, F. and Micelli, S. (2007). *I Distretti Industriali del Terzo Millenio: Dalle Economie di Agglomerazione Alle Strategie di Impresa*. Bologna: Il Mulino.

Guiso, L., Sapienza, P. and Zingales, L. (2006). Does culture affect economic outcome? *Journal of Economic Perspectives*, 20(2): 23–48.

Haggard, S. and Kaufman, S. (1994). Democratic institutions, economic policy and performance in Latin America. In C. I. Bradford, Jr. (ed.), *Redefining the State in Latin America*. Paris: OECD.

Hakansson, H. and Johanson, J. (1993). The network as a governance structure: interfirm cooperation beyond markets and hierarchies. In G. Grabher (ed.), *The Embedded Firm: On the Socioeconomics of Industrial Networks*. London: Routledge.

Hall, P. (1966). *The World Cities*. London: Weidenfeld & Nicolson.

——— (1993). Forces reshaping urban Europe. *Urban Studies*, 30: 883–898.

——— (1997). Megacities, world cities, and global cities. Mimeograph. The First Megacities Lecture, Rotterdam.

——— (1999). Creative cities and economic development. *Urban Studies*, 37(4): 639–649.

Hall, P. and Pain, K. (eds.) (2006). *The Polycentric Metropolis: Learning from Mega-City Regions in Europe*. London: Earthscan.

Hall, P. and Preston, P. (1988). *The Carrier Wave*. London: Unwin Hyman.

Harrod, R. F. (1939). An essay in dynamic theory. *Economic Journal*, 49(March): 14–33.

——— (1948). *Towards a Dynamic Economics*. London: Macmillan.

Hirschman, A. (1958). *The Strategy of Economic Development*. New Haven, CT: Yale University Press.

Hoff, K. (2000). Beyond Rosenstein-Rodan: the modern theory of coordination problems in development. In *Annual World Bank Conference on Development Economics*. Washington, D.C.: World Bank.

Hollingsworth, J. R., Schmitter, P. and Streeck, W. (eds.) (1994). *Governing Capitalist Economies: Performance and Control of Economic Sectors*. Oxford: Oxford University Press.

Hooghe, L. and Marks, G. (2001). *Multi-level Governance and European Integration*. Oxford: Rowman & Littlefield Publishers, Inc.

Hoover, E. M. (1937). *Location Theory and the Shoe and Leather Industries*. Cambridge, MA: Harvard University Press.

——— (1948). *The Location of Economic Activity*. New York: McGraw-Hill.

Hudson, J. (2004). Introduction: aid and development. *Economic Journal*, 114(496): 185–190.

Hudson, R. (1999). The learning economy, the learning firm and the learning region: a sympathetic critique of the limits of learning. *European Urban and Regional Studies*, 6: 59–72.

Humphrey, J. and Schmitz, H. (2004). Governance in global value chains. In H. Schmitz (ed.), *Local Enterprises in the Global Economy*. Cheltenham: Edward Elgar.

IMF (2009a). *World Economic Outlook, October 2009: Sustaining the Recovery*. Washington: International Monetary Fund.

———— (2009b). World economic crisis: stimulus measures bolstering demand amid crisis. *IMF Survey Magazine: Policy*, February 6. Washington: International Monetary Fund.

———— (2010). *World Economic Outlook, April 2010: Rebalancing Growth*. Washington: International Monetary Fund.

Johannisson, B. (1995). Paradigms and entrepreneurial networks — some methodological challenges. *Entrepreneurship & Regional Development*, 7: 215–231.

Kaufmann, A. and Tödtling, F. (2003). Innovation patterns of SMEs. In B. T. Asheim, A. Isaksen, C. Nauwelaers and F. Tödtling (eds.), *Regional Innovation Policy for Small-Medium Enterprises*. Cheltenham: Edward Elgar.

Kishimoto, C. (2004). Clustering and upgrading in global value chains: the Taiwanese personal computer industry. In H. Schmitz (ed.), *Local Enterprises in the Global Economy*. Cheltenham: Edward Elgar.

Kitching, G. N. (1982). *Development and Underdevelopment in Historical Perspective: Populism, Nationalism and Industrialization*. London: Methuen.

Konsolas, N. (ed.) (1990). *Local Development*. Athens: Regional Development Institute.

Kooiman, J. (1993). Findings, speculations and recommendations. In J. Kooiman (ed.), *Modern Governance: New Government–Society Interactions*. London: SAGE.

Krugman, P. (1990). *Geography and Trade*. Leuven, Belgium and Cambridge, MA: Leuven University Press and The MIT Press.

Kuznets, S. (1966). *Modern Economic Growth*. New Haven: Yale University Press.

Lacalle, M. C. (2002). *Microcréditos: De Pobres a Microempresarios*. Barcelona: Ariel.

Lambregts, B., Kloosterman, R., Werff, M., Roling, R. and Kapoen, L. (2006). Randstad Holland: multiple faces of a polycentric model. In P. Hall and K. Pain (eds.), *The Polycentric Metropolis: Learning from Mega-City Regions in Europe*. London: Earthscan.

Landes, D. S. (1969). *The Unbound Prometheus*. Cambridge: Cambridge University Press.

———— (1998). *The Wealth and Poverty of Nations*. New York: Norton & Company, Inc.

Lasuen, J. R. (1973). Urbanization and development: the temporal interaction between geographical and sectoral clusters. *Urban Studies*, 10: 163–188.

Lasuén, J. R. and Aranzadi, J. (2002). *El Crecimiento Económico y las Artes*. Madrid: Dataautor.

Lawson, C. and Lorenz, E. (1999). Collective learning, tacit knowledge and regional innovative capacity. *Regional Studies*, 33: 305–317.

Lester, K. R. and Piore, J. M. (2004). *Innovation — The Missing Dimension*. Cambridge, MA: Harvard University Press.

Lewis, A. (1954). Economic development with unlimited supplies of labour. *The Manchester School of Economic and Social Studies*, 22: 139–191.

——— (1955). *The Theory of Economic Growth*. London: George Allen & Unwin.

Londoño, C. (2001). Iniciativas de cooperación para el desarrollo económico local em Antioquia. In G. Aghon, F. Alburquerque and P. Cortés (eds.), *Desarrollo Económico Local y Descentralización en América Latina: Un Análisis Comparativo*. Santiago de Chile: CEPAL/GTZ.

Lucas, R. E. (1988). On the mechanics of economic development. *Journal of Monetary Economics*, 22(1): 129–144.

Lundvall, B. A. (ed.) (1992). *National Systems of Innovation: Towards a Theory of Innovation and Interactive Learning*. London: Pinter.

Lundvall, B. A. (1993). User–producer relationship, national systems of innovation and internationalization. In D. Foray and C. Freeman (eds.), *Technology and the Wealth of Nations*. London: Pinter.

Maddison, A. (2001). *The World Economy: A Millennial Perspective*. Paris: OECD Development Centre.

Madoery, O. (2008). *Otro Desarrollo: El Cambio Desde las Ciudades y Regiones*. Buenos Aires: UNSAM EDITA.

Maillat, D. (1995). Territorial dynamic, innovative milieus and regional policy. *Entrepreneurship & Regional Development*, 7: 157–165.

——— (2008). Local economic development: theory, models and experiences. Mimeograph. Paper presented to the AENL Meeting, Bogota, November.

Maillat, D., Nemeti, F. and Pfister, M. (1995). Distrito tecnológico e innovación: el caso del Jura Suizo. In A. Vázquez-Barquero and G. Garofoli (eds.), *Desarrollo Económico Local en Europa*. Madrid: Colegio de Economistas de Madrid.

Markusen, A. (1996). Sticky places in slippery spaces: a typology of industrial districts. *Economic Geography*, 72: 293–313.

——— (2000). Des lieux-aimants dans un espace mouvant: une typologie des districts industriels. In G. Benko and A. Lipietz (eds.), *La Richesse des Régions*. Paris: P.U.F.

Marshall, A. (1890). *Principles of Economics*. London: Macmillan.

Martin, R. and Sunley, P. (2003). Deconstructing clusters: chaotic concept or policy panacea? *Journal of Economic Geography*, 3: 5–35.

Martino, R., McHardy, D. and Zygliodopoulos, G. S. (2006). Balancing localization and globalization: exploring the impact of firm internationalization on a regional cluster. *Entrepreneurship & Regional Development*, 18: 1–24.

Maskell, P. (2001). Towards a knowledge-based theory of the geographical cluster. *Industrial and Corporate Change*, 10: 921–943.

Maskell, P., Eskelinen, H., Hannibalsson, I., Malberg, A. and Vatne, E. (1998). *Competitiveness, Localised Learning and Regional Development*. London: Routledge.

Massey, D. (1984). *Spatial Divisions of Labour: Social Structures and Geography of Production*. London: Macmillan.

Meier, M. G. (2005). *Biography of a Subject: An Evolution of Development Economics*. New York: Oxford University Press.

Meier, M. G. and Stiglitz, E. J. (eds.) (2001). *Frontiers of Development Economics*. New York: Oxford University Press.

Meijers, E. (2005). Polycentric urban regions and the quest for synergy: is a network of cities more than the sum of the parts? *Urban Studies*, 42: 765–781.

Messner, D. (2004). Regions in the world economic triangle. In H. Schmitz (ed.), *Local Enterprises in the Global Economy*. Cheltenham: Edward Elgar.

Metcalfe, S. (1995). The economic foundation of technology policy: equilibrium and evolutionary perspectives. In P. Stoneman (ed.), *Handbook of the Economics of Innovation and Technical Change*. Oxford: Blackwell.

Milanovic, B. (2001). World income inequality in the second half of the 20th century. Mimeograph. Washington, D.C.: World Bank.

Minian, I. (2007). Knowledge, obsolescence, and product segmentation. In A. J. Scott and G. Garofoli (eds.), *Development on the Ground*. London: Routledge.

Minsky, H. (1977). A theory of systemic fragility. In E. J. Alman and A. W. Sametz (eds.), *Financial Crisis: Institutions and Markets in a Fragile Environment*. New York: Wiley.

Mitchell, W. (1967). *Types of Economic Theory: From Mercantilism to Institutionalism*. New York: Augustus M. Kelley.

Muñoz, C. (2001). Programa "Rancagua Emprende": una experiencia de desarrollo económico local en Chile. In G. Aghon, F. Alburquerque and P. Cortés (eds.), *Desarrollo Económico Local y Descentralización en América Latina: Un Análisis Comparativo*. Santiago de Chile: CEPAL/GTZ.

Myrdal, G. (1957). *Economic Theory and Underdeveloped Regions*. London: Duckworth.

Nelson, R. (ed.) (1993). *National Systems of Innovation: A Comparative Study*. Oxford: Oxford University Press.

Nelson, R. (1999). How new is new growth theory? *Challenge*, 40(5): 29–58.

Nelson, R. and Winter, S. (1974). Neoclassical vs. evolutionary theories of economic growth. *Economic Journal*, 84: 886–905.

———— (1982). *An Evolutionary Theory of Economic Change*. Cambridge, MA: Harvard University Press.

North, D. C. (1981). *Structure and Change in Economic History*. New York: W. W. Norton.

——— (1986). The new institutional economics. *Journal of Institutional and Theoretical Economics*, 142(2): 230–237.

——— (1990). *Institutions, Institutional Change and Economic Performance.* Cambridge: Cambridge University Press.

——— (1994). Economic performance through time. *American Economic Review*, 83(3): 359–368.

Ocampo, J. A. (2009). Impactos de la crisis mundial sobre América Latina. *Revista CEPAL*, 97: 9–32.

OECD (1996). *Globalization and Linkages to 2020: Challenges and Opportunities for OECD Countries.* Paris: OECD.

——— (2009). *OECD Economic Outlook No. 85.* June. Paris: OECD.

O'Rourke, H. K. and Williamson, G. J. (1999). *Globalization and History: The Evolution of a Nineteenth-Century Atlantic Economy.* Cambridge, MA: The MIT Press.

Osborne, D. and Gaebler, T. (1992). *Reinventing Government: How the Entrepreneurial Spirit Is Transforming the Public Sector.* Reading: Addison-Wesley.

Ottati, G. D. (1994). Trust, interlinking transactions and credit in the industrial districts. *Cambridge Journal of Economics*, 18: 529–546.

Panico, C., Fleitas Ruiz, R. and Vázquez-Barquero, A. (2002). External evaluation report: Local Human Development Programme in Cuba. Mimeograph. Havana: UNDP.

Parr, J. B. (1979). Regional economic change and regional spatial structure: some interrelationships. *Environment and Planning A*, 11: 825–837.

——— (2004). The polycentric urban region: a closer inspection. *Regional Studies*, 38: 231–240.

——— (2005). Perspectives on the city-region. *Regional Studies*, 39: 555–566.

Pavitt, K. (1984). Sectoral patterns of technical change: towards a taxonomy and a theory. *Research Policy*, 13(6): 343–373.

Pérez, C. (1986). Las nuevas tecnologías, una visión de conjunto. In C. Ominami (ed.), *La Tercera Revolución Industrial.* México: Grupo Editor Latinoamericano.

Perroux, F. (1955). Note sur la notion de pôle de croissance. *Économie Appliquée*, 7: 307–320.

Piore, M. and Sabel, C. F. (1984). *The Second Industrial Divide.* New York: Basic Books.

Polanyi, K., Arensberg, M. C. and Pearson, W. H. (1957). *Trade and Market in the Early Empires: Economies in History and Theory.* Chicago: Henry Regnery Company.

Porter, M. (1990). *The Competitive Advantage of Nations.* New York: Free Press.

——— (1998). Clusters and the new economics of competition. *Harvard Business Review*, 76(November–December): 77–90.

Porter, M. E., Ketels, C. H. M., Miller, K. and Bryden, R. T. (2004). Competitiveness in rural U.S. regions: learning and research agenda. Report. Boston: Institute for Strategy and Competitiveness, Harvard Business School.

Pouder, R. and St. John, C. H. (1996). Hot spots and blind spots: geographic clusters of firms and innovation. *Academy of Management Review*, 21: 1192–1225.

Prats i Catala, J. (2003). *Instituciones y Desarrollo: Marco Conceptual Para la Reforma Institucional en America Latina*. Barcelona: Institut Internacional de Governabilitat de Catalunya, Universitat Oberta de Catalunya.

Precedo Ledo, A. (1996). *Ciudad y Desarrollo Urbano*. Madrid: Editorial Síntesis.

Priemus, H. and Zonneveld, W. (2004). Regional and transnational spatial planning: problems today, perspectives for the future. *European Planning Studies*, 12: 283–297.

Prieto Pérez, F. (2006). El papel de los mercados financieros en el desarrollo económico. Mimeograph. Report. Madrid: Universidad Autónoma de Madrid.

Putnam, R. (1993). *Making Democracy Work*. Princeton, NJ: Princeton University Press.

Quigley, J. M. (2002). Rural policy and the new regional economics: implications for rural America. Mimeograph. Berkeley: University of California.

Rabellotti, R., Carabelli, A. and Hirsch, G. (2009). Italian industrial districts on the move: where are they going? *European Planning Studies*, 17(1): 19–41.

Rasiah, R. (2007). Clusters and regional industrial synergies: the electronics industry in Penang and Jalisco. In A. Scott and G. Garofoli (eds.), *Development on the Ground*. London: Routledge.

Ray, D. (1998). *Development Economics*. New York: Princeton University Press.

Regidor, J. G. and Troitiño, M. A. (2008). El nuevo desafío rural. In J. G. Regidor (ed.), *Desarrollo Rural Sostenible: Un Nuevo Desafío*. Madrid: Mundi Prensa.

Reis, J. (1987). Os espaços da industrialização: notas sobre a regulação macroeconomica e o nivel local. *Revista Critica de Ciencias Sociais*, 22: 13–31.

——— (2007). *Ensaios de Economía Impura*. Coimbra: Almedina.

Richardson, H. (1978). *Regional and Urban Economics*. Harmondsworth: Penguin Books.

Romer, C. D. (2009). Lessons from the Great Depression for economic recovery in 2009. Mimeograph. Conference, March 9. Washington, D.C.: Brookings Institution.

Romer, P. M. (1986). Increasing returns and long-run growth. *Journal of Political Economy*, 94: 1002–1037.

Rosenfeld, S. A. (1997). Bringing business clusters into the mainstream of economic development. *European Planning Studies*, 5: 3–21.

Rosenstein-Rodan, P. N. (1943). Problems of industrialization of Eastern and South-Eastern Europe. *Economic Journal*, 53: 202–211.

Rostow, W. (1960). *The Stages of Economic Growth: A Non-communist Manifesto*. London: Cambridge University Press.

Rullani, E. (2008). I distretti industriali del terzo millenio: i mille modi com cui il nuovo nasce dal Vecchio, senza preavviso. *Rivista dell'Associazione Rossi-Doria*, 3–4: 183–199.

Saraceno, E. (2000). La experiencia Europea de desarrollo rural y su utilidad para el contexto latinoamericano. Mimeograph. Paper presented to the "Experiencias,

Políticas e Instrumentos Para el Desarrollo Rural en Europe y America" Workshop, San Fernando de Henares, Madrid, October.

——— (2006). Políticas rurales de la Unión Europea y proyectos territoriales de identidad cultural. Mimeograph. Paper presented to the "Territórios com Identidad Cultural" International Workshop, Cuzco, Perú, April.

Sassen, S. (1991). *The Global City: New York, London, Tokyo.* Princeton, NJ: Princeton University Press.

——— (2006). *Cities in a World Economy.* London: SAGE/Pine Forge.

Saxenian, A. (1994). *Regional Advantage: Culture and Competition in Silicon Valley and Route 128.* Cambridge, MA: Harvard University Press.

Schmitz, H. (2007). Regional systems and global chains. In A. J. Scott and G. Garofoli (eds.), *Development on the Ground.* Abingdon: Routledge.

Schumpeter, J. A. (1934). *The Theory of Economic Development.* Cambridge, MA: Harvard University Press (1st ed. in German, 1911).

——— (1939). *Business Cycles.* New York: McGraw-Hill.

Scott, A. J. (1988). *New Industrial Spaces.* London: Pion Ltd.

——— (2001). Globalization and the rise of city-regions. *European Planning Studies,* 9(7): 813–826.

——— (2005). The shoe industry of Marikina City, Philippines: a developing-country cluster in crisis. *Kasarinlan: Philippine Journal of Third World Studies,* 20(2): 76–79.

Scott, A. J., Agnew, J., Soja, E. W. and Storper, M. (2001). Global city-regions. In A. J. Scott (ed.), *Global City-Regions: Trends, Theory, Policy.* Oxford: Oxford University Press.

Scott, A. J. and Garofoli, G. (eds.) (2007). *Development on the Ground.* Abingdon: Routledge.

Scott, A. J. and Storper, M. (2003). Regions, globalization, development. *Regional Studies,* 37: 579–593.

Sen, A. (2001). *Development as Freedom,* 2nd ed. New Delhi: Oxford University Press.

Simmie, J. and Sennett, J. (1999). Innovative clusters: global or local linkages? *National Institute Economic Review,* 170(October): 87–98.

Simon, H. (1982). *Models of Bounded Rationality: Behavioral Economics and Business Organizations.* Cambridge, MA: The MIT Press.

Smith, A. (1776). *An Inquiry into the Nature and Causes of the Wealth of Nations.* Reprinted in 1937. E. Cannan (ed.). New York: Modern Library.

Soete, L. and Weel, B. (1999). Innovation, knowledge creation and technology policy in Europe. Mimeograph. Maastrich: MERIT, Maastrich University.

Solinas, G. (2006). Integrazione dei mercati e riaggiustamento nei distretti industriale. *Sinergie,* 69: 87–114.

Solow, R. (1956). A contribution to the theory of economic growth. *Quarterly Journal of Economics,* 78: 65–94.

———— (1994). Perspectives on growth theory. *Journal of Economic Perspectives*, 8: 45–54.

Staber, U. (1997). Specialization in a declining industrial district. *Growth and Change*, 28: 475–495.

Stiglitz, E. J. (1985). Economics of information and theory of economic development. Working Paper No. 1566. Cambridge, MA: National Bureau of Economic Research.

———— (1986). The new development economics. *World Development*, 14(2): 257–265.

———— (1989). Financial markets and development. *Oxford Review of Economic Policy*, 5(4): 55–68.

Stöhr, W. B. (1981). Development from below: the bottom-up and periphery-inward development paradigm. In W. B. Stöhr and D. R. Taylor (eds.), *Development from Above or Below?* Chichester: J. Wiley & Sons.

———— (1985). Selective self-reliance and endogenous regional development. In D. Nohlen and R.-O. Schultze (eds.), *Ungleiche Entwicklung und Regionalpolitik in Südeuropa*. Bochum: Studienverlag Dr. N. Brockmeyer.

Stöhr, W. B. and Taylor, D. R. F. (eds.) (1981). *Development from Above or Below?* Chichester: J. Wiley & Sons.

Summers, R. and Heston, A. (1991). The Penn World Table (Mark 5): an expanded set of international comparisons, 1950–1988. *Quarterly Journal of Economics*, 106(2): 327–368.

Sverrison, A. (2004). Local and global commodity chains. In C. Pierovelli and A. Sverrison (eds.), *Linking Local and Global Economies: The Ties That Bind*. London: Routledge.

Swan, T. W. (1956). Economic growth and capital accumulation. *Economic Record*, 32: 334–361.

Tallman, S., Jenkins, M., Henry, N. and Pinch, S. (2004). Knowledge, clusters and competitive advantage. *Academy of Management Review*, 29: 258–271.

Tamames, R. (2009). *Para Salir de la Crisis Global: Análisis y Soluciones*. Madrid: Editorial Edaf.

Taylor, P. J. (2004). *World City Network: A Global Urban Analysis*. London: Routledge.

Todaro, M. P. (2000). *Economic Development*. Harlow: Addison-Wesley.

Tomassini, L. (2000). El giro cultural de nuestro tiempo. In B. Kliksberg and L. Tomassini (eds.), *Capital Social y Cultura: Claves Estratégicas Para el Desarrollo*. Buenos Aires: Fondo de Cultura Económica.

Toscano Sánchez, F. (2000). Desarrollo local y economía social. In B. Pérez Ramírez and E. Carrillo Benito (eds.), *Desarrollo Local: Manual de Uso*. Madrid: ESIC Editorial.

UNCTAD (2008). World Investment Report 2008. *Transnational Corporations*, 17(3): 110–120.

—— (2009). *Global Economic Crisis: Implications for Trade and Development.* Geneva: UNCTAD secretariat.

United Nations (1987). *Our Common Future.* Report of the World Commission on Environment and Development. Oxford: Oxford University Press.

Valdés, B. (1999). *Economic Growth: Theory, Empirics and Policy.* Cheltenham: Edward Elgar.

Vázquez-Barquero, A. (1988). Small-scale industry in rural areas: the Spanish experience since the beginning of this century. In K. J. Arrow (ed.), *The Balance Between Industry and Agriculture in Economic Development.* Cambridge: Cambridge University Press.

—— (1993). *Política Económica Local.* Madrid: Editorial Pirámide.

—— (1999). Inward investment and endogenous development: the convergence of the strategies of large firms and territories? *Entrepreneurship & Regional Development*, 11: 79–93.

—— (2002). *Endogenous Development.* London: Routledge.

Vázquez-Barquero, A. and Sáez-Cala, A. (1997). The dynamics of local firm systems. In R. Ratti, A. Bramanti and R. Gordon (eds.), *The Dynamics of Innovative Regions.* Aldershot: Ashgate.

Veblen, Th. (1899). *The Theory of the Leisure Class: An Economic Study of Institutions.* New York: Macmillan.

Vegara, J. M. (1989). *Ensayos Económicos Sobre Innovación Tecnológica.* Madrid: Alianza Editorial.

Veltz, P. (1996). *Mondialisation, Villes et Territoires: L'economie D'archipel.* Paris: Press Universitaire de France.

Vence, X. (ed.) (2007). *Crecimiento y Políticas de Innovación.* Madrid: Pirámide.

Villanueva, M. (1998). Proyecto Quebrada de Catuche: programa de habilitación física de barrios (PROHABITAT). Mimeograph. Paper presented to the "Programas Sociales, Pobreza y Participación Ciudadana en Caracas" Seminar. Cartagena: Banco Interamericano de Desarrollo.

Weber, A. (1929). *Theory of the Location of Industries.* Chicago: University of Chicago Press (1st ed. in German, 1909).

Weber, M. (1905). *The Protestant Ethic and the Spirit of Capitalism.* London: Routledge.

Williamson, O. E. (1985). *The Economic Institutions of Capitalism: Firms, Markets, Relational Contracting.* New York: The Free Press.

Young, A. (1928). Increasing returns and economic progress. *Economic Journal*, 38: 527–542.

Index

.